FUN WITH THE FAMILY™ SERIES

fun WITH the
Family™

ARIZONA

HUNDREDS OF IDEAS FOR DAY TRIPS WITH THE KIDS

CARRIE MINER

SECOND EDITION

INSIDERS'GUIDE®

GUILFORD, CONNECTICUT
AN IMPRINT OF THE GLOBE PEQUOT PRESS

The prices, rates, and hours listed in this guidebook were confirmed at press time. We recommend, however, that you call establishments to obtain current information before traveling.

INSIDERS'GUIDE®

Copyright © 2002, 2004 by The Globe Pequot Press

Insiders' Guide is a registered trademark of The Globe Pequot Press.
Fun with the Family is a trademark of The Globe Pequot Press.

Text design by Nancy Freeborn and Linda Loiewski
Maps by Rusty Nelson © The Globe Pequot Press
Spot photography throughout © Photodisc

ISSN 1545-6498
ISBN 0-7627-2976-7

Manufactured in the United States of America
Second Edition/First Printing

To my eight-year-old twin sons, Hayden and Blake, without whom "family" travel would just be an abstract idea.

ARIZONA

Contents

Acknowledgments

"Choose a job you love and you will never have to work a day in your life."
—Confucius

I once had this quote pasted on my computer, along with other snippets of dubious wisdom and various cartoons on dieting, parenthood, and the plight of writing for a living. However, while working on this book, I often looked at that quote and snarled and grumbled, until I finally tossed it in the wastebasket. Never have to work—ha!

It all started when I took a college writing course. How could I have known that such a tiny thing would change my world? Bob Early, the editor of *Arizona Highways* magazine, was teaching that class in 1995. He made me write and rewrite and rewrite. I wrote jokes and a monologue and a short mystery. In return, Bob laughed at my humor, nodded at my attempt at stand-up comedy, and chastised me for killing my detective. At the end of that class he told me that I should be writing for a living, and in the next breath he scolded me for my lack of discipline. I started my love affair with words that winter and have never looked back. Bob still watches over my progress, pushes me, pokes me, and tells me to work harder. After I missed a deadline on this project, I stopped by his office bemoaning the tremendous task of creating a book and complaining at how far behind I was. He just looked at me for a moment and said in a gruff voice, "Well, what are you doing here? Go home and work!" So much for Confucius.

Of all of the things I have learned over the last several years, the most important one in my mind is that without my editors I wouldn't be a writer. I would like to thank all of those editors whose pens have touched my work and shaped my world. Special thanks goes to Bob Early, who has always believed in me, and to Mary Norris, for giving me the opportunity to create this book. I'd also like to thank my friends Theresa Mason and Cassie Scheideman, for their assistance in researching this project, and my sons, Hayden and Blake, for their endless patience and witty advice.

Introduction

rizona. The word brings to mind a forbidding place filled with rugged deserts, rocky terrain, rough-cut canyons—and little or no water. But Arizona is much more than that. It is a land of anomalies, a land of extremes, a land full of surprises. Here you'll find cities that see more sunshine than Florida, rivers of sand, trees of stone, snowy alpine mountaintops, thick ponderosa pine forests, the world's largest natural bridge, a bird that runs faster than it flies, night-blooming cactus, the only poisonous lizard found in the United States, ancient stands of thick-armed saguaros, islands in the sky, the world's deepest dam, the oldest continuously inhabited community in the nation, and the largest Native American reservation in the nation.

All seven of the Merriam Life Zones can be found in Arizona, which means that your travels here will take you through all of the habitats you'd encounter if you drove from the lower Sonoran Desert to the forests of the Canadian Zone. While traveling the state, you'll see spectacular sandstone cliffs, Sonoran highlands, snow-capped mountain ranges, broad valleys, rugged canyons, and stark badlands. Rainfall ranges from 3 inches a year in Yuma to more than 30 in the White Mountains. Arizona often records the highest and lowest temperatures in the nation on the same day. Record temperatures range from 128 degrees at Lake Havasu in 1994 to a low of 40 below zero at Hawley Lake in 1971.

Even though it ranks as the sixth largest state, Arizona averages only twenty-five people per square mile. Most of the state's population resides in the metro Phoenix area (also called the Valley of the Sun) and Tucson. The rest of the countryside is populated with quiet mountain hamlets, ghost towns, and tiny agricultural and ranching communities—which means you can literally explore hundreds of miles without seeing another soul.

During your travels you'll discover Native American ruins, ghost towns, old army forts, orchards and farms, more national parks and monuments than any other state, Spanish-Colonial missions, Victorian neighborhoods, mining towns, and a multitude of other historic sites. In addition to the cultural and natural attractions, you'll also find teams from all major sports—Major League Baseball's Arizona Diamondbacks, the National Hockey League's Phoenix Coyotes, the National Basketball Association's Phoenix Suns, the National Football League's Arizona Cardinals, and the Women's National Basketball Association's Phoenix Mercury.

Seat belts are the law here, so be sure to buckle up and make sure your toddlers are secured in car seats. Because of the distances involved and the sparseness of amenities, I'd strongly suggest being well prepared for emergencies by traveling with a complete road kit. Also, with the intense summer temperatures, you really need to have at least one gallon of water stashed in your car. Arizona can live up to its treacherous reputation, even though it is intensely beautiful. Just be aware of your surroundings and respect the land and its people, and your family will have a wonderful time discovering this land of contrasts and contradictions.

Lodging, Restaurant, and Attraction Fees

The dollar signs listed for lodgings and restaurants (in the Where to Eat and Where to Stay sections), as well as for attractions, offer a guide to each facility's prices. Lodgings include prices for rooms with a double bed and no meals, unless otherwise indicated, and the restaurant pricing structure is based on both lunch and dinner entrees. Be advised that prices for lodgings tend to fluctuate drastically depending on the season and, if you are traveling to either the Grand Canyon or Sedona in the summer months, reservations are a must.

Because admission fees change frequently, this book offers a general idea of the prices charged by each attraction. Keep in mind that even though many preserves and museums offer free admission, a donation is often expected to help the facility with the costs of keeping the lands and buildings open to the public.

Lodging

$	up to $50
$$	$51 to $75
$$$	$76 to $99
$$$$	$100 and up

Attractions

$	under $5
$$	$5 to $10
$$$	$11 to $20
$$$$	over $20

Restaurants

$	most entrees under $10
$$	most $10 to $15
$$$	most over $15 to $20
$$$$	most over $20

Attractions Key

The following is a key to the icons found throughout the text.

SWIMMING		**FOOD**	
BOATING / BOAT TOUR		**LODGING**	
HISTORIC SITE		**CAMPING**	
HIKING / WALKING		**MUSEUMS**	
FISHING		**PERFORMING ARTS**	
BIKING		**SPORTS/ATHLETICS**	
AMUSEMENT PARK		**PICNICKING**	
HORSEBACK RIDING		**PLAYGROUND**	
SKIING / WINTER SPORTS		**SHOPPING**	
PARK		**PLANTS / GARDENS / NATURE TRAILS**	
ANIMAL VIEWING		**FARMS**	

Help Us Keep This Guide Up to Date

Every effort has been made by the author and editors to make this guide as accurate and useful as possible. However, many changes can occur after a guide is published—establishments close, phone numbers change, hiking trails are rerouted, facilities come under new management, etc.

We would love to hear from you concerning your experiences with this guide and how you feel it could be improved and be kept up to date. While we may not be able to respond to all comments and suggestions, we'll take them to heart, and we'll make certain to share them with the author. Please send your comments and suggestions to the following address:

The Globe Pequot Press
Reader Response/Editorial Department
P.O. Box 480
Guilford, CT 06437

Or you may e-mail us at: editorial@GlobePequot.com

Thanks for your input, and happy travels!

Canyon Country

The Grand Canyon, known as one of the Seven Natural Wonders of the World, dominates the northwestern corner of the state. When Lt. Joseph Ives encountered this gaping crevice in 1857 during an exploration of the Arizona Territory, he said, "[The Grand Canyon] can be approached only from the south and after entering it there is nothing to do but leave. Ours has been the first and will doubtless be the last party of whites to visit this profitless locality. It seems intended by nature that the Colorado River, along with the greater portions of its lonely and majestic way, shall be forever unvisited and undisturbed." He was wrong. Today nearly five million people visit this impressive landmark each year.

The canyon, which reaches 227 miles long and gapes up to 18 miles at its widest point, neatly cuts off the northwestern corner of Arizona from the rest of the state. As a result, the North Rim is accessible only by looping around the divide near the Utah border and so remains fairly pristine. It is well worth the 210-mile drive and any inconvenience for

Carrie's
TopPicks for fun in Canyon Country

1. Grand Canyon National Park

2. Grand Canyon Deer Farm, Williams

3. Grand Canyon Railway, Williams

4. The Museum of Northern Arizona, Flagstaff

5. Lowell Observatory, Flagstaff

6. Arizona Snowbowl, Flagstaff

7. Agassiz Skyride, Flagstaff

8. Walnut Canyon National Monument, Flagstaff

9. Wupatki National Monument, Flagstaff

10. Sunset Crater Volcano National Monument, Flagstaff

CANYON COUNTRY

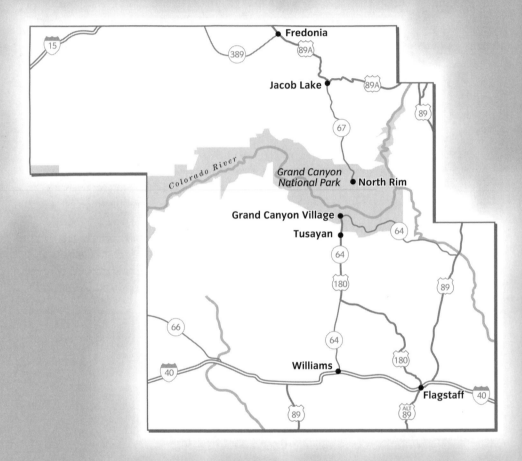

- Fredonia
- Jacob Lake
- North Rim
- Grand Canyon Village
- Tusayan
- Williams
- Flagstaff

Colorado River

Grand Canyon National Park

15 · 389 · 89A · 89A · 89 · 67 · 64 · 180 · 89 · 66 · 40 · 64 · 180 · 89 · ALT 89 · 40

families with older children. On the way you'll pass through Kaibab National Forest, known for its magnificent views, hiking trails, and backcountry camping, pass by the brilliant Vermilion Cliffs, and see sweeping vistas from the North Rim, which is about 1,000 to 1,500 feet higher than the South Rim.

The more accessible South Rim, which draws most of the canyon's visitors, is easily reached from Flagstaff or Williams. Prices climb as you near Grand Canyon National Park, so you're better off gassing up and doing any last-minute food shopping while passing through these two towns. A visit to this natural wonder can be done in a day, but for those who want to stay and explore, several lodges offer excellent packages for family travelers. Note that prices peak in the summer due to high demand, which means that for trips in the summer months you should generally make reservations at least six months in advance. And don't be too disappointed if your children aren't duly impressed by the grand spectacle once you arrive—the magnitude of nature's handiwork looks to many children like just a big hole in the ground.

Now that I–40 bypasses Williams, which is situated on Historic Route 66, this once busy city survives on tourist dollars. Billed as the Gateway to the Grand Canyon, it is only an hour ride from this quaint mountain town to Grand Canyon National Park. Flagstaff, 30 miles east of Williams, also sees its share of visitors heading north to the canyon, but this town holds a charm of its own and provides a great base to explore a variety of nearby natural attractions, including the ancient Native American dwellings at Walnut Canyon and an extinct volcano at Sunset Crater Volcano National Monument. Flagstaff is also the home to the observatory where Pluto was discovered, the state's third largest university, and the high-altitude training camp for the Arizona Cardinals.

Even though Canyon Country is the most highly visited region in the state, the drive between Flagstaff and the park is one of the least scenic byways in Arizona; however, the destination makes it all worthwhile.

Fredonia

Although this tiny village boasts a population of only 1,200 residents, it is the largest town on the 14,000 square miles of the isolated Arizona Strip. The Strip covers about the same amount of land as the state of New Jersey but is home to a mere 5,000 people. Hemmed in by Utah on the north, the Kaibab Plateau on the east, Nevada on the west, and the Grand Canyon on the south, a resident of Fredonia would have to drive nearly 350 miles across three states to get to the Mohave county seat in Kingman. This is also the reason this region is the least visited in the state. However, the long drive to this secluded part of the state yields panoramic views of pristine woodlands, colorful canyons, and mountain vistas. It is also the only way by land to reach the North Rim of the Grand Canyon, the viewpoints of which sit 1,500 feet higher than the heavily visited South Rim. It also gets 60 percent more rain and snow than the South Rim, which makes the area lush by comparison. Some of the state's last intact, old-growth ponderosa pine forests grace the canyon's North Rim, wildlife-watching opportunities are abundant, and scenic rim views make this trip worthwhile. On the down side, this jaunt is more suited to families with older children, as tiny tots are less likely to hold up to the rugged demands of this backcountry trip. Also keep in mind that the North Rim shuts down in the winter—usually from mid-October to mid-May—and that amenities are few and far between.

Pipe Spring National Monument (all ages) 🏛 🏵

401 North Pipe Spring Road, Fredonia; (928) 643–7105; www.nps.gov/pisp. Open daily 7:00 A.M. to 5:00 P.M. June through August, 8:00 A.M. to 5:00 P.M. September through May except Thanksgiving, Christmas, and New Year's Day. Adults $, children under 16 free.

Pipe Spring National Monument, located 14 miles southwest of Fredonia in northern Arizona, offers a glimpse of Western pioneer life with guided tours through a preserved Mormon ranch and demonstrations of everyday activities from the 1870s such as cheesemaking, cooking on a wood-burning stove, and making old-fashioned toys. Several tribal members from the surrounding Kaibab-Paiute Indian Reservation offer additional demonstrations on Native American arts and crafts. Kids will enjoy burning off some energy on the monument's ½-mile loop interpretive trail. The trail, which climbs to an overlook behind the weathered buildings, offers a great view of the property's garden and orchard.

The natural spring on the forty-acre national monument attracted civilization more than 1,000 years ago with Anasazi settlements and more recently by the nomadic Paiute now living on the surrounding reservation. In 1870 Mormon leader Brigham Young established the church's southern cattle operation in Pipe Spring and built the fortlike structure known as Winsor Castle, which earned its name from regal ranch superintendent Anson P. Winsor. President Harding proclaimed the site a national monument in 1923 to memorialize Western pioneer life.

Jacob Lake

Thirty miles south of Fredonia on State Route 67 at Highway 89A.

This hamlet, nestled high in the pine forest at an elevation of 7,925 feet, sits at the junction of Highway 89A and State Route 67 and is a great place to set up a base camp for

Condors **in Flight**

Those hoping to watch the endangered California condors in flight now have two locations to visit. In December 1996 the reintroduction program began at the Vermilion Cliffs in Grand Canyon National Park. In 1999 the Peregrine Fund released eight condors at a second Arizona location—Hurricane Cliffs—which is located 40 miles southeast of St. George, Utah. For more information on the California condors, such as recent sightings and habitats, call the Arizona Department of Game and Fish at (928) 774–5045 or visit www.azgfd.com.

Scenic **Drive**

Take a 23-mile drive along the paved road to Cape Royal to see some of the most spectacular viewpoints on the North Rim. About halfway there stop at Point Imperial, which at an elevation of 8,803 feet is the highest lookout on either rim. The view embraces Nankoweap Creek below, the Vermilion Cliffs to the north, the Painted Desert to the east, the Little Colorado River Canyon to the southeast, and Navajo Mountain (one of the four sacred mountains of the Navajo) to the northeast. Picnic tables at the point provide a great place for lunch. A few additional lookouts along the way to Cape Royal offer views of such legendary landmarks as Freya Castle, Vishnu Temple, and Wotan's Throne.

exploring the Kaibab Plateau. Kaibab, pronounced "KY-bab," is a Paiute Indian word meaning "mountain lying down." Also referred to as "an island in the sky," the plateau is home to a diverse set of wildlife, including mule deer, mountain lions, and the Kaibab squirrel, which can be found only on the Kaibab Plateau. This is also the last stop before heading the final 45 miles to Grand Canyon National Park, so make sure you're stocked up here before heading on. Although there's not much going on around town, stop at the **Kaibab Plateau Visitor Center** (928–643–7298), which offers information on nearby viewpoints, trails, and historic sites, including a 1910 forest cabin overlooking the lake. The visitor center is closed from the end of December through the end of April.

Bright Angel Point (ages 5 and up) 🏛 👫 ⊜
Forty-five miles south of Jacob Lake on State Route 67, Grand Canyon National Park; (928) 638–7888. Open daily from mid-May to mid-October. $$$ per private vehicle for admission to the park.

Well, this is the end of the road—literally—and the only North Rim location with services within the park boundaries. Unless you plan on camping out at the North Rim Campground, you'd best make reservations well in advance at the Grand Canyon Lodge, the only accommodations on the North Rim. Near the west entrance is a bronze statue of the famous burro Brighty, who used to roam the area after his days as a pack animal were at an end. Even though the location isn't the most convenient, there is plenty of elbowroom to enjoy dramatic views of the Colorado River from the rim. A paved footpath will lead you and your family on an easy ½-mile loop trail to the tip of Bright Angel Point. Here you will be able to see shells and fossils embedded in an outcropping of Kaibab limestone as well as stupendous views of the canyon.

North Rim Visitor Center (ages 4 and up)
Grand Canyon National Park; (928) 638–7864; www.nps.gov/grca. Open daily 8:00 A.M. to 6:00 P.M. from mid-May to mid-October. Free.

This center makes life a bit easier for families traveling to the North Rim than in the past. Located across from the Grand Canyon Lodge on the Bright Angel Peninsula, the center hosts a few exhibits and offers information on nature walks, children's programs, and other activities. Public restrooms are located in the back of the building.

Canyon Trail Rides (ages 7 and up)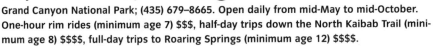

Grand Canyon National Park; (435) 679–8665. Open daily from mid-May to mid-October. One-hour rim rides (minimum age 7) $$$, half-day trips down the North Kaibab Trail (minimum age 8) $$$$, full-day trips to Roaring Springs (minimum age 12) $$$$.

With offices located in the lobby of the Grand Canyon Lodge, this outfitter takes families on mule rides along the North Rim and down into the canyon. Children must be at least seven and be able to mount and dismount by themselves. In addition, all riders must be of good health, less than 200 pounds, and at least 4'7'' in height. Reservations are highly recommended.

Where to Eat

Grand Canyon Lodge Dining Room. Grand Canyon National Park; (928) 638–2612, ext. 160. Fabulous views; children's menu; open daily for breakfast, lunch, and dinner. $$$–$$$$

Marble Canyon Lodge. ¼ mile west of Navajo Bridge on US 89A, Marble Canyon; (928) 355–2225 or (800) 726–1789. This Arizona Strip lodge serves up steaks, seafood, pasta, and sandwiches. $$–$$$

Where to Stay

Grand Canyon Lodge. Grand Canyon National Park; (928) 638–2611 for same-day reservations, (303) 297–2757 for advance reservations; www.grandcanyonlodges.com. A 1936 national landmark overlooking Transept Canyon near Bright Angel Point. $$$–$$$$

Grand Canyon Motel. 175 South Main Street, Fredonia; (928) 643–7646. Motel rooms with kitchenettes. $

Jacob Lake Inn. Junction of Highway 89A/State Route 67, Jacob Lake; (928) 643–7232; www.jacoblake.com. This rustic lodge offers cabins, family units, and rooms with no telephone or televisions. Even if you don't stay here, you should stop for one of the famous milk shakes. $$–$$$

Area Campgrounds

Jacob Lake Campground. North Kaibab Ranger District, Highway 89A/State Route 67, Jacob Lake; (928) 643–7770. Fifty-three first-come, first-serve RV and tent sites. Rangers present programs on summer evenings. Open mid-April to late October. $

Kaibab Lodge Camper Village. Off State Route 67, Jacob Lake, 1 mile southwest of Jacob Lake Inn; reservations (928) 643–7804. Eighty full hookup sites and 50 tent sites complete with fire pits and picnic tables. Open May to November. $

North Rim Campground. Grand Canyon National Park, 1½ miles northwest of the Grand Canyon Lodge; (800) 365–2267; www.reservations.nps.gov. Reservations required, no hookups. $

For More Information

Fredonia Chamber of Commerce. 130 North Main, P.O. Box 217, Fredonia 86022; (928) 643–7241.

North Kaibab Ranger District. 430 North Main Street, Fredonia 86022; (928) 643–7395.

Grand Canyon National Park– South Rim

The grandest of canyons pays tribute to the human imagination with landforms named after mythic heroes and deities from around the world. From the rim you can see such landmarks as Wotan's Throne, Brahma Temple, Isis Temple, and Cheops Pyramid. The gorge, two billion years in the making, exposes layers of rock reaching a mile deep. The Grand Canyon, which is completely contained within the state lines, plummets into the earth 1 mile deep and gapes an average width of 10 miles across from rim to rim. You can push it and "do the canyon" in a day, but with so much to do and see in the park you're better off taking a couple of days dedicated to exploration, especially since the admission fee ($$$) is good for a week.

The first Europeans to encounter this natural divide were members of Coronado's party in 1540–41 on their search of the Seven Cities of Cibola. It remained unexplored until 1869, when the tenacious, one-armed Civil War veteran John Wesley Powell tackled the Colorado River, charting its tumultuous course through the giant chasm. President Teddy Roosevelt established it as a national park in 1908, and it was later dedicated as a World Heritage Site in 1979. Make sure to wear good, sturdy shoes and keep a close eye on the kids. Even though rails guard against people getting too close to the rim's edge, several people are injured and killed each year from ignoring the warnings and bypassing the park's safety measures.

Canyon View Information Plaza (all ages)

Grand Canyon National Park, Mather Point; (928) 638–7644. Open daily 8:00 A.M. to 6:00 P.M. in the summer and 8:00 A.M. to 5:00 P.M. in the winter. Free.

This plaza, which opened in 2000, provides a plethora of information for Grand Canyon visitors. Exhibits, both indoors and outdoors, will give you a great orientation to Grand Canyon National Park. The center also offers the informative video program *Lure of the*

Canyon at 4:00 P.M. daily. Other facilities at this stopping point include restrooms and a bookstore, where you can pick up your copy of *The Guide*, the newspaper detailing events and activities held in the park. Best of all, your family's first look at the canyon is just a short stroll away down a paved path. Be sure to ask about **free** ranger-led programs, which are offered year-round.

Yavapai Observation Station (all ages)

Grand Canyon National Park, 5 miles north of the park's south entrance. Open daily 8:00 A.M. to 5:00 P.M. Free.

This overlook has informative panels that identify many of the Grand Canyon's landmarks, just beyond the building's large glass viewing windows. The station also houses educational exhibits and a bookstore run by the nonprofit Grand Canyon Association, which has put more than twenty-five million dollars back into the park since the association's inception. Public restrooms are located next to the station parking lot.

Mule Rides (ages 8 and up)

Grand Canyon National Park, Bright Angel Lodge; (928) 638–3283. Open daily. Day trips leave at 7:15 A.M. and return at 3:30 P.M. $$$$

The Bright Angel Lodge offers mule rides down to Plateau Point, about halfway into the canyon. Children must be able to mount and dismount by themselves, be in good health, and reach the minimum height requirement of 4'7''. Reservations required.

Tusayan Museum (all ages)

Grand Canyon National Park, located 3 miles west of Desert View and 22 miles west of the Grand Canyon Village on Desert View Drive; (928) 638–2305. Open daily 9:00 A.M. to 5:00 P.M. Free.

A stop at this small museum will orient you to the lifestyles of the prehistoric people that lived in the adjacent ruins, a pueblo dating back to A.D. 1185. Along the self-guided tour, interpretive signs give a glimpse of how these ancient people farmed and gathered wild food along the rim and nearby uplands. For a more in-depth tour, sign up for one of the daily forty-five-minute, ranger-guided tours. Times vary.

Amazing Arizona Facts

For more than 700 years, the Havasupai Indians have lived on their ancestral lands at the bottom of one of the chasm's side canyons, which can only be reached by foot, mule, or helicopter. This remote reservation's only village, Supai, is the last location in the United States where mail is still delivered by mule.

Become a Grand Canyon
National Park Junior Ranger

Kids ages four to fourteen can be sworn in as junior park rangers after completing the following requirements:

To become a Raven (ages four to seven), Coyote (ages eight to ten), or Scorpion (ages eleven to fourteen), you need to complete the requirements listed in the *Junior Ranger* magazine, including completing word puzzles, answering questions about the park, and attending a ranger-led program.

To be a Dynamic Earth Junior Ranger (ages nine to fourteen), you will need to attend the Dynamic Earth Program, which is offered at 10:00 A.M. on Sunday, Tuesday, and Thursday between May 27 and September 3. Activities include a ranger-led hike along the rim and hands-on experiments detailing how the Grand Canyon was formed from uplift and erosion.

Desert View Information Center (all ages)

Grand Canyon National Park, located at the east entrance station, 25 miles east of the Grand Canyon Village; (928) 638–7893. Open daily 9:00 A.M. to 6:00 P.M. in the summer, 9:00 A.M. to 5:00 P.M. in the winter. Free.

This center introduces visitors to the canyon with historical dioramas and interpretive exhibits. For a quarter (the same price of admission since opening in 1933) the kids can climb the 70-foot-tall **Desert View Watchtower.** This overlook, at 7,500 feet, marks the highest viewpoint on the South Rim and affords a panoramic look at the canyon and surrounding landmarks, including the colorful, 43,000-acre Painted Desert.

Three miles up the road, **Lipan Point** offers views of more of the Colorado River than any other lookout point on the South Rim.

Rivers and Oceans (ages 8 and up)

12620 North Copeland Lane, Flagstaff; (928) 526–4575 or (800) 473–4576; www.grand-canyon.az.us/R&O. Open Monday through Friday 8:30 A.M. to 4:30 P.M. Free.

With the multitude of river-running companies traveling down the Colorado River through the Grand Canyon, your best bet is to call this operator. It will hook you up with the different companies, offer information on the many different river trips, and even make reservations. Trips range from one day to a week and range in price from $260 to $2,200. The rafting season runs from March to mid-September. If this is something you decide to do, make sure to make your reservations well in advance. Some trips require hiking either in or out of the canyon. Suggested items to take include a camera, rainwear, a bathing suit, sunscreen, and a hat that ties under the chin.

Where to Eat

The Arizona Room. Grand Canyon National Park, located in the Bright Angel Lodge; (928) 638–2631. Dinner service only, beginning at 4:30 P.M. Serving steak and seafood on a first-come, first-serve basis. $$$

Bright Angel Fountain. Grand Canyon National Park, located in the Bright Angel Lodge; (928) 638–2631. An old-fashioned ice cream fountain located on the lodge patio. $

Bright Angel Restaurant. Grand Canyon National Park, located in the Bright Angel Lodge; (928) 638–2631. Family-oriented restaurant serving cuisine with a Southwestern flair. $$–$$$

El Tovar Fine Dining Room. Grand Canyon National Park, located in the El Tovar Hotel; (928) 638–2631. Continental menu with a Southwestern flavor. Dinner reservations required. $$$–$$$$

Maswik Cafeteria. Grand Canyon National Park, located in the Maswik Lodge; (928) 638–2631. Cafeteria dining. $

Where to Stay

Grand Canyon National Park Lodges. P.O. Box 699, Grand Canyon 86023; (928) 638–2631; www.grandcanyonlodges.com. Operates eight lodges on the South Rim, including the historic 1905 El Tovar Hotel, the Kachina Lodge, the Maswik Lodge, the Yavapai Lodge, the Moqui Lodge, the historic 1936 Bright Angel Lodge, and Phantom Ranch. The Bright Angel Lodge and El Tovar are favorites for families. Children under sixteen stay **free.** $$$–$$$$

Area Campgrounds

Mather Campground. Grand Canyon National Park; (800) 365–2267. Ninety-seven RV and 190 tent sites. No hookups available. Reservations available from March to November. $

For More Information

Grand Canyon Chamber of Commerce. P.O. Box 3007, Grand Canyon 86023; (928) 638–2901; www.grandcanyon chamber.com.

Grand Canyon Information. (800) 635–2212.

Tusayan

This compact town on State Route 64, 9 miles south of the Grand Canyon Village, is the last stop for services before entering Grand Canyon National Park. There's only one road going through town, and that's the highway, which is why there are no street addresses for any of the businesses. Even though these facilities aren't in the park proper, prices are just about as high for lodging and other services. So if you want to stock up or stay cheap, your best bet is to stay 60 miles farther south in Williams.

Grand Canyon IMAX Theatre (ages 3 and up)

Two miles south of the park entrance, Tusayan; (928) 638–2468. Showing daily on the half hour 8:30 A.M. to 8:30 P.M. from March to October and 9:30 A.M. to 6:30 P.M. in the winter months. Adults and children ages 6–12 $$, under 6 free.

Although rafting the rugged inner canyon is for older children and adults, the younger set can still enjoy the experience, thanks to the thirty-four-minute movie *Grand Canyon—The Hidden Secrets* showing on the six-story-high IMAX screen. Along with action-packed scenes of river runners and aircraft tours, the movie informs as well as entertains with segments on the Grand Canyon's natural history and wildlife. Even though three-year-olds can get in to watch the show, dizzying aerial views from soaring planes and the crashing sound as river runners battle class 10 rapids might overwhelm a timid toddler.

Apache Stables (ages 8 and up)

One mile north of Tusayan on State Route 64 near the Moqui Lodge, Tusayan; (928) 638–2891; www.apachestables.com. Open daily from March to November, weather permitting. One-hour ride (ages 8 and up) $$$$, two-hour ride (ages 10 and up) $$$$.

Children taking these guided trail rides through the Kaibab National Forest must be of the minimum age and at least 48 inches tall. Beginners quickly learn on the stable's gentle horse stock and become trail blazers under the guidance of the experienced cowboys leading the rides. Reservations are recommended at least two weeks in advance during the busy summer months.

Grand Canyon Airlines (all ages)

Grand Canyon Airport, Tusayan; (928) 638–2407; www.grandcanyonairlines.com. Adults and children 2–12 $$$$, under 2 free.

This forty-five- to fifty-five-minute loop flight takes passengers over 100 miles of the canyon with views of the North and South Rims and the Little Colorado River confluence in a high-wing, two-engine plane. The spectacular sights and narrated passes over both the well-known and more obscure formations will thrill young and old alike.

Papillon Grand Canyon Helicopters (all ages)

Grand Canyon Airport, Tusayan; (928) 638–2419 or (800) 528–2418; www.papillon.com. Adults and children 2–11, $$$$, under 2 free for thirty- or fifty-minute ride.

Both tours travel across to the North Rim. In addition, the fifty-minute tour covers parts of the eastern portion of the Grand Canyon. For those that have never ridden in a helicopter before, this tour is a real treat. However, keep an eye on the tots—airsickness is more prevalent in helicopters than in regular airplanes due to the nature of its up-and-down, side-to-side type of travel.

Where to Eat

The Steak House. State Route 64, Tusayan; (928) 638–2780. Steak, chicken, and shrimp entrees. Open for lunch and dinner. $$$

We Cook Pizza and Pasta. State Route 64, Tusayan; (928) 638–2278. Pizza, pasta, and sandwiches. $

Where to Stay

Best Western Grand Canyon Squire Inn. State Route 64, Tusayan; (928) 638–2681 or (800) 622–6966. Exercise room, heated pool, video arcade, gift shop, and cowboy museum. Children under twelve stay **free.** $$$–$$$$

Grand Canyon Quality Inn & Suites. State Route 64, Tusayan; (928) 638–2673 or (800) 221–2222. There are 176 deluxe rooms and 56 two-room suites. Children under eighteen stay **free.** $$$$

Holiday Inn Express Grand Canyon. State Route 64, P.O. Box 3245, Tusayan 86023; (928) 638–3000 or (800) HOLIDAY. Complimentary continental breakfast. Children under nineteen stay **free.** $$$–$$$$

The Grand Hotel. State Route 64, P.O. Box 3319, Tusayan 86023; (928) 638–3333 or (888) 63–GRAND. Indoor pool, 120 rooms, and Native American gift store. Children under eighteen stay **free.** $$$

Area Campgrounds

Grand Canyon Camper Village. Located 1 mile south of Grand Canyon National Park; State Route 64, Box 490, Tusayan 86023; (928) 638–2887. Two hundred RV hookups and fifty tent sites. $

Williams

Self-billed as the Gateway to the Grand Canyon, this railroad and lumber town takes its name from mountain man Bill Williams, a well-known trapper, trader, and guide who roamed the West until he died in 1849 at the hands of Ute Indians. Although tiny in size, Williams is home to the famous Grand Canyon Railway and offers less-expensive accommodations than those at the park. In addition, this picturesque community provides great scenery and an opportunity to stretch your legs among grassy meadows and forested hill country.

Grand Canyon Deer Farm (all ages) 🐘

6752 East Deer Farm Road, Williams; (928) 635–4073 or (800) 926–DEER; www.deerfarm. com. Located 8 miles east of Williams off I–40. Open daily except Thanksgiving and Christmas Day 8:00 A.M. to 7:00 P.M. June through August, 9:00 A.M. to 6:00 P.M. March through May and September through October, and 10:00 A.M. to 5:00 P.M. November through February, weather permitting. Adults $$, children ages 3–13 $, under 3 free.

Kids get up-close and personal with deer, llamas, pronghorn, wallabies, and miniature donkeys at this large petting zoo. In addition to hand-feeding these tame animals, visitors also get a chance to see buffalo, goats, potbellied pigs, exotic birds, and reindeer.

Grand Canyon Railway (all ages) 🏛 ⊖

Williams Depot, 233 North Grand Canyon Boulevard, Williams; (928) 773–1976 or (800) 843–8724; www.thetrain.com. Departs daily from the depot at 10:00 A.M. Five classes of service are available, all $$$$ for adults and children. Prices don't include tax and park admission fees.

The railway offers a great way to travel the last 65 miles to the Grand Canyon in style. In 1901 the Grand Canyon Railroad Company originally built the short line railroad to haul copper ore from a promising mine at Anita, just 15 miles south of the rim. Although the mine played out by the time the rails arrived, the Santa Fe Railroad acquired the track to provide access to the canyon, which soon became a national destination for visitors.

You and your family should plan on checking in an hour before departure. Don't worry about keeping the kids out of mischief—the railroad hosts a Wild West show every day at 9:30 A.M. Along the way, the train is chased by train robbers on horseback, which should keep even toddlers entertained. The train arrives at the South Rim at 12:15 P.M., and visitors are given three hours to explore the majesty of the Grand Canyon before the train departs back to Williams at 3:30 P.M. Families can save some money on this trip by asking for the Family Getaway package, which includes round-trip train fare, lodgings in Williams at the historic Fray Marcos Hotel, and breakfast and dinner at Max & Thelma's Restaurant. A holiday favorite is the Polar Express train ride to the "North Pole," an "elf city" made up of lights, held on selected December evenings.

Amazing
Arizona Facts 🔍

Although Arizona's most famous moniker is the Grand Canyon State, it also goes by the Copper State (because it produces most of our nation's copper) and the Valentine State (because it became the last of the contiguous territories to gain statehood, on February 14, 1912).

Flagstaff holds the honor as the world's first "International Dark-Sky City" for preserving its dark skies for future generations of stargazers.

A Miner Family
Adventure

For a Christmas surprise I bundled up my seven-year-old twin boys and we headed north for a magical trip on the Polar Express train ride, hosted by the Grand Canyon Railway. When we finally arrived at the train depot, the boys engaged in a snowball fight. After picking up our tickets, we climbed aboard with other families, dressed in winter flannels, bulky coats, and bobbing red caps.

As we sped off to the "North Pole," elves served chocolate chip cookies the size of plates and "hot cocoa as thick and rich as melted chocolate bars," and a lady dressed in green read the story of *The Polar Express*, written and illustrated by Chris Van Allsburg.

Soon the city lights receded as the Polar Express carried us toward the North Pole. Hayden looked outside into the chilly dark and exclaimed that he could see wolves running through the forest. Thirty minutes out of the depot, the train arrived at the "North Pole." Children wiped the mist from the windows and stared at the bright lights of the elf city. Santa stood in his sleigh, which was harnessed to the most famous reindeer in history, and he waved merrily as the train slowed to pick him up.

As the train turned around and headed back to the depot, Santa walked down the aisle of each cozy car and handed out silver sleigh bells to the children. When Santa reached Hayden and Blake, the boys threw their arms around the jolly fellow and pressed their smiling faces against his red coat.

"I love you, Santa," Blake said, his eyes shining from the magic of it all.

Williams Ski Area (all ages)

Approximately 4 miles southwest of I–40 off South Fourth Street, Box 953, Williams; (928) 635–9330; www.williamsskiarea.com. Open Thursday through Monday from 9:30 A.M. to 4:30 P.M. mid-December through March, weather permitting. Adults and children $$$–$$$$.

This family-oriented winter play area features four groomed downhill ski runs including a beginner's slope. There is also a snowy hillside set aside for tubing fun. A log canyon lodge has a potbellied wood-burning stove to warm up next to and an indoor children's play area. The ski area offers ski and snowboard lessons for varying ages and skill levels. The lodge also provides inner tube, snowboard, and ski rentals.

Grand Canyon Caverns (all ages)

Twenty-five miles northwest of Seligman. Historic Route 66, mile marker 115, P.O. Box 180, Peach Springs; (928) 422–3223. Open daily except Christmas Day 9:00 A.M. to 5:45 P.M. summer hours and 10:00 A.M. to 4:45 P.M. winter hours. Adults $$$, children 5–12 $$, under 5 free.

A dinosaur posted out front like some prehistoric sentry quickly gets the attention of young children. Guided forty-five-minute tours, down ¾ mile of stairs, lead into the vast underground chambers. The caverns stay at fifty-six degrees year-round, so a sweater or light coat is a good idea for the young ones. Children especially love the crystals and marine fossils embedded in the cavern walls. You'll also come across a replica of a prehistoric ground sloth, which looks somewhat like a giant bear.

Planes of Fame Air Museum (ages 5 and up)

Located at the junction of State Route 64 and Highway 180, Valle; (928) 635–1000; www.planesoffame.org. Open daily except Christmas Day and Thanksgiving 9:00 A.M. to 6:00 P.M. in summer; 9:00 A.M. to 5:00 P.M. in winter. Adults $$, children ages 5–12 $, under 5 free. Bataan tours additional fee.

Historic aircraft, replicas, and aviation oddities are all featured in this quaint sister museum to the Planes of Fame Air Museum in Chino, California. Housed in a 31,000-square-foot hangar, the museum is home to everything from model airplanes to a World War I British fighter. You'll discover an exhibit detailing the history of aviation, open cockpit biplanes, and an early commercial airliner. Kids especially enjoy sitting in the real F86 cockpit simulator pilots once used to learn how to eject from a doomed plane. Outside you'll see jets and get the chance to board Gen. Douglas MacArthur's restored Lockheed Constellation C-121A named *Bataan*. And if you're in the area on the last weekend of May, stop by for the museum's High Country Warbirds Air Display, which features vintage plane flybys.

Where to Eat

Cruisers Café 66. 233 West Route 66, Williams; (928) 635–2445. Standard American cuisine including burgers, steaks, and pasta served with style in a renovated gas station, complete with Route 66 memorabilia. $

Miss Kitty's Steakhouse & Saloon. 642 East Route 66, Williams; (928) 635–9161. Families will enjoy the hearty dishes on the menu at this Western-style steakhouse. Live music and entertainment in the evenings on a seasonal basis. $$–$$$

Pancho McGillicuddy's Mexican Cantina. 141 Railroad Avenue, Williams; (928) 635–4150. Mexican cuisine and live entertainment on evenings and weekends. $–$$

Pine Country Restaurant. 107 North Grand Canyon Boulevard, Williams; (928) 635–9718. This local favorite, across from the Grand Canyon Railway Depot, serves up homemade pies and country cooking. $–$$

Rod's Steak House. 301 East Route 66, Williams; (928) 635–2671. A Western-style steak house serving steak, seafood, and sandwiches. Offers a children's menu for kids ten and under. $$–$$$

Where to Stay

The Canyon Motel. 1900 East Rodeo Road, Williams; (928) 635–9371 or (800) 482–3955. This 1948 remodeled motor lodge offers eighteen rooms in six flagstone cottages. But kids will especially love staying in the 1929 or 1934 historic cabooses or one of the three rail car suites. The motel is situated on ten acres, giving kids plenty of places to burn off a little steam. $$–$$$

Fray Marcos Hotel. 235 North Grand Canyon Boulevard, across from the Williams Depot, Williams; (928) 635–4010 or (800) 843–8724; www.thetrain.com. A modern hotel built in the same style as the 1908 depot. Children under sixteen stay **free.**

Mountainside Inn Gateway to the Grand Canyon. 642 East Route 66, Williams; (928) 635–4431 or (800)

462–9381. Heated outdoor pool, American food served at Miss Kitty's Steakhouse, and live dinner music. Children under sixteen stay **free.** $$–$$$

Quality Inn Mountain Ranch and Resort. 6701 East Mountain Ranch Road (6 miles east of town), Williams; (928) 635–2693 or (800) 228–5151; www.mountainranchresort.com. Restaurant, heated outdoor pool, horseback rides, and hayrides with cookouts. Children under twelve stay **free.** Closed from November to April. $$–$$$

For More Information

Kaibab National Forest. 800 South Sixth Street, Williams 86046; (928) 635–8200; www.fs.fed.us/r3/kai.

Williams–Grand Canyon Chamber of Commerce. 200 West Railroad Avenue, Williams 86046; (928) 635–4061 or (800) 863–0546; www.williamschamber.com. Stocks maps and brochures for Williams and the Grand Canyon.

Flagstaff

This mountain town, with a population of 64,000, possesses a small-town charm despite its size. It is home to Northern Arizona University, the world-renowned Museum of Northern Arizona, and a variety of other attractions, including a major observatory, three nearby national monuments, and several ski runs. Outdoor recreation is a favorite in this town, situated at 7,000 feet. Unlike some other areas of the state, Flagstaff enjoys four distinct seasons, which makes for year-round outdoor recreation opportunities. Phoenicians flock north to Flagstaff in the summer, where highs reach into the eighties, to enjoy the nearby meadows, canyons, and lakes. Boston colonists founded Flagstaff in hopes of farming the area but soon turned away in search of gentler climes. However, before they left they gave the rustic settlement the name Flagstaff, or "Flag," when they skinned the branches from a tall pine to raise the American flag on the nation's centennial in 1876.

Even though Flagstaff has been a trade and lumber town, today it mainly serves college students, hippies, and environmentalists. Like many of the state's mountain villages, Flagstaff's appeal to families is primarily that of outdoor recreation.

The Museum of Northern Arizona (all ages) 🖼️

3101 North Fort Valley Road, Flagstaff; (928) 774–5213; www.musnaz.org. Open daily 9:00 A.M. to 5:00 P.M. except Thanksgiving, Christmas, and New Year's Day. Adults $$, children ages 7–17 $, under 7 free.

Founded in 1928 by zoologist Dr. Harold S. Colton and artist Mary-Russell Ferrell Colton, the Museum of Northern Arizona continues to preserve the history and cultures of the Colorado Plateau. In addition to the regular exhibits, this world-renowned institution also offers a behind-the-scenes look at the museum's natural history and anthropology collections with special tours. The galleries feature geology, native plants and wildlife, and the art and culture of the Native Americans of the Colorado Plateau region, including the Hopi, Pai, Zuni, Navajo, and the prehistoric people of the region. Kids will especially enjoy the fossil exhibits, where they can ogle a life-size model of the carnivorous dinosaur Dilophosaurus.

Lowell Observatory (ages 5 and up) 🏛️

1400 West Mars Hill Road, Flagstaff; (928) 774–3358; www.lowell.edu. Daytime hours are noon to 5:00 P.M. daily November through March; 9:00 A.M. to 5:00 P.M. daily April through October. Nighttime hours begin at 7:30 P.M. Friday and Saturday November through March; 7:30 P.M. Wednesday, Friday, and Saturday in April, May, September, and October; 8:00 P.M. Monday through Saturday from June through August. Closed on Thanksgiving, Christmas Eve, Christmas Day, and New Year's Day. Adults and children 5–17 $, under 5 free. Separate admissions are charged for day and evening programs.

This observatory, founded in 1894 by Percival Lowell, takes amateur astronomers on a trip through space with lectures, slide shows, and a look at the stars through a telescope.

Amazing Arizona Facts

State motto: Ditat Deus (God Enriches)
State flower: saguaro blossom
State colors: blue and gold
State tree: palo verde
State gem: turquoise
State reptile: ridge-nosed rattlesnake
State fossil: petrified wood
State mammal: ring-tail cat
State neckwear: bolo tie

Although Lowell never found signs of intelligent life on Mars, another astronomer, Clyde Tombaugh, discovered Pluto from the observatory in 1930. The observatory features the 24-inch Clark refractor telescope that Lowell used more than one hundred years ago. Family activities abound at the facility, including an astronomy series and several workshops. Some family favorites include National Astronomy Day in April, Halloween Spooky Skies, the Annular Solar Eclipse, Holiday Skies Program, and the Winter Solstice.

During one of these special programs, the kids will learn about constellations and the Native American stories that go with them. For instance, the Hopi attribute the haphazard placement of the stars to Coyote's cosmic bungling. They say Coyote disobeyed and opened the lid to the jar in which the stars were stored. All of the stars rushed out, singeing his nose as they escaped into the sky. Coyote caught a few and hung them in their proper place, but he quickly grew impatient and let the others stay where they were. Some of the stars, not securely fastened in place, still occasionally fall back to Earth. This is why, the Hopi explain, there are only a few constellations, why there are shooting stars, and why the coyote's nose is black.

Downtown Flagstaff—Historic Railroad District (all ages) 🏛 🅰 🍴
Flagstaff Visitors Center, 1 East Route 66, Flagstaff; (928) 774–9541 or (800) 842–7293. Open daily 7:00 A.M. to 7:00 P.M. Free.

You can still see the trains whistling by on the tracks near the visitor bureau located in the 1926 Amtrak building. The historic downtown district has a distinct rustic charm and offers an array of shopping opportunities for young and old alike. Here you'll find mountain outfitters, bookstores, galleries, eclectic boutiques, eateries, coffeehouses, and even an ice cream shop. For more information about the district, stop at the visitor center for a tour map.

Amazing
Arizona Facts

Flagstaff almost became the country's motion-picture hub when Jesse Laskey and Cecil B. DeMille, intrigued by the area's forested countryside and dramatic scenery, decided to unloaded their movie company at the town's train depot. A sudden snowstorm quickly changed their minds and sent the duo packing for the warmer weather of the West Coast, where Hollywood was born.

Coconino County, of which Flagstaff is the county seat, is large enough to hold the states of Massachusetts, Rhode Island, and Connecticut with a few miles to spare.

The Arboretum at Flagstaff (all ages)

4001 South Woody Mountain Road (3⅘ miles south of Route 66), Flagstaff; (928) 774–1442; www.thearb.org. Open daily 9:00 A.M. to 5:00 P.M. from April 1 through December 15. Adults and children ages 6–12 $, under 6 free.

More than 700 species of plants and trees flourish in the protected 200 acres sitting at a lofty 7,150 feet. The kids will enjoy the interactive displays as you travel through a children's garden, wildflower meadow, herb garden, wetlands, display gardens, and greenhouse. After experiencing this diverse landscape, take a time-out and enjoy the scenery as you lunch at one of the arboretum's picnic tables. Call ahead for special programs and information on guided tours, which are offered daily at 11:00 A.M. and 1:00 P.M.

Jay Lively Activity Center (all ages)

1650 North Turquoise Drive, Flagstaff; (928) 774–1051. Public ice-skating sessions held from July through April 30. Hours vary for public skating sessions. Adults and children ages 5–17 $, under 5 free. Skate rental $1.

This indoor center offers public ice-skating sessions on an NHL-size rink. Other features include skating lessons, open hockey times, and a small pro shop. The ice gets pretty cold even in the warmer months, so make sure to bring a sweater, gloves, and a thermos of hot chocolate.

Bushmaster Park (all ages)

Alta Vista and Lockett Roads, Flagstaff Parks and Recreation, Flagstaff; (928) 779–7690; www.flagstaff.az.gov. Open daily. Free.

This community favorite features picnic tables, footpaths, playgrounds, basketball and tennis courts, and a BMX park. Within the park boundaries is Bark Park, a fenced-in area for furry friends to socialize with other canines and their owners.

High-Altitude Sports Training Complex at Northern Arizona University (all ages)

Northern Arizona University, Lumberjack Stadium, Building 34, Flagstaff; (928) 523–4444 or (800) 628–5038; www.nau.edu/hastc. Open 8:00 A.M. to 5:00 P.M. Monday through Friday. Free.

Children, especially those interested in professional sports, will enjoy watching professional and amateur athletes from all over the world train at this world-renowned high-altitude training camp. Since it opened in 1994, the center has hosted more than 4,000 athletes from nearly forty countries, including Japan, Germany, Australia, Italy, The Netherlands, and Brazil.

Curious as to why athletes want to train at Flagstaff's 7,000-foot altitude? Sports scientists have determined that by training at high altitudes, athletes' bodies will adjust by increasing the oxygen-carrying capacity of their blood, which they retain when returning to lower elevations. In the past, this proven method has led to record breakers, championships, and gold medals. That might motivate the kids for a footrace of their own when you get out into Flagstaff's open areas.

NFL's Arizona Cardinals **Training Camp**

From late July to mid-August, the Arizona Cardinals, the state's professional football team, holds its summer training camp on the campus of Northern Arizona University. Most practices are open to the public free of charge. An intrasquad scrimmage game, youth clinics, and autograph sessions are also held during camp. For practice times and field locations, call the Flagstaff Visitor Center at (800) 842–7293.

Pioneer Historical Museum (all ages) 🏛 🖼

Fort Valley Park Complex, 2340 North Fort Valley Road, Flagstaff; (928) 774–6272; www.infomagic.net/~ahsnad. Open 9:00 A.M. to 5:00 P.M. Monday through Saturday. Adults $, children under 12 free.

Housed in a 1908 building created from the area's surrounding volcanic rock, this museum once served as Coconino County's hospital for the poor. Some of the historical exhibits display items once used in the old hospital, including an old iron lung and a re-created doctor's office. Other displays feature artifacts from Flagstaff's pioneering past. The museum also hosts three annual events, including a Wool Festival in June, where the kids will learn all about wool production and sheep shearing; a Fourth of July Festival, where artisans dressed in historical costumes demonstrate early crafts such as blacksmithing, weaving, spinning, quilting, and candlemaking; and Playthings of the Past, held November through January, featuring historical children's toys and games.

Riordan Mansion State Historic Park (ages 5 and up) 🏛 🚫

409 Riordan Road, Flagstaff; (928) 779–4395; www.pr.state.az.us/Parks/parkhtml/riordan.html. Open daily 8:30 A.M. to 5:00 P.M. May through October and 10:30 A.M. to 5:00 P.M. November through April. Adults $$, children ages 7–13 $, under 7 free.

Built for the Riordan brothers in 1904, this 13,300-square-foot, forty-room log-and-stone mansion was designed by renowned architect Charles Whittlesey. A wonderful example of the Arts and Crafts style, it houses one of the largest collections of Stickley furniture in the country. In the mid-1880s Timothy and Michael Riordan took control of the Arizona Lumber and Timber Company, becoming northern Arizona's most successful lumber barons. Guided tours begin every hour on the hour from 9:00 A.M. to 4:00 P.M. In December the mansion takes on a festive appearance with Christmas decorations from the early 1900s. Because the tours are an hour long, younger children might have difficulty staying interested, and due to limited space, reservations are strongly encouraged.

Heritage Square (all ages) 🪑

On Aspen Avenue between Leroux and San Francisco Streets, Flagstaff; (928) 779–7685; www.heritagesquaretrust.org. Open daily year-round. Free.

This community plaza in downtown Flagstaff offers music, movies, and events in the large square and outdoor amphitheater. Kids can walk down a winding redbrick path that details the history, biology, geology, and anthropology of Flagstaff. For another fun history lesson, check out the flagpole base that reconstructs the geological strata of the Grand Canyon with actual rocks taken from the depths of Arizona's greatest gorge. Some of the regularly featured events at Heritage Square include Friday's Movies on the Square, First Friday Art Walk!, Flagstaff Live's Thursdays on the Square, Heritage Square Trust's Music and Dance Series, Heritage Square Trust's Educational Series, and the Jumpin' Jubilee Bounce House. There is even a relaxed picnic area for families looking to sit back and unwind.

Arizona Snowbowl (ages 4 and up) ⛷️

Seven miles north on Snowbowl Road off Highway 180, P.O. Box 40, Flagstaff 86002; (928) 779–1951; www.arizonasnowbowl.com. Snow report, (928) 779–4577. Adults and children ages 8–12 $$$$, under 8 free.

With more than thirty slopes and an average snowfall of 260 inches a year, this alpine region hosts the majority of Arizona skiers. The slopes feature 2,300 feet of vertical drop on thirty-two different trails. Snowbowl offers a children's ski school for different ages. Ski-wee, for ages four to seven, and the Ridgerunner program, geared for ages eight to twelve, range in price from $48 to $65 for half- and full-day sessions. Both school sessions include equipment rental. As an added bonus, parents get a few free minutes to run Snowbowl's more challenging slopes. In addition to downhill skiing, the **Flagstaff Nordic Center** offers more than 25 miles of cross-country trails through the Coconino National Forest. Keep in mind that because of Flagstaff's high altitude, sunburns can happen much faster than at lower elevations. If you forget your sunscreen, check out the facility's sport shop.

Agassiz Skyride (all ages)

Arizona Snowbowl. Open daily 10:00 A.M. to 4:00 P.M. from Memorial Day through Labor Day, 10:00 A.M. to 4:00 P.M. Friday, Saturday, and Sunday in the fall through mid-October. Adults and children ages 8–12 $$, under 8 free.

Just because it's summer doesn't mean you shouldn't consider spending the morning at a ski resort. The chairlifts, at San Francisco Peaks overlooking Flagstaff, will take you and your family on a twenty-five-minute ride, which will take you from 9,500 feet to an 11,600-foot prominence on Mt. Humphreys, whose 12,633-foot summit marks the highest point in the state. The slumbering remains of a massive volcano, Mt. Humphreys features slopes that harbor thick pine, fir, and spruce forests plus delicate alpine vegetation and several unique plant species that survive above the timberline. Best of all, the panoramic views reach as far as 70 miles, and if it's a clear day and you look carefully, you'll even be able to see the North Rim of the Grand Canyon.

Hart Prairie Preserve (all ages) 🍁

Northern Arizona Office of the Nature Conservancy, 2601 North Fort Valley Road, Flagstaff; (928) 774–8892. Nature walks are held at 10:00 A.M. Wednesday and Sunday mid-June through mid-October. Walkers meet in the Grand Canyon Trust Building in Suite 1. Free.

Explore aspen groves and mountain meadows while walking the paths of the 245-acre Hart Prairie Preserve, 14 miles north of Flagstaff near the San Francisco Peaks. During these ninety-minute, guided nature walks, visitors learn about the wildlife, botany, and forest ecology in this globally rare wetland. The preserve, at an elevation of 8,600 feet, protects many species of rare and threatened plants such as the delicate bloomer stock and the globally rare Bebb's willow trees. While visiting the preserve, check out the original homestead, which dates from 1877. You can also rent one of the historic cabins at the preserve; call (928) 607–1167.

Elden Pueblo Archaeological Project (all ages) 🏛

Coconino National Forest, 1½ miles north of the Flagstaff Mall off Highway 89, P.O. Box 3496, Flagstaff 86003; (928) 526–0866; www.fs.fed.us/r3/coconino/volcanic/elden_special.html. Open daily. Free.

This Sinagua Indian ruin, dating from A.D. 1150, is still being excavated by archaeologists. Accessible via the self-guided tour of the pueblo, redware and brownware pottery, shells, and jewelry are just a few of the artifacts you can see that have been discovered at the site. A couple of weekends a year the forest service opens up the ruin to give families an opportunity for kids to do what they like best—digging in the dirt. Call ahead for times and reservations.

On the **Lookout**

A wildlife-viewing guide put out by the Arizona Game and Fish Department will lead you to ninety of Arizona's premier wildlife-viewing areas over five geographic regions, including the Canyonlands, Sky Island Mountains, Central Mountain Region, Rivers and Deserts Region, and White Mountains. Travel to the Canyonlands Region north of Flagstaff to the Raymond Buffalo Ranch, where eighty-five bison roam, or head south of Tucson to the Sky Island Mountain Region, where the Buenos Aires National Wildlife Refuge, established to recover the endangered masked bobwhite quail, offers eye-catching views of mule deer, pronghorn antelope, and neo-tropical migrant songbirds.

The *Arizona Wildlife Viewing Guide* by John N. Carr is available at local bookstores or from the Arizona Game and Fish Department, 2221 West Greenway Road, Phoenix 85023-4399; (602) 942–3000.

Walnut Canyon National Monument (ages 5 and up) 🏃 🏛

3 Walnut Canyon Road (7½ miles east of Flagstaff on I–40), Flagstaff; (928) 526–3367; www.nps.gov/waca. Visitor center open daily 8:00 A.M. to 6:00 P.M. June through August, 9:00 A.M. to 5:00 P.M. December through February (except Christmas Day), 8:00 A.M. to 5:00 P.M. March through May and September through November. Trails close an hour before the visitor center. Adults $$, children under 16 **free.**

A steep staircase leads hikers down on a self-guided tour into Walnut Canyon, where you can peek into single-story cliff dwellings once occupied by the prehistoric Sinagua Indians more than 900 years ago. Interpretive displays add to the experience, and a small museum in the visitor center shows children how these ancient people lived. Although the Island Trail has handrails and concrete steps, climbing 185 feet in a mile tuckers out even the most agile. Benches along the way give you a chance to rest, but make sure to carry water for the trip, especially during the summer. Rangers also lead a two-hour hike (Tuesday and Sunday from June to August), for ages nine and up, to the first ranger cabin built in the area. Call ahead for times and reservations. Remember that your receipt is good for admission for seven days from the time of purchase.

Wupatki National Monument (all ages) 🏃 🍽 🏛

Thirty-nine miles north of Flagstaff on Highway 89, and then 14 miles on Forest Service Road 545 at the Wupatki exit; H.C. 33 Box 444A, Flagstaff 86004; (928) 679–2365; www.nps.gov/wupa. Visitor center open daily 8:00 A.M. to 6:00 P.M. June through August, 9:00 A.M. to 5:00 P.M. December through February, 8:00 A.M. to 5:00 P.M. March through May and September through November. Closed Christmas Day. Extended hours in the summer. Adults $$ for seven days, children under 17 **free.**

A visitor center complete with a small museum orients you to Wupatki ("tall house" in Hopi), the best-preserved cliff dwelling in the area. Eight hundred years ago, ancestors of the Hopi farmed on this volcanic plateau. A ½-mile walk will take you and the kids to the prehistoric Indian ruin, where you will see the impressive three-story cliff dwelling that houses nearly one hundred rooms. Most visitors spend only a couple of hours here, and a

Hiking **Arizona**

As soon as the snow melts, hikers of all ages lace up their boots and ascend the many mountain trails in the area. In the summer, the U.S. Forest Service (Coconino National Forest Supervisor's Office, 2323 East Greenlaw Lane, Flagstaff; 928–527–3600; www.fs.fed.us/r3/coconino) offers maps on nearby hiking trails in the Coconino National Forest, which is the world's largest contiguous ponderosa pine forest. While exploring this natural wonderland, which ranges in elevation from 2,600 to 12,633 feet, keep an eye out for such wildlife as the American bald eagle and the black bear as well as plants ranging from desert cactus to alpine tundra groundsel.

few picnic tables, back at the center, make a good place for lunch before continuing on to Sunset Crater National Monument. Admission fees include both national monuments, and the 35-mile loop road reconnects with Highway 89 after Sunset Crater.

Sunset Crater Volcano National Monument (all ages) 👫

Fifteen miles north of Flagstaff on Highway 89, and then 2 miles on Forest Service Road 545 at the Sunset Crater exit; Route 3 Box 149, Flagstaff 86004; (928) 526–0502; www.nps.gov/sucr. Visitor center open daily 8:00 A.M. to 6:00 P.M. June through August, 9:00 A.M. to 5:00 P.M. December through February, 8:00 A.M. to 5:00 P.M. March through May and September through November. Closed Christmas Day. Extended hours in the summer. Adults $$ for seven days, children under 17 free.

It is almost certain that the Native Americans living at Wupatki in A.D. 1064–1065 witnessed the eruption of Sunset Crater Volcano. The remaining cinder cone, which today rises 1,000 feet above the surrounding landscape, was named by the famous explorer John Wesley Powell for the red-orange cinders around the rim.

Around it, odd-looking lava formations with names like squeeze-ups and hornitos create a jagged, surreal landscape covering 120 miles of countryside. Children get up close to these formations on the self-guided, 1-mile Lava Flow Trail. Older kids might enjoy the more difficult 1-mile trip up a cinder cone on the Lenox Crater Trail. Call ahead for information on the summer programs, which are held from June through August.

Where to Eat

Black Bart's Steakhouse Saloon and Old West Theater. 2760 East Butler Avenue, Flagstaff; (928) 779–3142 or (800) 574–4718. Serves steak, seafood, and chicken. Children's menu. $$$

Brandy's Restaurant & Bakery. 1500 East Cedar Avenue #40, Flagstaff; (928) 779–2187. A European bakery serving award-winning breakfasts, lunch, and dessert. $

Bun Huggers East. 3012 East Route 66, Flagstaff; (928) 526–0542. Locals flock to this grill to partake of the mesquite-grilled burgers, hot dogs, and sandwiches. $

Buster's Restaurant & Bar. 1800 South Milton Road, Flagstaff; (928) 774–5155. A steak and seafood restaurant rated the

"Best Flagstaff Restaurant" by the *Arizona Daily News Sun*. $$

The Crown Restaurant and Railroad Café West. 2700 South Woodlands Village Boulevard #620 (in the Wal-Mart shopping center), Flagstaff; (928) 774–6775. Dishes up hearty American home-cooked favorites. Highlights include a children's menu and the largest electric train display in northern Arizona. $

Galaxy Diner. 931 West Route 66, Flagstaff; (928) 774–2466. This nostalgic 1950s-style diner serves old-fashioned American entrees. $

Mamma Luisa Italian Restaurant. Kachina Square, 2710 North Steves Boulevard, Flagstaff; (928) 526–6809. Italian specialties in a family dining environment. Open for dinner only. $$

Roma Pizza. 1800 South Milton Road #500, Flagstaff; (928) 779–4425. Hand-tossed specialty pizzas and Italian dinners. $–$$

Where to Stay

Econolodge. 914 South Milton Road, Flagstaff; (928) 774–7326. Complimentary continental breakfast. $$

Fairfield Inn by Marriott. 2005 South Milton Road, Flagstaff; (928) 773–1300 or (800) 574–6395. Complimentary continental breakfast, heated outdoor pool, and spa. $$$–$$$$

Inn Suites Hotel. 1008 East Route 66, Flagstaff; (928) 774–7356 or (800) 898–9124. Children under sixteen stay free. Complimentary continental breakfast. $$

Radisson Woodlands Hotel. 1175 West Route 66, Flagstaff; (928) 773–8888 or (800) 333–3333. Two restaurants, heated outdoor pool, and exercise room. Children under seventeen stay free. $$$$

Ski Lift Lodge. 6355 Highway 180 and Snowbowl Road, Flagstaff; (928) 774–0729 or (800) 472–3599; arizonasnowbowl. com/skiliftlodge.htm. Twenty-five single-room cabin units with front porches and gas fireplaces. Also operates a full-service restaurant serving homemade meals. $$$

Sled Dog Inn. 10155 Mountainaire Road, Flagstaff; (928) 525–6212 or (800) 754–0664; www.sleddoginn.com. Cozy rooms, common areas, and visits with sled dogs. $$

Weatherford Hotel. 23 North Leroux Street, Flagstaff; (928) 779–1919; www.weatherfordhotel.com. Established in 1897, this historic downtown landmark has had such famous guests as lawman Wyatt Earp, President Theodore Roosevelt, and Western author Zane Grey. $$

Area Campgrounds

Fort Tuthill Coconino County Park. Three miles south of Flagstaff, exit 337 off I–17; (928) 774–3464. Fifteen RV spaces with hookups and ninety tent sites. Open May 1 through September 30. $

Montezuma Lodge at Mormon Lake. Twenty-five miles southeast of Flagstaff, H.C. 31, Box 342, Mormon Lake 86038; (928) 354–2220; www.arizonamountain resort.com. This rustic retreat in the Coconino National Forest rents cabins with full kitchens. Children under fifteen stay free. $$$$

Woody Mountain Campground and RV Park. 2727 West Route 66, Flagstaff; (928) 774–7727 or (800) 732–7986. Forty tent sites and 106 RV spaces with hookups. Open March 15 through November 1. $

For More Information

Flagstaff Visitor Center. 1 East Route 66, Flagstaff 86001; (928) 779–7611 or (800) 842–7293.

The Flagstaff Convention and Visitor Bureau. 211 West Aspen Drive, Flagstaff 86001; (928) 779–7611 or (800) 217–2367; www.flagstaffarizona.org.

Annual Events

FEBRUARY

Winterfest. Flagstaff; (928) 774–4505 or (800) 842–7293. Entire month of February.

More than one hundred winter events, including a parade, sled-dog races, ski competitions, sleigh rides, broom ball, snowmobile drag racing, ice skating, winter stargazing, and snow sculpture. Winterfest is recognized as one of the top 200 winter events in North America.

MAY

Rendezvous Days. Williams; (928) 635–4061. Memorial Day weekend. A reenactment of the springtime mountain men gathering complete with a black-powder shoot, parade, carnival, live music, and street dances.

Route 66 Fun Run. Seligman/Topock; (928) 753–5001. Early May. A celebration of Arizona's claim to this nostalgic stretch of highway with a road rally.

JUNE

Chili Cook-off. Flagstaff; (928) 526–4314. Third weekend in June. An all-day event, which doubles as a qualifying event for the World Championship Chili Cook-off.

Pine Country Pro Rodeo. Flagstaff; (800) 842–7293. Third weekend in June. Top rodeo contenders compete in this favorite Southwestern sport of cowboys held at the Coconino County Fairgrounds.

Flagstaff Heritage Days. Flagstaff; (928) 774–9541 or (800) 842–7293. Fourth week of June. Twelve days of events including Route 66 Festival, Arizona Dream Cruise, and Route 66 Car Rally.

JULY

Small Town Celebration and Fireworks Spectacular. Williams; (928) 635–4061. July 4th. An old-fashioned parade, live entertainment, and a fireworks display against the backdrop of Bill Williams Mountain.

Old-Fashioned Fourth. Fredonia; (928) 643–7241. July 4th. This day-long event starts off with a pancake breakfast and a parade. Other activities include a patriotic program, a softball tournament, horseshoe competition, a Western outdoor dance, and fireworks at dusk.

Flagstaff's Fabulous 4th Festivities. Flagstaff; (928) 774–9541 or (800) 842–7293. July 4th. An old-fashioned Fourth with a parade, live entertainment, and fireworks.

The Arizona Highland Celtic Festival. Flagstaff; (928) 774–9541 or (800) 842–7293. Second weekend in July. A Celtic celebration honoring the people of Brittany, Cornwall, Ireland, Isle of Man, Scotland, and Wales.

AUGUST

Summerfest. Flagstaff; (480) 968–5353 or (800) ART–FEST. First weekend in August. Juried artwork, live entertainment, and arts and craft activities for children at Coconino County Fairgrounds.

Zuni Marketplace. Flagstaff; (928) 774–5213. Last weekend in August. Dance performances, Zuni art, pottery demonstrations, a native plants nature trail, and children's activities at the Museum of Northern Arizona.

SEPTEMBER

Labor Day PRCA Rodeo. Williams; (928) 635–4061. Labor Day weekend. A traditional professional rodeo, Western celebration, parade, and barn dances.

Coconino County Fair. Flagstaff; (928) 774–5130. Labor Day weekend. Northern Arizona's largest county fair, featuring exhibits, livestock, entertainment, a demolition derby, and carnival at the Fort Tuthill Coconino County Fairgrounds.

Flagstaff Festival of Science. Flagstaff; (800) 842–7293. End of September. A ten-day family-oriented event promoting science awareness. Activities include hands-on exhibits, interactive displays, field trips, and scientific lectures.

Grand Canyon Chamber Music Festival. Grand Canyon; (928) 638–9215; www. grandcanyonmusicfest.org. Select dates throughout September. This monthlong tribute to chamber music is held in the Shrine of Ages auditorium at the South Rim.

NOVEMBER

Mountain Village Holiday. Williams; (928) 635–4061. Thanksgiving through New Year's Day. More than a million Christmas lights, holiday activities, arts and crafts, and a parade of lights on the second Saturday of December.

Annual Holiday Lights Festival. Flagstaff; (928) 779–7979 or (800) 435–2493. Saturday after Thanksgiving through New Year's Day. Light displays, tree-lighting ceremony, parade, live entertainment, and appearances by Santa.

Other Things to **See and Do**

- **Air Grand Canyon,** Grand Canyon; (928) 638–2686 or (800) 247–4726.
- **AirStar Airlines,** Grand Canyon; (928) 638–2606 or (800) 962–3869.
- **Flintstones Bedrock City,** Valle; (928) 635–2600.
- **The Flying Heart Barn,** Flagstaff; (928) 526–2788.
- **Fred Harvey Transportation Co.,** Grand Canyon; (928) 638–2401.
- **Grand Canyon Field Institute,** Grand Canyon; (928) 638–2485.
- **Grand Canyon Helicopters,** Grand Canyon; (928) 638–2412 or (800) 541–4537.
- **Grand Canyon Jeep Tours,** Grand Canyon; (928) 638–5337 or (800) 320–5337.
- **Hitchin' Post Stables,** Flagstaff; (928) 774–1719.
- **MacDonalds Ranch Trail Rides,** Flagstaff; (928) 774–4481.
- **Mormon Lake Ski Center,** Flagstaff; (928) 354–2240.
- **Nava-Hopi Tours,** Flagstaff; (928) 774–5003 or (800) 892–8687.
- **Thorpe Park,** Flagstaff; (928) 779–7690.
- **Windrock Airlines,** Grand Canyon; (800) 24–ROCKY.
- **Woods Canyon Lake,** Flagstaff; (877) 444–6777.

Central Strip

I n Arizona's central region, located between Flagstaff and metro Phoenix, you'll find ancient ruins, a historic military fort, a mining town turned arts colony, the historical capital of Arizona Territory, and the agricultural plains of the fertile Verde Valley. Because of its diversity and easy access, this area receives a good portion of Arizona's adventurers. While heading south from Flagstaff, you'll first encounter the sweeping red vistas of Arizona's Red Rock Country. The surreal landscape of jutting pinnacles and rough-cut monoliths was created millions of years ago when geological forces uplifted the area, leaving Oak Creek to carve into the soft, sandstone shelves. The intense contrasts of reddish-pink rock formations, deep green forests, and startlingly blue skies make Sedona one of the most beautiful locations in the state. Children will enjoy playing in Oak Creek, ambling around in Sedona's canyons, or taking one of the many offered tours.

Carrie's
Top Picks for fun in the Central Strip

1. Slide Rock State Park, Oak Creek

2. Red Rock State Park Nature Center, Sedona

3. Jerome State Historic Park, Jerome

4. Verde Canyon Railroad, Clarkdale

5. Tuzigoot National Monument, Clarkdale

6. Montezuma Castle National Monument, Camp Verde

7. The Sharlot Hall Museum, Prescott

8. Desert Caballeros Western Museum, Wickenburg

9. Hassayampa River Preserve, Wickenburg

10. Vulture Mine, Wickenburg

CENTRAL STRIP

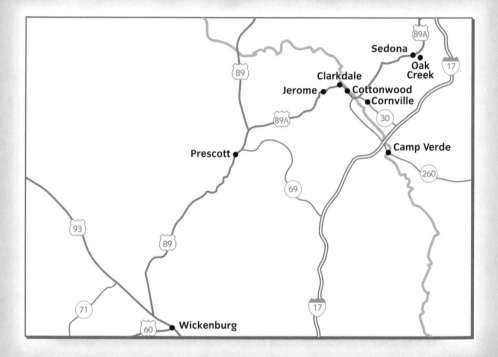

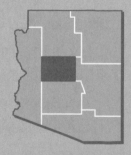

Farther south, you'll come to the Verde Valley and its outlying communities. Here you'll find more activities for the family to enjoy, including a trip to Historic Fort Verde, Montezuma's Castle, and the Verde Canyon Railroad. Things are more relaxed in the Verde Valley. Even though Jerome—a ghost town turned arts colony—isn't as highbrow as Sedona, it's still not a fabulous choice for kids. However, if shopping is on your mind, there's enough here to keep them entertained long enough for you to hit a few galleries. Your best bet is to get them homemade ice-cream cones and send them down to the common area to shoot hoops.

A little farther west and you'll come to the mountain country at Prescott—the first capital of Arizona before it was relocated. Unlike most of the state's lumber and mining towns, Prescott grew under a master plan, which is reflected in its Victorian architecture and structured street design. The stylish historic districts, towering pine trees, and old-fashioned charm make Prescott a great place to stop and learn some history before heading out to play in the forested mountains. For a more Western flavor, head down to Wickenburg, where the discovery of the Vulture Gold Mine eventually led to the development of nearby Phoenix. Cowboy cookouts, horseback riding, and cattle drives are featured activities in this Western town, which bills itself as the Dude Ranch Capital of the World. Just be prepared for action-packed adventure while visiting the Central Strip. You won't be sitting in a room watching John Wayne reruns—you'll be giving him a run for his money.

Sedona

Towering spires, dramatic pinnacles, and weather-worn canyon walls create the picturesque beauty of Arizona's Red Rock Country. Although prehistoric Native Americans raised corn, beans, and squash on the banks of nearby Oak Creek, it wasn't until the late 1800s that white settlers began farming and ranching in this remote region. In 1902 T. C. Schnebly petitioned for a post office and named it after his wife, Sedona, making this city one of the few Arizona towns named after a lady. Since its humble beginnings, Sedona has flourished into a renowned art colony, spiritual retreat, and popular resort town.

The dramatic landscape, carved by Oak Creek, attracts outdoor enthusiasts and art lovers alike. The town of Sedona sprawls out around the juncture of Highways 89A and 179 and is home to more than 16,500 people. Zane Grey first brought attention to Sedona's legendary beauty with his novel *Call of the Canyon,* which was then brought to the silver screen. Since then, artists of all mediums have flocked to Sedona to experience its magical allure. Although you might not want to take younger children shopping at Sedona's many upscale galleries and boutiques, a plethora of outdoor activities in the surrounding countryside await even the most rambunctious child. Hiking trails, hatchery fishing, and swimming in Oak Creek Canyon top the list of family favorites in the area. For more photo ops take the drive up Schnebly Hill Road or an airborne adventure in a helicopter or a biplane. Best of all, Sedona offers four mild seasons and plenty of options for a relaxing family weekend.

Fun Fall **Color**

Because varied autumnal weather makes fall color difficult to forecast, the U.S. Department of Agriculture's Forest Service offers an automated fall color hotline with weekly updates on peak color in different regions of the country, from September through November. Call (800) 354–4595 or visit www.fs.fed. us/news/fallcolors.

Sedona Supervue Theater (all ages)

Prime Outlet Stores on Highway 179, Oak Creek; (928) 284–3214; www.supervue.com. Showing daily every hour from 10:00 A.M. to 6:00 P.M. Adults and children ages 3–11 $$, under 2 free.

This is a great place to start your trip in the Sedona area. The thirty-three-minute motion picture *Sedona: The Spirit of Wonder* takes you on a journey of Sedona's mystical Red Rock Country. The film, shown on a spectacular big screen, includes aerial sights from a helicopter and a hot-air balloon as well as views taken from a train, a jeep, and on horseback. Additional footage takes viewers back in time with information on Sedona's Native American and pioneering history and even further back to the area's geologic formation. Afterward a quick stop at the Arizona Visitor Information Center will give you a great chance to stock up on tour maps, hiking-trail information, and other outdoor recreation opportunities.

Sedona Heritage Museum (all ages)

735 Jordan Road, P.O. Box 10216, Sedona 86339; (928) 282–7038. Open daily 11:00 A.M. to 3:00 P.M. except all major holidays. Adults $, children ages 12 and under free.

Housed in the apple-packing shed and family home of the 1930 Jordan farmstead, the Sedona Heritage Museum takes visitors on a nostalgic trip to the past with displays on pioneering life. The homestead was once the biggest business in the area and supplied fresh fruit and produce to the boomtown of Jerome and the nearby Verde Valley. Today a few apple trees still stand in the orchard, and kids will enjoy checking out the vintage apple-sorting machine and other apple-picking equipment in the red rock packing shed. Inside the house you'll see displays on Sedona's movie-making history from the 1940s and '50s, a hundred years of Forest Service memorabilia, an exhibit on cowboys and cattle ranching, and photos of the town's namesake, Sedona Schnebly. The homestead's four and a half acres offer a great place for kids to run, and the picnic tables provide a perfect place for lunch before heading off to your next destination.

Amazing **Arizona Architecture**

You don't have to be religious to enjoy a quick visit to the *Chapel of the Holy Cross*, built by architect Marguerite Brunwige Staude in 1956. Marguerite studied under famed architect Frank Lloyd Wright and incorporated many of Wright's naturalistic ideals in this modern landmark. You can see it just off Highway 179, where it rises majestically between two russet peaks. The chapel is at 780 Chapel Road, and admission is free. For more information call (928) 282–4069.

Tlaquepaque Arts and Crafts Village (ages 8 and up) 🍴🔒
336 Highway 179, P.O. Box 1868, Sedona 86399; (928) 282–4838; www.tlaquepaque.net. Open daily 10:00 A.M. to 5:00 P.M. Free.

Modeled after a suburb of Guadalajara, Mexico, Tlaquepaque's charming courtyards, shops, galleries, and restaurants bring a Spanish-Colonial style to Sedona's rustic landscape. You will find artifacts nestled in little niches, hand-painted tiles, and an abundance of flowers and greenery while walking the romantic streets between the shops. Here you can find the **How Sweet It Is** (928–282–5455), which offers sugary sweets and fine chocolates. **Esteban's** (928–282–4686) showcases functional and decorative art by area artists. Kids will especially love the **Storyteller** (928–282–2144), which is brimming with Southwestern books, music, and videos. Tlaquepaque, pronounced "T-lockey-pockey," also hosts the annual Festival of Lights, held on the second Saturday in December. This holiday celebration involves the lighting of 6,000 luminarias, music, entertainment, and holiday-themed activities for children of all ages.

Pink Jeep Tours (all ages)
204 North Highway 89A, Sedona; (928) 282–5000 or (800) 873–3662; www.pinkjeep.com. Open daily 7:00 A.M. to 6:00 P.M. except Christmas Day. Adults $$$$, under 12, 20 percent discount.

Pink Jeep Tours has been operating in the area for more than forty years and has five distinct narrated off-road adventures through Red Rock Country. Broken Arrow, the original jeep tour in the United States, offers two hours of some of the best scenery in the Southwest. Ancient Ruin Tour features 700-year-old Native American ruins; the Scenic Rim Tour travels up 200 feet to the Mogollon Rim; Canyon West Tour highlights some of Sedona's most famous landmarks; and the Rock Art Expedition takes you to one of the best Native American rock-art sites in Arizona.

Sedona Red Rock Jeep Tours (all ages)
270 North Highway 89A, Sedona; (928) 282–6826 or (800) 848–7728; www.redrockjeep.com. Open daily 7:30 A.M. to 5:30 P.M. with extended hours in the summer. Adults $$$$, under 11, 25 percent off.

Although this touring company offers several different packages, the family favorite is the Soldier Pass Trail—an exclusive four-wheel-drive adventure on the historic trail once traveled by General Crook. This trail also passes the legendary Devil's Kitchen, a giant sinkhole that rumbles each time a chunk of rock peels off to fall 600 feet to the bottom of the immense pit. Other tours include Canyons and Cowboys, a relaxing trip to Dry Creek Basin and its seven surrounding canyons, and Old Bear Wallow, which follows an old stagecoach route up Schnebly Hill Road.

Sedona Red Rock Jeep Tours also offers a three-hour jeep-horseback combo for ages six and up ($$$$). You and the kids travel in style in one of the company's jeeps past Cathedral Rock to the stables and then will spend two hours on horseback, riding through the breathtaking beauty of Coconino National Forest before returning to the headquarters in Sedona.

Red Rock Biplane Tours (ages 6 and up)

1225 Airport Road, Sedona; (928) 204–5939 or (888) TOO–RIDE; www.sedonaairtours.com. Open daily 8:00 A.M. to 5:00 P.M. Adults $$$$, ages 6–12, 15 percent discount.

Although it may seem a bit pricey, the airborne thrill of exploring this region from the open cockpit of a Waco biplane makes it all worthwhile. The pilot takes the controls in the back and two passengers sit in the front cockpit for the tours, which range from ten to forty-five minutes. Cameras record your own personal tour as a keepsake of your aerial adventure as you pass by Native American cliff dwellings, the Chapel of the Holy Cross, the sweeping Verde Valley, the ghost town of Jerome, Mund's Canyon, Red Rock Crossing, the Devil's Kitchen, and such famous rock formations as Bell Rock, the Three Nuns, the Fin, Submarine Rock, and Cathedral Rock.

Great Ventures Charter Tours (ages 6 and up)

95 Hohokam Drive, Sedona; (928) 282-4451 or (800) 578-2643; www.greatventures.net. Open daily year-round. Adults and children ages 6 to 12 $$$$.

Every Tuesday this charter operator offers a "Trail Ride to the Stars." The action-packed

Take a Walk **on the Wild Side**

Hiking trails around Sedona attract all levels and all ages of outdoor enthusiasts. The Sedona Ranger District (250 Brewer Road, Sedona; 928–282–4119) provides a free brochure and map of maintained hiking trails in the Sedona and Oak Creek areas. Several of them—Allens Bend, Boynton Canyon, Fay Canyon, Long Canyon, and Vultee Arch—are especially suited to children and provide wonderful opportunities for wildlife watching, plenty of fresh air, and stupendous scenic vistas.

evening adventure begins with a two-hour sunset trail ride, which returns to the ranch in time for a hearty, all-you-can-eat, western-style cookout. Dinner is followed by ninety minutes of stargazing with renowned astronomer Dennis Young. Young treats guests to telescope views of the clear night sky and its many treasures, including galaxies, star clusters, planets, and other celestial objects.

The tour company also offers trips to the Grand Canyon, Colorado River rafting expeditions, and trips to the Verde Valley.

Slide Rock State Park (all ages) 🌊 🧍 🏕

6871 North Highway 89A (7 miles north of Sedona), Oak Creek; (928) 282–3034; www.pr.state.az.us/Parks/parkhtml/sliderock.html. Open daily 8:00 A.M. to 5:00 P.M. in the winter, 8:00 A.M. to 6:00 P.M. in the spring and fall, and 8:00 A.M. to 7:00 P.M. in the summer. $$ per vehicle (maximum four adults), $ each additional adult, under 13 free.

A natural 30-foot water slide leads the attractions found at this forty-three-acre recreation hot spot. In addition to swimming in Oak Creek, the park also offers great hiking trails, picnic spots, and a historic apple orchard. Even though the park gets jam-packed in summer, it still attracts a diverse set of birds, which you can keep track of on the area checklist available at the park office. One note of caution: Because of the slide's popularity, bacteria levels occasionally rise to a point where the swimming area closes to visitors. To check on the water quality, call the park's Phoenix hotline at (602) 542–0202 or check for posted warnings at the park.

Red Rock **Pass**

The Red Rock Pass, which has daily ($), weekly ($$$), or annual ($$$) admission, admits cars to U.S. Forest Service land in Red Rock Country, including Banjo Bill Picnic Area, Call of the Canyon, Grasshopper Point, Honanki and Palatki Indian Ruins, and Red Rock Crossing. The pass also admits hikers to the Forest Service trails in the Red Rock preservation areas. Passes can be purchased at several locations, such as the Sedona–Oak Creek Canyon Chamber of Commerce, the West Gateway Visitor Information Center at the Sedona Cultural Park, the South Gateway Visitor Information Center in the village of Oak Creek at Tequa Festival Market Place, and the North Gateway Visitor Information Center at Oak Creek Vista. For more information on the pass or to purchase online, check out www.redrockcountry.org.

Honanki and Palatki Ruins (ages 5 and up) 🏛

Twelve miles northwest of Sedona on Forest Service Road 795 in Red Canyon, Sedona; (928) 282–3854. Open daily 9:30 A.M. to 4:00 P.M. Admission is $$ per car or free with a Red Rock Pass. Reservations required.

These two ruins, built more than 700 years ago, are the largest prehistoric structures in the Red Rocks region. Palatki, which means "red house" in the Hopi language, has two pueblos that once housed between thirty and fifty people. Honanki, or "bear house," once had sixty rooms and was built during the same time—between A.D. 1100 and 1300. Although prehistoric Sinagua pictographs have been discovered in the area, older rock art dating back nearly 8,000 years can also be seen. The loop road passes by both ruins, and a visitor center at Palatki offers additional information on the sites.

Rainbow Trout Farm (all ages) 🎣🍴

3500 North Highway 89A (3 miles north of Sedona), Oak Creek; (928) 282–5799. Open daily 9:00 A.M. to 6:00 P.M. from Memorial Day to Labor Day and 9:00 A.M. to 5:00 P.M. in the off-season except Thanksgiving, Christmas, and New Year's Day. $$.

Admission includes a five-gallon storage bucket, bait, and a pole. However, those who want to bring their own poles are welcome to do so. This isn't a catch-and-release site, so you catch it, you keep it. The nice thing is you can pretty much guarantee your children won't get skunked in these two ponds. The average size of the trout you'll pull from these waters is about 11 to 13 inches, and the farm charges between $ and $$ per fish depending on its size. Best of all, for an extra 50 cents a fish, the guys on duty will gut and gill

Amazing
Arizona Facts

Draped in the colors of an Arizona sunset, Sedona's sandstone monoliths, spires, and pinnacles have been determined to have a sacred power by many over the ages. The Yavapai Indians believe that the goddess Komwida Pokwee once lived in **Boynton Canyon.** Other legends tell stories about an ancient, mystical city that lies buried beneath the rich, red soil. And modern spiritualists flock to the region, attesting that it is one of the two strongest locations in the world for spiritual energy vortexes.

In the 1980s seven vortexes were mapped in the area, some of which are said to be electrical and others that are magnetic in nature. Interestingly enough, New Agers and the ancient Native Americans agree on the sacredness of Boynton Canyon, which is believed to have the strongest vortex of all—an electromagnetic vortex combining both the electrical and magnetic forces into a perfect balance.

A Miner Family **Adventure**

After months of watching my twin boys, Hayden and Blake, fishing in the bathtub with anything that even remotely resembled a fishing pole, I decided to initiate them into the real world of angling. My brief experiences with catching grasshoppers for my father's bait (which I now suspect was a diversionary tactic on his part) didn't prepare me for the task of teaching two boys how to fish in the wild, so I opted for the more comforting atmosphere of a trout farm.

I remember catching my first fish on a string attached to a stick; however, Hayden and Blake insisted on real fishing poles, which quickly transformed into makeshift swords for an impromptu backseat fencing match on the drive from Phoenix to Oak Creek.

Once we reached our destination, I asked for directions at the shop in front, where a man was busily gutting someone's catch and another was handing out Styrofoam cups of some grayish puttylike bait. Relieved at the bait, yet mortified at the bloody business going on behind the glass, I took the children to a nearby table and struggled hopelessly with the tangled mess of line and bobbers and hooks before resignedly returning to the counter for help. We were in luck. One of the guys came out from behind the counter, set up the boys' poles, and gave them an introductory casting lesson.

I told them to watch their bobbers and plopped down on a bench, where I hoped I could make sure no one got hooked. Within minutes, Blake caught his first real fish, which we both hopelessly watched writhe on the hook. I admit I panicked. Luckily, a kind boy saved me from the squeamish responsibility of unhooking the fish, and before a half hour had passed, our bucket was teeming with five good-size trout.

To my exasperation, that night Blake refused to cook his catch, saying that the gutted, half-frozen fish only had an "owie" and we should set it free. Nowadays, I leave the fishing to their grandfather. I'm sure he has them out catching grasshoppers, playing with worms, and cavorting in the mud—only now I don't have to know about it.

your catch and even pack it in ice if you have a ways to travel. Or, if you're in the mood, you can pay an additional $1.00 a fish for a grill kit (foil, salt and pepper, butter, lemon, paper plate, and plastic flatware) and cook up your trout on one of the farm's gas grills.

Red Rock State Park (all ages) 🧗 🏕 🖼

4050 Red Rock Lower Loop Road, Sedona; (928) 282–6907; www.pr.state.az.us/Parks/parkhtml/redrock.html. Open daily 8:00 A.M. to 5:00 P.M. October through March, 8:00 A.M. to 6:00 P.M. April and September, and 8:00 A.M. to 8:00 P.M. May through August. Admission is $$ per vehicle (maximum four persons), $ each additional person.

Check out this 286-acre park, which focuses on environmental education. Among its attractions are nature activities, education displays, and wildlife watching.

Six miles of hiking trails lead to overlooks where you and the kids can spot many of Sedona's famous rock formations, including Cathedral Rock and Bell Rock. Ranger-guided nature hikes leave the visitor center at 10:00 A.M. on Wednesday and Sunday, and guided birding hikes leave at 9:00 A.M. Wednesday and Saturday.

Where to Eat

Café and Cattle Company. 771 Highway 179, P.O. Box 1774, Sedona 86339; (928) 282–2188. Steak, chicken, seafood, and vegetarian dishes. Standard children's menu. $$

Dahl and DiLuca Ristorante Italiano. 2321 West Highway 89A, P.O. Box 3846, Sedona 86340; (928) 282–5219. Pasta and seafood. $$

Dairy Queen Oak Creek Canyon. 4551 North Highway 89A, Sedona; (928) 282–2789. Burgers, hot dogs, sandwiches, and desserts. $

Fournos Restaurant. 3000 West Highway 89A, P.O. Box 3748, Sedona 86340; (928) 282–3331. Mediterranean food. Open only for dinner. $$

Hitching Post Restaurant and Bakery. 269 North Highway 89A, Sedona; (928) 282–7761. Steaks, burgers, salads, and daily specials. Children's menu. $

Mesquite Grill and BBQ. 250 Jordan Road #9, Sedona; (928) 282–6533. Barbecue, steaks, ribs, and hamburgers. $

Oaxaca Restaurante and Cantina. 231 North Highway 89A, Sedona; (928) 282–4179. Mexican and Southwest cuisine. Diverse kids' menu with everything from hot dogs to enchiladas. $$

Pago's Pizzeria. 6446 Highway 179, Sedona; (928) 284–1939. Pasta and pizza. $$

Shugrue's Hillside Grill. Hillside 671, Highway 179, Sedona; (928) 282–5300. Specialty restaurant offering lamb, beef, chicken, and vegetarian dishes. Children's menu. $$$$

Where to Stay

Bell Rock Inn and Suites. 6246 Highway 179, Sedona; (928) 282–4161 or (800) 521–3131. Two pools, two spas, barbecue fire pit, restaurant, and nearby hiking trails. $$$$

Desert Quail Inn. 6626 Highway 179, Sedona; (928) 284–1433 or (800) 385–0927. Outdoor heated pool. Children under twelve stay **free.** $$–$$$$

Enchantment Resort. 525 Boynton Canyon Road, Sedona; (928) 282–2900 or (800) 826–4180; www.enchantment resort.com. Located in Boynton Canyon. Hiking trails, tennis courts, mountain-bike trails, pool, full-service spa, and three restaurants. Children under twelve stay **free.** $$$$

Hampton Inn of Sedona. 1800 West Highway 89A, Sedona; (928) 282–4700 or (800) HAMPTON. Refrigerators, microwaves, outdoor pool and spa, and **free** continental breakfast. $$$

Iris Garden Inn. 390 Jordan Road, Sedona; (928) 282–2552 or (800) 321–8988. A small inn decorated like a bed-and-breakfast. Eight units and iris gardens. Children under twelve stay **free.** $$$

Kokopelli Suites. 3119 West Highway 89A, Sedona; (928) 204–1146 or (800) 789–7393. Outdoor heated pool, spa, and refrigerators. $$$$

Oak Creek Terrace Resort. 4548 North Highway 89A, Sedona; (928) 282–3562 or (800) 224–2229; www.oakcreekterrace. com. Two family units, Jacuzzi, fireplace, access to Oak Creek. Children under twelve stay **free.** $$$–$$$$

Sugar Loaf Lodge. 1870 West Highway 89A, Sedona; (928) 282–9451 or (877) 282–0632; www.sedonasugarloaf.com. Outdoor heated pool, spa, and kitch-enettes. $$

Area Campgrounds

Oak Creek Canyon Campgrounds. Coconino National Forest Service; (877) 444–6777; www.oakcreekcanyon.net. Six campgrounds with 173 total sites available on a first-come, first-serve basis. Campgrounds are open from Memorial Day to Labor Day. No electrical hookups or shower facilities. Campgrounds fill up fast on summer weekends, so plan on getting there early.

For More Information

Sedona–Oak Creek Canyon Chamber of Commerce. 331 Forest Road, P.O. Box 478, Sedona 86339; (928) 282–7722 or (800) 288–7336; www.VisitSedona.com.

Sedona Ranger District. 250 Brewer Road, Sedona 86336; (928) 282–4119.

Verde Valley

This high desert region affords sweeping views and a multitude of outdoor recreation opportunities. Home to several linked communities, the Verde Valley offers a look at ancient Native American dwellings, a historic military fort, and a mining bonanza. The boomtown of Jerome, once known as "the billion dollar camp," created commerce in this 1,200-square-mile tract of land with its rich strikes of gold, silver, and copper. Enjoy a nostalgic trip to the past in nearby Clarkdale, visit the Native American ruins at Tuzigoot National Monument, and take a historic train ride along the Verde River. Cottonwood, just a couple of miles north of Clarkdale, began as a farming settlement and then developed into the area's trade and population center as Jerome grew. Camp Verde, just east of Cottonwood, is the home to Fort Verde State Park, where the military established a camp in 1865 to protect the area's settlers from fierce Apache raids. Life proceeds slowly in this relaxed region, so sit back and enjoy the ride.

Jerome State Historic Park (ages 5 and up) 🏛 🖢 🚗

100 Douglas Road, Jerome; (928) 634–5381; www.pr.state.az.us/Parks/parkhtml/ Jerome.html. Open daily 8:00 A.M. to 5:00 P.M. except Christmas Day. Adults and children ages 7–13 $, under 7 **free.**

You can see Jerome's tumultuous history chronicled at the whitewashed adobe mansion of mine owner James S. "Rawhide Jimmy" Douglas, which now houses a comprehensive museum of Jerome's boisterous mining days. Preserved as a state park, this 1916 mansion was built using more than 80,000 adobe blocks at a cost of $150,000. The 8,700-square-foot structure documents Jerome's raucous past with historical photographs, mining artifacts, and a 3-D model of Douglas's Little Daisy Mine, which returned $125 million before closing in 1934.

Jerome Historical Society Mine Museum (ages 5 and up) 🖢

200 Main Street, Jerome; (928) 634–5477. Open daily 9:00 A.M. to 4:30 P.M. Adults $, under 12 **free.**

Amazing
Arizona Facts

In its heyday, the historic mining town of Jerome—known as the Wickedest Town in the West—once was the third largest city in Arizona, with more than 15,000 residents. But two years after the mines shut down in 1953, Jerome was a virtual ghost town with fewer than one hundred residents. Today, this "ghost town" attracts more than 90,000 tourists a year, who come to see this funky hamlet's art galleries, specialty shops, and restaurants. Kids can shoot hoops at an old basketball court in town; toss coins into the ore cars, outhouse, and old bank vault in the courtyard of the Bartlett Hotel; or mine for treats at Copper Country Fudge, the town's classic candy store, or at Zips, an old-fashioned ice cream fountain.

In 1925 Jerome's jail slid several hundred feet down Cleopatra Hill. Jerome's residents took it all in stride and adopted a new slogan: Jerome—a Town on the Move.

A huge flywheel off an old air compressor marks the entrance to this museum, dedicated to Jerome's mining history. You'll discover all sorts of mining memorabilia tucked away in the back of the storefront and historical photos of Jerome's glory days.

Gold King Mine Museum and Ghost Town (ages 5 and up)

One mile northwest of Jerome on Perkinsville Road, P.O. Box 125, Jerome 86331; (928) 634–0053. Open daily 9:00 A.M. to 5:00 P.M. except Christmas Day. Adults and children ages 5–12 $, under 5 free.

While wandering the dusty streets of this little ghost town, keep an eye out for the town's wild burro. The hamlet, once known as Hayes, boasts an assay office, a blacksmith shop, a 1930s gas station, an antique sawmill, and an assortment of mining equipment used during the town's boom in the early 1900s.

Verde Canyon Railroad (all ages)

300 North Broadway, Clarkdale; (928) 639–0010 or (800) 293–7245; www.verdecanyonrr.com. Departs daily at 1:00 P.M. and returns at 5:00 P.M. Admission $$$$, children under 2 free.

This train, which originally catered to the local mining industry, now operates as a tourist train, taking visitors on a narrated, four-hour sight-seeing excursion through one of the nation's last remaining cotton-willow riparian habitats. Make sure to watch for wildlife along the river as you travel to the abandoned town of Perkinsville, before returning back through the rough-cut canyon to Clarkdale.

Tuzigoot National Monument (all ages)

Two miles west of Clarkdale on Tuzigoot Road, P.O. Box 68, Clarkdale 86324; (928) 634–5564; www.nps.gov.tuzi. Open daily 8:00 A.M. to 5:00 P.M. in winter and 8:00 A.M. to 6:00 or 7:00 P.M. in summer. Closed Christmas Day. Adults $, children under 17 free.

This two-story pueblo, with more than one hundred rooms, housed 225 Sinagua Indians from A.D. 1125 to 1425. A ¼mile loop trail will take you through the maze of ruins. Back at the visitor center, you'll see exhibits on the way of life for these ancient farmers and displays of stone tools, pottery, jewelry, and other artifacts.

Page Springs Hatchery (all ages)

1600 North Page Springs Road, Cornville; (928) 634–4805. Open daily 7:00 A.M. to 3:30 P.M. Free.

A visitor center offers exhibits on the fish native to Oak Creek. Back outside, you can take a self-guided tour of the grounds. Children will especially enjoy tossing food pellets into the show pond, where large trout gobble up the tidbits as soon as they hit the water.

Dead Horse Ranch State Park (all ages)

675 Dead Horse Ranch Road, Cottonwood; (928) 634–5283; www.pr.state.az.us/Parks/park html/deadhorse.html. Open daily 8:00 A.M. to 5:00 P.M. except Christmas Day. Admission $ per vehicle for day use, $$ for tent campsites, and $$$ for RVs.

Bird-watching, biking, hiking, and fishing make this 423-acre state park an outdoor enthusiast's dream come true. Forty miles of hiking and mountain-biking trails, wildlife-viewing platforms at Tavasci Marsh, bird-watching along the forested coastline along the Verde River, and a fishing lagoon teeming with largemouth bass, catfish, and bluegill will make this a place where you'll want to stay for a while. Check out the campfire programs at 2:00 and 4:00 P.M. Saturdays and Sundays.

Blazin' M Ranch (all ages)

Located adjacent to Dead Horse Ranch State Park, 1875 Mayberry Ranch Road, Cottonwood; (928) 634–0334 or (800) 937–8643; www.blazinm.com. Open 5:00 A.M. to 8:30 P.M. Closed in January and August. Adults $$$$, children under 12 $$$. Fees include admission and dinner.

Pony up for a Wild West experience at this authentic ranch. Start off with a chuckwagon supper complete with barbecue beef and chicken, cowboy beans, and biscuits. After dinner you can browse the many shops set up in the Western-style town. Other attractions include Western stage shows, cowboy music and poetry, old-time photos, a shooting gallery, a mechanical horse, horseshoe pits, and pony rides.

Clemenceau Heritage Museum (ages 6 and up)

1 North Willard, Cottonwood; (928) 634–2868. Open 9:00 a.m. to noon on Wednesday and 11:00 A.M. to 3:00 P.M. Friday through Sunday. Closed holidays. Free. Donations accepted.

Housed in the 1923 historic Clemenceau school building, this little museum features rotating exhibits and a vintage classroom. Events include an American craft show on the second Saturday of February and the Zeke Taylor barbecue on the second Saturday of November.

Fort Verde State Historic Park (all ages)

125 East Hollamon, Camp Verde; (928) 567–3275; www.pr.state.az.us/Parks/parkhtml/fortverde.html. Open daily 8:00 A.M. to 5:00 P.M. except Christmas Day. Adults and children ages 7–13 $, under 7 free.

This twelve-acre park preserves the historic buildings of the fort, which was used as a supply post and a base for soldiers fighting Native Americans in the late 1800s. Several of the buildings have been restored and furnished. Exhibits on army and pioneering life introduce visitors to the history of the soldiers, prospectors, and settlers that came to the region more than one hundred years ago. If you are in the area the second weekend of October, make sure to stop by and celebrate Fort Verde Days, which includes living-history presentations and military reenactments.

Montezuma Castle National Monument
(all ages)

2800 Montezuma Castle Highway, Camp Verde 86322; (928) 567–3322; www.nps.gov/moca. Open daily 8:00 A.M. to 5:00 P.M. with extended summer hours from 8:00 A.M. to 6:00 P.M. Adults $, children under 16 free.

Known as one of the best-preserved cliff dwellings in the country, this monument was named after the famous Aztec ruler by early European settlers. In truth, the pueblo has nothing to do with Montezuma's empire, nor is it a castle. The five-story structure was actually built by the prehistoric Sinagua Indians more than 600 years ago. The monument's visitor center orients travelers on the history of the ruins and offers displays of ancient Sinagua artifacts.

Montezuma Well, part of Montezuma Castle National Monument, is located 11 miles northeast of the monument at exit 293 off I–17. This limestone sinkhole formed when an immense underground cavern collapsed. The Sinagua Indians used the water to irrigate their farmlands. An easy 1/3-mile loop trail will take you to the rim and past ancient irrigation ditches and other remnants of this prehistoric culture. Both locations offer shaded picnic tables for a relaxed lunch.

Where to Eat

The Asylum. 200 Hill Street, Jerome; (928) 639–3197. This "restaurant on the fringe" serves up soups, salads, sandwiches, burgers, pasta, seafood, and steak. $$–$$$$

Jerome Palace's Haunted Hamburger. 410 North Clark Street, Jerome; (928) 634–0554. Steaks, pasta, fish, and salads. $$

Manzanita Restaurant. 11425 East Cornville Road, Cornville; (928) 634–8851. American and continental food. $$

Page Springs Restaurant. 1975 North Page Springs Road, Cornville; (928) 634–9954. Steak, seafood, and barbecue ribs. Children's menu. $$

Storytellers Steakhouse. 555 Middle Verde Road, Camp Verde; (928) 567–7905. Reservations required. Children's menu. $$$

Where to Stay

Best Western Cottonwood Inn. 993 South Main Street, Cottonwood; (928) 634–5575 or (800) 350–0025. Heated outdoor pool, spa, and restaurant. Children under twelve stay **free.** $$$

Conner Hotel of Jerome. 164 Main Street, Jerome; (928) 634–5006 or (800) 523–3554. Victorian rooms and great views in a historic 1898 building. $$$$

Jerome Grand Hotel. 200 Hill Street, Jerome; (928) 634–8200 or (888) 817–6788. The only National Historic Landmark hotel in the Verde Valley. Great views and a bed-and-breakfast atmosphere in a five-story Spanish Mission building. $$$–$$$$

The Lodge at Cliff Castle. 333 Middle Verde Road, Camp Verde; (928) 567–6611 or (800) 524–6343; www.cliffcastle casino.net. Kids Quest, bowling, heated outdoor pool and spa, child care, casino, and four restaurants. $$–$$$

Quality Inn. 301 West Highway 89A, Cottonwood; (928) 634–4207 or (800) 228–5151. Restaurant on-site. $$–$$$

For More Information

Camp Verde Chamber of Commerce. 385 South Main Street, P.O. Box 3520, Camp Verde 86322; (928) 567–9294; www.campverde.org.

Clarkdale Chamber of Commerce. P.O. Box 161, Clarkdale 86324; (928) 634–4296.

Cottonwood–Verde Valley Chamber of Commerce. 1010 South Main Street, Cottonwood; (928) 634–7593; cottonwood. verdevalley.com.

Jerome Chamber of Commerce. P.O. Drawer K, Jerome 86331; (928) 634–2900; www.jeromechamber.com.

Prescott

The mile-high town of Prescott (pronounced Pres-KIT) offers a decorum not found in most of Arizona's cities, which more often than not sprawl haphazardly near mining strikes, agricultural lands, or old military posts. Prescott was designed with a master plan as the state's capital in 1864. The capitol building resided at this mountain town, designed with a New England atmosphere, until the legislature had a change of heart and moved it to Tucson, returned it to Prescott, and then moved it for good to Phoenix in 1889. Although the politicians departed with the capitol, the streets had already been laid and were taken over by miners striking gold in the Bradshaw Mountains and ranchers taking advantage of Prescott's mild seasons and rich ranges.

Named after historian William Hickling Prescott, this historic settlement gives visitors an up-close look at some of the state's oldest buildings, including the Yavapai County Courthouse, built in the Neoclassical Revival style; Arizona's oldest restaurant and saloon, the Palace on Prescott's racy Whiskey Row; and the first Territorial Governor's Mansion, which is now part of the Sharlot Hall Museum. Rich in the lore of the Old West, Prescott claims more than 500 buildings listed on the National Register of Historic Places, ranging from Victorian homes in the Mount Vernon District to Fort Whipple, an army fort dating back to 1863.

Situated amid the largest stand of ponderosa pines in the world, Prescott is known officially as Arizona's Christmas City. Nearby are 450 miles of hiking trails, five lakes, and a multitude of opportunities for fishing, hiking, camping, biking, and gold panning. Whatever your fancy—from outdoor recreation to historical heritage—you are sure to find it in this "capitol" city.

The Sharlot Hall Museum (all ages)

415 West Gurley Street, Prescott; (928) 445–3122; www.sharlot.org. Open 10:00 A.M. to 5:00 P.M. (until 4:00 P.M. October through April) Monday through Saturday and 1:00 to 5:00 P.M. Sunday. Free. Donations welcome.

Founded in 1927 by pioneer, poet, and historian Sharlot Hall, the museum complex features ten historic buildings including the 1934 Sharlot Hall Building; the first Territorial Governor's Mansion; the 1875 Fremont House, built by Arizona's fifth territorial governor; and Fort Misery, an 1864 general store. A rose garden on the grounds commemorates the state's women pioneers, a transportation building houses stagecoaches and wagons from Arizona's territorial days, and the Museum Center provides a look at Prescott's early years in comprehensive displays and exhibits. The Folk Arts Fair, held the first weekend in June, showcases traditional folk arts, including soap making, weaving, and blacksmithing. The Prescott Indian Market, held the second weekend in July, features Native American arts

Prowling **Whiskey Row**

Courthouse Plaza in historic downtown Prescott often hosts concerts, festivals, and other entertainment on summer nights under the bronze statue of William "Bucky" O'Neill, a Spanish-American War hero. Also part of the downtown square is Whiskey Row, which once boasted twenty-six saloons. In 1900 a fire caused by an exploding whiskey barrel swept through the district, and patrons at The Palace Saloon carried the bar across the street to continue drinking and carousing as the fire destroyed the rest of Whiskey Row (on Montezuma Street between Goodwin and Gurley Streets). But you don't have to worry about bringing the kids here—the modern incarnation of Whiskey Row is much tamer than it was in its notorious days, and most of the saloons have been transformed into boutiques, galleries, and restaurants.

and crafts, and the Arizona Cowboy Poets Gathering, the third week of August, features cowboy folklore and music.

Smoki Museum (all ages)

147 North Arizona Street, Prescott; (928) 445–1230; www.smokimuseum.org. Open 10:00 A.M. to 4:00 P.M. Monday through Saturday and 1:00 to 4:00 P.M. Sunday in summer; closed Tuesday through Thursday in winter from January 1 to April 14. Adults $, children under 12 free.

Built in 1935 out of native rock and wood, this Native American museum resembles a Native American pueblo. Archives and exhibits reflect Native American culture and history of both prehistoric and modern tribes. Collections include pottery, baskets, jewelry, kachinas, photographs, and stone artifacts. Children will especially enjoy trying their luck at grinding corn with a matate.

The Phippen Museum of Western Art (all ages)

4701 North Highway 89, Prescott; (928) 778–1385; www.phippenartmuseum.org. Open 10:00 A.M. to 4:00 P.M. Monday through Saturday and 1:00 to 4:00 P.M. Sundays. Adults $$, children 12 and under free.

This museum honors the works of renowned Western artist George Phippen, cofounder of the Cowboy Artists of America, and also features paintings, sketches, and bronzes of several other acclaimed Western artists, including Joe Beeler, Olaf Weigehorst, Frank Polk, and Ernest Chiriacka. On Memorial Day weekend the museum hosts an annual Western art show featuring more than 150 world-renowned Western artists and a "quick-draw" contest that's sure to amaze the kids.

Ghosts and **Ghost Towns**

It doesn't have to be Halloween to get a good chill in Prescott. Locals claim that several of the town's historic buildings are haunted, including the Hotel Vendome, Coyote Joe's, and Prescott Fine Arts Gallery and Performance Hall. After exploring the local haunts you can also check out some of the area's many ghost towns, such as Bumblebee, Cleator, Crown King, Congress, Stanton, and Weaver—all just a short drive from Prescott. For more information, call (928) 708–9336.

Heritage Park Zoo (all ages) 🐘

1403 Heritage Park Road, Prescott; (928) 778–4242; www.heritageparkzoo.org. Open daily 9:00 A.M. to 5:00 P.M. in summer and 10:00 A.M. to 4:00 P.M. November though April. Adults $$, children ages 3–12 $, under 3 free.

Local wildlife, exotic animals, and domestic farm critters occupy this small but growing zoo. The zoo also acts as a rescue facility for injured, orphaned, and nonreleasable wildlife, including Abbey, a mountain lion who was rescued as a cub by a ranger from her hiding place in a slash and burn pile, and Shash, an orphaned American black bear who was brought to the zoo when he was three months old. Kids will especially enjoy trick-or-treating at the annual Boo at the Zoo held on Halloween. They'll also get a kick out of having Christmas with the Animals, held the first Sunday in December, when Santa delivers his presents to the zoo's denizens.

Prescott National Forest—Bradshaw District (all ages) 🧍🏃🚴

344 South Cortez Street, Prescott; (928) 443–8000. Open 8:00 A.M. to 4:30 P.M. Monday through Friday. Free.

Stop by and get information on the many outdoor opportunities in the nearby recreation areas of the Prescott National Forest. The forest boasts more than 450 miles of groomed trails, including the popular Thumb Butte Trail, Groom Creek Loop, and the Prescott Peavine Trail. Five area lakes—Granite Basin, Lynx, Goldwater, Willow, and Watson—and several nearby rivers and creeks provide a great place for fishing, canoeing, and gold panning. The more adventurous families will enjoy tackling the Granite Basin Recreational Area, which offers rock climbing, hiking, and backpacking. Wildlife watching is another favorite activity here, so bring your binoculars and keep an eye out for antelope, javelina, elk, beaver, black bear, fox, wild turkey, and bald eagle.

Where to Eat

Gurley Street Grille. 230 West Gurley Street, Prescott; (928) 445–3388. Pasta, salads, and roast chicken. $$

Murphy's. 201 North Cortez Street, Prescott; (928) 445–4044. Steak and seafood offered in a historic 1890 mercantile building. Children's menu. $–$$

The Palace Restaurant and Saloon. 120 South Montezuma Street, Prescott; (928) 541–1996. The state's oldest restaurant and saloon. Steaks, seafood, and daily specials. Children's menu. $$–$$$

Zuma's Woodfire Café. 124 North Montezuma Street, Prescott; (928) 541–1400. Sante Fe–style Mexican food and regional entrees. Children's menu. $

Where to Stay

Best Western Prescottonian Motel. 1317 East Gurley Street, Prescott; (928) 445–3096 or (800) 528–1234. Heated outdoor pool, spa, and refrigerators. Kids under twelve stay **free.** $$–$$$

Hassayampa Inn. 122 East Gurley Street, Prescott; (928) 778–9434 or (800) 322–1927; www.hassayampainn.com. Historic 1927 hotel. $$$

Hotel Vendome. 230 South Cortez Street, Prescott; (928) 776–0900 or (888) 468–3583; www.vendomehotel.com. **Free** continental breakfast. Children under twelve stay **free.** $$$

For More Information

Prescott Area Convention and Visitor Bureau. 117 West Goodwin, P.O. Box 1147, Prescott 86302; (928) 445–2000; www.visit-prescott.com.

Prescott Valley Chamber of Commerce. 3001 North Main Street, Suite 2A, Prescott Valley 86314; (928) 772–8857.

Wickenburg

In 1863 Henry Wickenburg discovered what became one of Arizona's richest mines—the Vulture, which eventually yielded more than $200 million in gold. Legend has it that old Wickenburg discovered the rich cache when he noticed vultures circling the knobby quartz outcropping. Other stories say he found the strike when he threw a rock at his ornery burro. Without water in the immediate vicinity, the ore had to be taken down to the Hassayampa River for processing, and old Wickenburg sold his share of the mine. Near the river, the town of Wickenburg sprung up to meet the needs of the Vulture Mine and the other eighty mines that soon struck up in the area. Some prospectors still roam the hills "Out Wickenburg Way," but this quiet little hamlet now caters mostly to tourists seeking a Western-style adventure, which is how it got its nickname as the Dude Ranch Capital of the World.

A Miner **Adventure**

One late summer weekend, my sons, Hayden and Blake, and I ventured out for some adventure at the Hassayampa River Preserve. Being only three years old at the time, the boys merrily skipped along ahead of me, shrilly claiming that they could see monkeys in the trees. All I could think about were the poor birders that were probably wishing I'd just stayed home. We walked along one sandy trail, and the boys thrilled at the many lizards that scampered across our path. Finally, certain I'd tired them out, we turned around and began to make our way back to the car. We came upon a corner when Blake stopped, pointed, and said in his squeaky toddler voice, "Snake." At that moment I saw a large diamondback rattlesnake just a few feet away from Blake. In a frantic fit I grabbed him and pulled him several feet back down the path. I'm certain herpetologists love parents like me, parents that scare their children half to death with their own unreasonable fears. Anyway, we waited for a few minutes until the snake finished slithering across the path, and then I carried the boys to "safety" around the corner. Startled and not too sure, the boys hung close, holding my hand in their chubby little fists. Hayden looked up at me with big brown eyes and said, "Mom, I want to go home and watch TV."

Desert Caballeros Western Museum (all ages)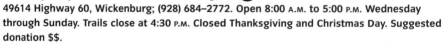
21 North Frontier Street, Wickenburg; (928) 684–2272; www.westernmuseum.org. Open 10:00 A.M. to 5:00 P.M. Monday through Saturday and noon to 4:00 P.M. Sunday except major holidays. Adults $$, children ages 6–18 $, under 6 free.

Take a trip back to Wickenburg's Wild West days at this museum, which chronicles the history of the Vulture Mine and the early mining community of Wickenburg. Prehistoric Native American artifacts, modern Native American arts, and cowboy paintings and sculptures complete this very Western museum experience.

Hassayampa River Preserve (all ages)
49614 Highway 60, Wickenburg; (928) 684–2772. Open 8:00 A.M. to 5:00 P.M. Wednesday through Sunday. Trails close at 4:30 P.M. Closed Thanksgiving and Christmas Day. Suggested donation $$.

This 300-acre preserve, located 5 miles east of Wickenburg, provides bird-watchers a paradise of mesquite, cottonwood, and willows filled with 227 avian species. During the fall and winter months, bird-watchers can expect to see a diverse set of birds such as blue heron, red-tailed hawks, and Gila woodpeckers along the preserve's 4 miles of trails. A naturalist leads visitors on a two-hour trip along the meandering river every Saturday at 10:00 a.m. Reservations are required for the guided hike.

Drive through a **Funky Forest**

If you're traveling on Highway 93 from Wickenburg, you'll get the opportunity to travel through Arizona's **Joshua Tree Forest**. These trees are actually part of the yucca family and are named so because the pointy branches resemble the Biblical Joshua's arm, raised with spear in hand, when he pointed to the city of Ai in ancient Greece. Joshua trees (*Yucca brevifolia*) are found in the Mojave Desert, which extends into California, where you'll find Joshua Tree National Park. These odd-looking plants grow to an impressive height of 30 feet and, from early February to early April, bloom with large clusters of pale-green flowers. Have the kids look for the first one about 22 miles northwest of Wickenburg. The forest extends on both sides of the highway for about 18 miles, between mileposts 180 and 162.

Robson's Arizona Mining World (all ages)

Thirty-one miles northwest of Wickenburg on State Route 71, P.O. Box 3465, Wickenburg 85358; (928) 685–2609. Open 10:00 A.M. to 4:00 P.M. Monday through Friday and 8:00 A.M. to 6:00 P.M. Saturday and Sunday from October through April. Adults $$, children under 10 free.

This attraction, at the old Nella-Meda gold mining camp, is a reconstructed ghost town with twenty-six buildings crammed full with artifacts. Check out an antique print shop, a mineral museum, an assay office, blacksmith shop, and a mercantile. Along with the self-guided walking tour of the town, you can take the 3-mile round-trip nature trail leading back to the Black Tanks petroglyph sites. Other attractions include gold panning, the world's largest collection of antique mining equipment, a bed-and-breakfast, an old-fashioned ice cream parlor, a restaurant, and cowboy cookouts.

Vulture Mine (ages 6 and up)

36610 North 355 Avenue, Wickenburg; (602) 859–2743. Open daily 8:00 A.M. to 4:00 P.M. Closed in the summer. Adults and children ages 6–12 $$, children under 6 free.

Make sure to wear sturdy shoes while touring this abandoned ghost town and keep an eye out for roving rattlesnakes while walking through the abandoned buildings. This is not recommended for tiny tots as the dirt paths are bumpy, snakes roam, and the buildings are not completely safe, but older siblings will enjoy the self-guided, ¼-mile loop trail that will take you past the town's assay office, blacksmith shop, ball mill, power plant, and other structures. Many of the buildings have been well preserved, complete with furniture, clothing, and other remnants from Vulture City's glory days.

Rancho De Los Caballeros (all ages) 🌊 🍴 🛏

1551 South Vulture Mine Road, Wickenburg; (928) 684–5484. Open October through May. Room rates include three meals a day and use of the ranch facilities. Double-occupancy rates $$$$ with an additional fee ($$$) for each extra person. Children under 5 stay free.

Dude ranches aren't just for adults anymore, especially not at this historic guest ranch. Although there is golf, a shooting range, tennis courts, and horseback riding for adults, children have just as much to do in the children's programs, which are offered at no charge. Children older than eight go on trail rides, whereas the younger set takes pony rides in the corral. Additional children's activities include swimming, nature hikes, and crafts. The ranch also offers special family trail rides in the afternoon.

Flying E Ranch (all ages) 🌊 🍴 🛏

2801 West Wickenburg Way, Wickenburg; (928) 684–2690 or (888) 684–2650; www.flying eranch.com. Open November through May. Double-occupancy rates $$$$, children 17 and over $$$$, ages 13–16 $$$, ages 7–12 $$, ages 6 and under $. Room rates include three family-style meals and use of the ranch facilities. Day horse rates $ for guests only.

For a relaxed riding vacation, check out this small ranch, which accommodates only thirty-four guests. Known as a "riding ranch," this family-owned operation prides itself on its casual atmosphere, excellent horses, and trails on 20,000 acres of rolling hills. A heated pool, spa, and gardens add to the Western experience.

Amazing Arizona Facts

Legend says that if you drink from the Hassayampa River, you can never tell the truth again—so a polite way to call someone a liar is to call him a "Hassayamper."

Alamo Lake State Park (all ages) 🦌🏕️

Thirty-five miles northwest of Wenden, P.O. Box 38, Wenden, 85357; (928) 669–2088; www.pr.state.az.us/Parks/parkhtml/alamo.html. Open daily. Day-use $.

Fighting forces most likely weren't thinking of this tiny fishing lake when they shouted the famous battle cry, "Remember the Alamo!" However, Davy Crockett would have enjoyed the peaceful solitude at this often overlooked desert oasis. Here you can catch a plethora of fish: largemouth bass, channel catfish, bluegill, sunfish, tilapia, and crappie. If you don't mind bushwhacking your own trail, hiking and bird-watching are other options for outdoor recreation you can explore while you're here. A small store at the lake provides a place to stock up on groceries and fishing supplies. The store also rents fishing boats, if you'd rather try your luck in the interior of the lake. Other features at the park include picnic tables, a campground with hookups, and the chance to see roaming wild burros.

Where to Eat

Anita's Cocina. 57 North Valentine, Wickenburg; (928) 684–5777. Mexican food and regional dishes. $

Charley's Steak House. 1187 West Wickenburg Way, Wickenburg; (928) 684–2413. Steak, seafood, and chicken. Dinner only. Children's menu. $$

Cowboy Café. 686 North Tegner, Wickenburg; (928) 684–2807. Famous for chicken-fried steak. $$

Sangini's Pizza and Subs. 107 East Wickenburg Way, Wickenburg; (928) 684–7828. Pizza, subs, and salads. $$

Screamers Drive In. 1151 West Wickenburg Way, Wickenburg; (928) 684–9056. A 1950s-style drive-in hamburger stand. $

Where to Stay

Americinn Motel. 830 East Wickenburg Way, Wickenburg; (928) 684–5461. Outdoor heated pool, spa, and continental breakfast. $$

Best Western Rancho Grande. 293 East Wickenburg Way, Wickenburg; (928) 684–5445. Outdoor heated pool, spa, continental breakfast, and mini suites. Children under 16 stay **free.** $$$–$$$$

Los Viajeros Inn. 1000 North Tegner, Wickenburg; (928) 684–7099. Outdoor heated pool, continental breakfast, and refrigerators. $$$–$$$$

For More Information

Wickenburg Chamber of Commerce. 216 North Frontier Street, Wickenburg 85390; (928) 684–5479; www.wickenburgchamber.com.

Annual Events

FEBRUARY

Gold Rush Days. Wickenburg; (928) 684–5479. Second weekend in February. Three fun-filled days of Western activities, including shootouts in the streets, a parade, gold panning, a mucking and drilling contest, rodeo, carnival, and arts and crafts.

MARCH

Sedona International Film Festival. Sedona; (928) 282–0747. First weekend in March. Features new experimental and mainstream movies from around the world.

APRIL

Southwest Days. Camp Verde; (928) 567–9294. Third weekend of April. Mule races, equestrian events, and arts and crafts.

MAY

Sedona Chamber Music Festival. Sedona; (928) 204–2415. Mid-May. A ten-day event featuring musicians from around the world.

Verde Valley Fair. Cottonwood; (928) 634–3290. First weekend in May. An old-time fair complete with carnival, arts and crafts, and a livestock show.

Other Things to **See and Do**

- **A Day in the West,** Sedona; (928) 282–4320.
- **Arizona Botanical Garden,** Clarkdale; (928) 634–2166.
- **BC Jeep Tours,** Wickenburg; (928) 684–7901.
- **Date Creek Ranch,** Wickenburg; (928) 776–8877.
- **Granite Mountain Stables,** Sedona; (928) 771–9551 or (800) SADDLEUP.
- **Hoel's Indian Shop,** Sedona; (928) 282–3925.
- **Marvelous Mary's Private Grand Canyon Tours,** Grand Canyon; (928) 635–4948 or (800) 655–4948.
- **Native Visions Van Tours**—Yavapai Apache, Camp Verde; (928) 567–3035.
- **Nellie Bly Kaleidoscopes and Art Glass,** Jerome; (928) 634–0255.
- **Red Rock Balloon Adventures,** Sedona; (928) 284–0040.
- **Red Rock Crossing,** Sedona; (928) 282–7722 or (800) 288–7336.
- **Rubicon Outdoors,** Prescott; (800) 903–6987.
- **Sedona Arts Center,** Sedona; (928) 282–3809.
- **Sedona Cultural Park,** Sedona; (928) 282–0747.
- **Sedona Fudge Company,** Sedona; (928) 282–1044.
- **Sedona Trolley Tours,** Sedona; (928) 282–5400.
- **Trails West Horseback Adventures,** Wickenburg; (928) 684–2600.

JUNE

Prescott Bluegrass Festival. Prescott; (928) 778–2193. Mid-June. Live bluegrass performances, arts and crafts, and food at Courthouse Plaza.

JULY

Clarkdale's 4th of July Celebration. Clarkdale; (928) 634–9591. July 4th. Pancake breakfast, children's parade, and ice cream social at Clarkdale Town Park.

Cornfest. Camp Verde; (928) 567–9294. Fourth Saturday in July. A celebration of the harvest season, featuring a corn roast, hog-calling contest, corniest joke contest, arts and crafts, and dancing at the "Corn Ball."

Fourth of July Celebration. Wickenburg; (928) 684–5479. July 4th. Fireworks, a watermelon bust, and family-oriented activities.

Frontier Days and World's Oldest Rodeo. Prescott; (928) 445–3103. Fourth of July weekend. Parade, fireworks, and Professional Rodeo Cowboys Association (PRCA) rodeo (a tradition dating back to 1888) at the Yavapai County Fairgrounds.

AUGUST

Arizona Cowboy Poets Gathering. Prescott; (928) 445–3122 or (877) 928–4253. Second weekend in August. Traditional and contemporary poetry readings, cowboy yodeling, and old-time Western singing sessions at the Sharlot Hall Museum.

SEPTEMBER

Fiesta de Tlaquepaque. Sedona; (928) 282–4838. First weekend in September.

Latino and Native American musical performances, Southwestern cuisine, and art displays.

Fiesta Septiembre. Wickenburg; (928) 684–5479. First Saturday in September. Ethnic foods, folklorico dance performances, mariachi music, arts and crafts, and a salsa-making contest.

Sedona Jazz on the Rocks Festival. Sedona; (928) 282–1985. End of September. A four-day event featuring top jazz performers.

Yavapai County Fair. Prescott; (928) 775–8000. End of September. Exhibits, entertainment, and carnival rides at the Yavapai County Fairgrounds.

OCTOBER

Young's Farm Pumpkin Festival and Craft Show. Dewey; (928) 632–7272. Every weekend in October. Pumpkin picking, wagon rides, pony rides, children's activities, face painting, and a critter corral.

Sedona Arts Festival and Artist Invitational. Sedona; (928) 204–9456. Mid-October. Art show, live entertainment, Kidzone, Kids Only shop, and food booths at Sedona Red Rock High School.

NOVEMBER

BlueGrass Festival. Wickenburg; (928) 684–5479. Second weekend in November. Music festival featuring the fiddle, guitar, banjo, and mandolin.

Red Rock Fantasy. Sedona; (928) 282–1777. End of November through the first week of January. More than fifty light displays, caroling, and visits with Santa Claus at Los Abrigados Resort.

DECEMBER

Cowboy Poetry Gathering. Wickenburg; (928) 684–5479. First weekend in December. Three days of cowboy poetry and Western music.

Holiday Festival of Lights and Parade. Prescott Valley; (928) 772–8857. First Friday in December. Light parade, holiday music, and tree-lighting ceremony.

Arizona Christmas Parade and Courthouse Lighting Ceremony. Prescott; (928) 445–2000 or (800) 266–7534. First Saturday in December. Christmas carols, parade, lighting ceremony, and a retelling of *The Christmas Story* in Arizona's "Official Christmas City."

Arizona's Largest Gingerbread Village. Prescott; (928) 776–1666. Entire month of December. Children get in on the fun by decorating the gingerbread residents for this village made up of more than one hundred gingerbread houses, estates, and castles.

Children's Christmas Party. Flagstaff; (928) 779–4395. Second Saturday in December. Festivities include Victorian-era arts and crafts projects, refreshments, and a visit from Mr. and Mrs. Claus.

Navajolands

The Navajo Nation—the largest Native American reservation in the United States—occupies most of the upper northeastern corner of the state. The Hopi Reservation, situated on three mesas, is also in this region and is completely surrounded by the Navajo Nation. Together, the tribal lands of these two peoples encompass more mass than some states. While driving across this dramatic terrain, your family will encounter a forest where the trees have turned to stone, a lake with more shoreline than the entire West Coast, and a desert Mother Nature painted all of the dramatic colors of a sunset. On the Hopi Reservation, you can visit the oldest continuously inhabited community in the United States and watch ceremonies that have been performed virtually

Carrie's
TopPicks for fun in Navajolands

1. Glen Canyon National Recreation Area, Page

2. Lake Powell, Page

3. Canyon de Chelly National Monument, Chinle

4. Four Corners National Monument, Teec Nos Pos

5. Monument Valley Navajo Tribal Park, Monument Valley, UT

6. Navajo National Monument, Tonalea

7. Meteor Crater, Winslow

8. Rock Art Canyon Ranch, Winslow

9. Homolovi Ruins State Park, Winslow

10. Petrified Forest National Park, Holbrook

NAVAJOLANDS

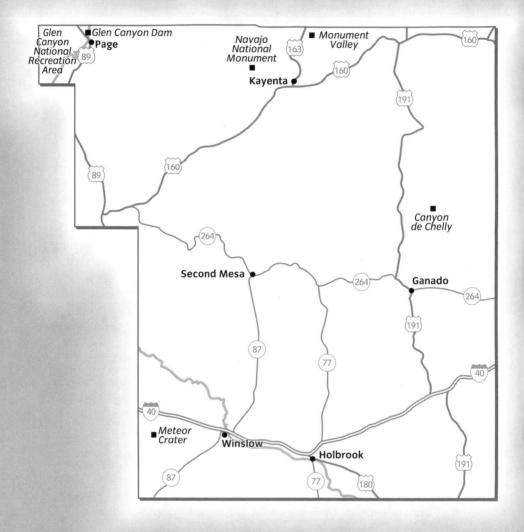

unchanged for centuries. The sparsely populated Navajo Nation encompasses one of the largest Anasazi cliff dwellings in the state, the oldest continuously operating trading post, and Monument Valley's dramatic buttes and spires. While exploring this corner of the state, you'll also have a great opportunity to introduce the kids to Historic Route 66. On the down side, you'll need to come to Navajolands prepared for long drives and the fact that accommodations are basic and hard to come by. It gets dreadfully hot in the summer months here, so be sure to bring water, hats, and sturdy shoes. Even though the badlands are beautiful, they hold many dangers. Use common sense and keep the kids from picking up stones, climbing on rocks, and straying from your supervision.

Page

Although fairly small in size with a population of 8,500, Page is the biggest community in the far reaches of northern Arizona. Built in the wake of the construction of Glen Canyon Dam, this cozy hamlet provides a great base camp for exploring the narrow slot canyons at Lake Powell, the remote Arizona Strip, and the Navajo Nation, reaching to the east and south. Plan on taking your time in this magical realm. Stand under the soaring sandstone arch of Rainbow Bridge, discover hidden petroglyphs, visit the isolated ruins that were once home to the ancient Anasazi, and relax on the placid blue lake behind Glen Canyon Dam. One tip: If you plan on taking one of the many tours offered in the area, your best bet is to book it at the Page–Lake Powell Chamber of Commerce and make reservations in advance, as more than two and a half million people visit Lake Powell each year.

Glen Canyon Dam (all ages)
Three miles north of Page on Highway 89, P.O. Box 581, Page 86040; (928) 608–6404; www.nps.gov/glca. Open daily 8:00 A.M. to 6:00 P.M. in the summer and 8:00 A.M. to 5:00 P.M. in the winter, except Thanksgiving, Christmas, and New Year's Day. Free.

Take a tour of the second-largest gravity arch dam in the United States while visiting Lake Powell in north-central Arizona. Rangers lead **free** tours down into the Glen Canyon Dam and power plant from the Carl Hayden Visitor Center. The center features historical exhibits relevant to the Glen Canyon area, ranging from the mammals that inhabited the canyon during the Ice Age to the construction of the dam and the birth of Lake Powell. A large viewing window at the center provides spectacular views of the canyon, dam, and lake. While you are here, you can pick up a map detailing the recreation options in the **Glen Canyon National Recreation Area** such as visiting Lees Ferry, exploring the canyons of the Escalante River, or taking a trip to Rainbow Bridge National Monument—the world's largest natural bridge. Water sports, camping, backcountry adventure, mountain biking, and fishing are just a few ways to enjoy this natural wonderland of clear water and colored stone.

Lake Powell (all ages) ⬳ 🐟 🚌 🍽

Wahweap Marina, Page; (800) 528–6154; www.visitlakepowell.com. Open daily. $$$$ for the one-and-a-half-hour Canyon Cruises tour, the two-and-a-half-hour Sunset Dinner Cruise, and the Rainbow Bridge Boat Tour; adults $$$, children 11 and under $$ for the one-hour Wahweap Bay Paddle Wheeler tour.

Lake Powell was created by the Glen Canyon Dam in 1963 and takes its name from John Wesley Powell, the explorer who first mapped the Colorado River through the Grand Canyon. Surreal salmon-colored buttes, crystalline blue waters, and more than 1,960 miles of shoreline make Lake Powell America's Natural Playground. Here you will see such stone formations as Castle Rock, the Cathedral in the Desert, and Rainbow Bridge. Boat tours include everything from an authentic 95-foot paddle wheeler to a tour past some of the lake's most famous features. If you'd rather take your time, you can rent a powerboat or even a houseboat. Other amenities include Colorado River float trips, three restaurants, and both lodges and three-bedroom family units. Lake Powell is within the boundaries of Glen Canyon National Recreation Area, which charges a fee of $10 for a seven-day pass or $20 for an annual pass.

Powell Museum (all ages) 🏛

6 North Lake Powell Boulevard, Page; (928) 645–9496. Open Monday through Friday 9:00 A.M. to 5:00 P.M. Closed mid-December to mid-February. Adults and children 6 and older $, under 6 free.

Like the lake, this small museum honors John Wesley Powell, the explorer who led the first expedition down the raging Colorado River in 1869. What many don't realize is that Powell named most of the spectacular sections along the Grand Canyon on his second trip in 1871–72. Exhibits include photographs of Powell and his journeys, fossils and minerals found in the canyons carved out by the Colorado River system, and artifacts from Southwestern Native American tribes.

Amazing Arizona Facts

Arizona is nearly square in shape and at its farthest point stretches 393 miles north to south and 338 miles west to east. The total area of the state is 113,909 square miles and, even though it is mostly known as a desert state, boasts about 500 square miles of surface water from its many lakes and rivers.

Native American reservations occupy 27 percent of Arizona lands.

Arizona has more parks and national monuments than any other state.

Wilderness River Adventures (ages 6 and up) ⚠

50 South Lake Powell Boulevard, Page; (928) 645–3279 or (800) 528–6154. Half-day trips leave at 11:00 A.M. March through mid-May and mid-September through mid-October; 7:30 A.M. and 1:30 P.M. mid-May through mid-September. $$$$

Take a relaxed 15-mile float trip down the Colorado River from Glen Canyon Dam to Lees Ferry. Along the way you'll see the beautiful colors of canyon's Navajo sandstone, stop to inspect ancient Native American petroglyphs, and will have the chance to see a variety of birds and waterfowl. Make sure to make reservations in advance as these trips fill up fast.

Navajo Village Heritage Center (ages 6 and up)

Vermillion Down, Page; (928) 660–0304 or (928) 645–2741. Open daily 4:00 to 8:00 P.M. $$$$

Experience an evening with the Navajo in this grand tour, which encompasses art demonstrations, native foods, traditional dance performances, and stories told around a campfire.

Where to Eat

Kerr's Old West. 718 Vista, Page; (928) 645–5160. Salads, barbecue, steaks, and seafood. Children's selections include sandwiches, shrimp, chicken, and the salad bar. $–$$

Pepper's Restaurant. Courtyard by Marriott, 600 Clubhouse, Page; (928) 645–5000. A simple but diverse menu that includes salads, sandwiches, prime rib, Navajo tacos, and daily specials. Children's menu offers variety, with prime rib and spaghetti options. Open April through October. $

Rainbow Room. Wahweap Lodge, 100 Lake Shore, Page; (928) 645–2433. Southwest cuisine in a relaxed atmosphere. Children's menu. $$

Ranch House Grille. 819 North Navajo, Page; (928) 645–1420. Sandwiches and burgers. Open for lunch only. Children's menu. $

Strombolli's Pizzeria. 711 North Navajo, Page; (928) 645–2605. Pizza, pasta, and sandwiches. Children's menu. $

Where to Stay

Bashful Bob's. 750 South Navajo, Page; (928) 645–3919. Basic budget rooms. $

Best Western Arizona Inn. 716 Rimview, Page; (928) 645–2466. Outdoor pool and **free** continental breakfast. Children under twelve stay **free.** $$–$$$

Best Western Lake Powell. 208 North Lake Powell, Page; (928) 645–5988. Outdoor pool, spa, and **free** continental breakfast. Children under twelve stay **free.** $$$

Courtyard by Marriott. 600 Clubhouse Drive, Page; (928) 645–5000. Outdoor pool. $$

Area Campgrounds

Wahweap Lodge. 100 Lake Shore, Page; (800) 528–6154. Tent and RV sites with full hookups. $

For More Information

Page–Lake Powell Chamber of Commerce and Visitor Bureau. 644 North Navajo Drive, P.O. Box 727, Page 86040; (928) 645–2741 or (888) 261–7243; www.pagelakepowellchamber.org.

Navajo Indian Reservation

The Navajo Nation has more than 260,000 members and occupies 25,000 square miles, making it the largest Native American reservation in the United States. Navajo country encompasses many of Arizona's wonders, including Navajo National Monument, Canyon de Chelly National Monument, and Monument Valley. The reservation covers most of the northeastern corner of Arizona and extends out into Utah and New Mexico as well. The Navajo live in hogans scattered across the vast Colorado Plateau; however, there are a few population centers on the reservation lands, including the capital city of Window Rock, Chinle, Kayenta, and Tuba City. Near the center of the Navajo Reservation, you'll find the Hopi Reservation, which is home to 10,000 tribal members. The Hopi tend to congregate on the three mesas, which are their ancestral homes. Old Oraibi on Third Mesa, dating back from A.D. 1150, is the oldest continuously occupied habitation in the United States. The Hopi have attracted many visitors to come and see their elaborate ceremonies, which are held year-round and incorporate the colorful kachinas treasured by Southwestern collectors. Keep in mind while traveling the Navajo Reservation that information can be hard to come by and that the Navajo Nation, unlike the rest of Arizona, follows daylight savings time from early April to late October. Be advised that lodging can be a bit pricey due to the lack of competition. Respect is the key while traveling through Native American territory. Keep in mind that photography and recording are forbidden by the Hopi and, although the Navajo are a little more relaxed about photographs, be prepared to ask permission and pay a posing fee.

Canyon De Chelly National Monument (all ages) 🧑‍🤝‍🧑 ⛰ 🏛
Two miles east of Chinle off Highway 191, P.O. Box 588, Chinle 86503; (928) 674–5500; www.nps.gov/cach. Open daily 8:00 A.M. to 5:00 P.M. except Thanksgiving, Christmas, and New Year's Day. Free.

White House Ruin Trail, the only hike in the canyon permitted without a guide, leads the curious from the overlook on a 2½-mile round-trip hike that dead-ends 30 feet from the ruin. Rangers say to allow two hours for the hike and suggest that you take plenty of water. The hike provides an up-close look at the cliff dwelling inhabited by the Anasazi from A.D. 1060 to 1275. Portions of sixty rooms and four kivas remain in the upper and lower sections of the village. The White House Overlook on the rim drive, where canyon walls reach to 550 feet, provides a stunning view of the dwelling's original white plaster as it contrasts with the reddish hues of the surrounding sandstone. White House Ruin continues to attract attention as one of the largest ruins in the monument. The monument's visitor center provides information on the two scenic rim drives traveling along the sheer sandstone cliff walls. The best time to visit is from April to October; be sure to take raincoats if you venture this way in the summer, when afternoon rainstorms are commonplace.

Four Corners National Monument (all ages) 🏕

A quarter mile west of Teec Nos Pos off Highway 160, Navajo Nation Parks and Recreation, P.O. Box 2520, Window Rock 86515; (928) 871–6647. Open daily 7:00 A.M. to 8:00 P.M. from May to August and 8:00 A.M. to 5:00 P.M. from September to April. $

An unimposing concrete slab marks the only place in the United States where four states meet—Arizona, New Mexico, Colorado, and Utah. Kids will enjoy standing in all four states at once, and parents get a chance to stretch their legs. During fair weather you'll also get an opportunity to look at Navajo wares displayed for sale in impromptu arts and crafts booths.

A Tangled **Web**

Tucked away in the sacred realm of Canyon de Chelly, an 800-foot-tall sandstone monolith looms from the depths. The Navajo believe that the sharp monolith, called Spider Rock, is the home to the mysterious Spider Woman. This deity is credited with instructing the People in the craft of weaving, among other things. Despite her benevolent teachings, this powerful creature is the Navajo equivalent of the Boogey Man. Daniel Staley, a Navajo guide, recalls his grandmother telling him that, if he kept ignoring her and didn't do as he was told, Spider Woman would swoop down from her lofty perch and take him to the top of Spider Rock. There, she would gobble him up and toss his bones down to the canyon floor. "That's what happens to naughty children," she said. Years later, Staley tried the traditional tactic on some children that weren't listening to him. He told them the story just as his grandmother had told him on that long-ago summer day. He told them he would call Spider Woman down from her towering rock and that she would take them away and eat them alive. But in a modern world filled with television and comic books, Spider Woman has lost some of her edge. The children he was chastising just smiled at him, and his son looked at him defiantly. "Well then, I'm going to call Spider Man," he said.

Drum to a **Different Beat**

Hear the timeless sounds of Native American drumming each Thursday evening during KTNN's Drums of Summer. Broadcast from the radio station's studios at Window Rock or on location, the program features continuous live performances of powwow drums and intertribal singing styles from 8:00 to 11:00 P.M. Mountain Daylight Savings Time.

The Drums of Summer broadcasts to eleven states from June through August on station AM 660. For more information call the Navajo Nation Radio Station at (928) 871–3552 or (928) 871–3553.

Hubbell Trading Post National Historic Site (ages 6 and up) 🏛️ 🚗 🔒

Off Highway 191 in Ganado, P.O. Box 150, Ganado 86505; (928) 755–3475; www.nps.gov/hutr. Open daily 8:00 A.M. to 5:00 P.M. October through April and 8:00 A.M. to 6:00 P.M. May through September except Thanksgiving, Christmas, and New Year's Day. Free.

This historic site is the nation's oldest continuously operating trading post. Trader John Lorenzo Hubbell established the post as a link to the outside world in 1876. You can tour Hubbell's house and the grounds or visit the trading post proper, which looks much like it did one hundred years ago. Navajos still trade their goods here, and you can find rugs, jewelry, and other Native American products sitting side-by-side with grocery items, horse tack, and household essentials. While you're here, make sure to stop by the visitor center and watch a Navajo weaver working on her loom. But as tempting as it may be, don't attempt to pose the kids with her or any other Native Americans without first asking permission, and keep an eye on the little ones—you break it, you buy it. Some of the specialty items for sale can cost several thousand dollars.

Monument Valley Navajo Tribal Park (ages 6 and up) 🚫 🏕️

Four miles east of Monument Valley off Highway 163, P.O. Box 360289, Monument Valley, UT 84536; (435) 727–5870. Open daily 7:00 A.M. to 7:00 P.M. from May through September and 8:00 A.M. to 5:00 P.M. from October through April, except Thanksgiving and Christmas. (Call ahead; hours vary from one year to the next.) Adults $$, children under 9 free.

This surreal valley lies on the border of Arizona and Utah and offers enchanting views of sand-swept plains, towering buttes, and jagged pinnacles of eroded sandstone. The Navajo believe it to be an ancient battleground where Monster Slayer destroyed the enemies of the People. Whatever their origin, these sandstone monoliths have graced the silver screen countless times, since John Ford filmed Stagecoach in 1938. Preserved as a tribal park, Monument Valley can be seen only along the 17-mile, scenic Monument Valley Drive or on a tour accompanied by a Navajo guide. Several Navajo operations at the tribal park offer jeep trips, horseback rides, backcountry trips, and hiking and photography tours. Check with the visitor center for tour operators. Also, keep in mind that water is scarce in this desolate expanse and that only the visitor center and the campground have water.

Navajo National Monument (ages 6 and up) 🏃 🅰 🚗

Ten miles north of the Black Mesa Junction on State Route 564, HC 71, Box 3, Tonalea 86044; (928) 672–2700; www.nps.gov/nava/. Open daily 8:00 A.M. to 5:00 P.M. except Thanksgiving, Christmas, and New Year's Day. Free.

Take a hike through history at this monument, which protects three of Arizona's largest Native American ruins. Betatakin, which contains 135 rooms and one kiva tucked up neatly in the red sandstone cliffs, can be reached daily on a 5-mile round-trip guided hike held from May to September. Be aware that this trail is fairly primitive and drops 700 feet to the canyon floor. Groups are limited to the first twenty-five people, so be sure to arrive at the visitor center early. Those not up to the hike can catch a glimpse of the Betatakin ruins from a viewpoint near the visitor center. Families with older children might also consider taking the 16-mile round-trip hike to Keet Seel, Arizona's largest Anasazi ruin with 160 rooms and several kivas. This isolated cliff dwelling is well worth the strenuous overnight trip, as a ranger at Keet Seel will actually take you up a ladder to the alcove, where you can walk the streets built more than 700 years ago. This hike, also offered only between May and September, is restricted to twenty persons a day and requires a permit. Make sure to take plenty of water for either trip and stay on the marked trails, as the open countryside is privately owned. The visitor center has good restroom facilities and a small museum detailing the lives of the ancient peoples who once inhabited these canyons.

Hopi Cultural Center and Museum (all ages) 🍴 🅰 🛍 🔒

Five miles west of Highway 87 on State Route 264, Box 67, Second Mesa 86043; (928) 734–2401 or (928) 734–6650. Open daily 6:00 A.M. to 9:00 P.M. March 15–October 14; daily 7:00 A.M. to 8:00 P.M. October 15–March 14. The Hopi Museum is open 8:00 A.M. to 5:00 P.M. Monday through Saturday and 8:00 A.M. to 4:00 P.M. Sundays. $

The center, on Second Mesa, is a good place to start when exploring the Hopi Reservation. Here you can check out Hopi culture and customs in the center's museum, buy Hopi arts and crafts at the gift shop, and try traditional Hopi foods like noqkwivi (a corn and lamb stew) or blue corn pancakes at the restaurant. Children will especially enjoy looking at the brilliantly colored kachinas; just make sure to enforce the "look, but don't touch" rule. While the kachina dolls look sturdy, they are carved from cottonwood, and the detailed figurines can easily break.

Dinosaur **Tracks**

If you happen to be traveling along Highway 160, between mile markers 316 and 317, stop and check out dinosaur tracks preserved in the sandstone.

Where to Eat

Amigo Café. One mile north of Highway 160 on Highway 163, P.O. Box 1530, Kayenta 86033; (928) 697–8448. This popular local hangout serves homemade Mexican, American, and Navajo entrees. Children's menu. $

Blue Coffee Pot Café. At the junction of Highways 160 and 163, P.O. Box 652, Kayenta 86033; (928) 697–3396. A diverse selection of Mexican and Navajo specialties. Children's menu. $–$$

Golden Sands Café. One mile north of Highway 160 on Highway 163, P.O. Box 458, Kayenta 86033; (928) 697–3684. Hearty meals of barbecue chicken, hamburgers, and Navajo tacos served in a Western-theme restaurant. Traditional children's menu. $$

Pizza Edge. On Highway 160, P.O. Box 7, Kayenta 86033; (928) 697–8427. Pizza, subs, and wings. $–$$

Tuba City Truck Stop Café. At the junction of Highway 160 and State Route 264, Tuba City; (928) 283–4975. Small cafe serving some of the best Navajo tacos in the Southwest. Regular and child-size. $

Where to Stay

Anasazi Inn. Ten miles west of Kayenta on Highway 160, P.O. Box 1543, Kayenta 86033; (928) 697–3793; www.anasaziinn. com. Basic budget rooms and a restraunt. $

Canyon de Chelly Motel. Three miles west of Canyon de Chelly, P.O. Box 295, Chinle 86503; (800) 327–0354. Restaurant and an indoor pool. Children under twelve stay free. $$

Kayenta Holiday Inn. At the junction of Highways 160 and 164, P.O. Box 307, Kayenta 86033; (928) 697–3221 or (800) HOLIDAY. Restaurant and outdoor pool. Children under twelve stay and eat free. $$

Thunderbird Lodge. Three miles east of Highway 191 on State Route 7, P.O. Box 548, Chinle 86503; (928) 674–5841 or (800) 679–2473; www.tbirdlodge.com. A hotel and restaurant in a renovated 1896 trading post. The lodge also provides six-wheel-drive tours into the national monument with experienced Navajo guides. $$$–$$$$

Area Campgrounds

Goulding's Monument Valley Campground. 2000 Main Street, Monument Valley, UT; (435) 727–3235; www.gouldings. com. Tent and RV sites with full hookups. Amenities include an indoor pool, showers, laundry, and a convenience store. Open March 15 to October 15. $

Spider Rock RV Park and Camping. P.O. Box 2509, Chinle 86503; (928) 674–8261. Tent and RV sites with water hookups. $

For More Information

First Mesa Consolidated Villages. Hopi Tribe, P.O. Box 260, Polacca 86042; (928) 737–2262.

Hopi Office of Public Information. One mile south of State Route 264, P.O. Box 123, Kykotsmovi 86039; (928) 734–3283; www.hopi.nsn.us.

Navajo Nation Tourism Office. P.O. Box 663, Window Rock 86515; (928) 871–6436; www.discovernavajo.com.

Navajo Parks and Recreation Department. P.O. Box 9000, Window Rock 86515; (928) 871–6647.

Winslow

Founded as a railroad terminal in 1882, Winslow quickly became a shipping hub for ranchers. By the early 1900s, Route 66 finally connected Chicago with the West Coast and traveled through Winslow's busy downtown. A few years later Charles Lindbergh designed Winslow Airfield as a midway stop for continental flights, which made it the busiest airport in Arizona at the time. But by the 1970s, I–40 was built to the side of the town, commercial flights bypassed the airfield, and train passenger travel all but disappeared. The once busy town lay nearly forgotten until recently. Portions of Old Route 66 survived, as did the airfield and the town's elite La Posada—all revamped to cater to a new generation of travelers taking the easy road through Winslow. Located near the remote Navajo Indian Reservation, Petrified Forest National Park, and Homolovi Ruins State Park, Winslow is a great place to set up base while exploring the northeast region of the state. Such celebrities as Howard Hughes, John Wayne, Bob Hope, Albert Einstein, and the Crown Prince of Japan visited the legendary La Posada, designed by architect Mary Colter as the last and most elegant of the Fred Harvey hotels. Reopened in 2001 in all of its grandeur, this is the place to stay while checking out the region. While in Winslow, you might also want to take a moment to get a photo at "Standin' On a Corner" park in downtown. The corner, made famous by the Eagles' hit "Take It Easy," features a life-size bronze statue and a mural commemorating the famous song.

Meteor Crater (ages 5 and up)

Forty miles east of Flagstaff on I-40 at exit 233, P.O. Box 70, Flagstaff 86002; (928) 289–2362 or (800) 289–5898; www.meteorcrater.com. Open daily 6:00 A.M. to 6:00 P.M. May 15 through September 15 and 8:00 A.M. to 5:00 P.M. September 16 through May 14. Adults $$$, children ages 6–17 $$, under 6 free.

Visit this immense crater, which was created by a meteorite striking the ground about 49,500 years ago. The meteorite was traveling more than 40,000 miles per hour when it hit Earth, leaving a pit measuring 570 feet deep and nearly 1 mile wide. Since it is the best-preserved crater on Earth, it is still studied by scientists and was designated by NASA as an official training site for the Apollo astronauts. To get the best vantage sites of the crater, take the guided rim trail hike. While at the visitor center, make sure to check out the Museum of Astrogeology and the Astronaut Hall of Fame. Be advised that this is a privately owned site and not a national park, and it is therefore a bit more pricey than a government operation.

Rock Art Canyon Ranch (all ages)

Fifteen miles east of Winslow; P.O. Box 224, Joseph City 86032; (928) 288–3260. Open Monday through Saturday. Closed Easter, Thanksgiving, and Christmas. Reservations are required. Prices vary.

Take a guided tour of Chevlon Canyon, where the Anasazi left their mark in the form of petroglyphs at Rock Art Canyon Ranch. Along with the access to the canyon walls filled with the ancient designs, visitors can travel the 8,000-acre working cattle ranch astride a horse and even join authentic cowboys on a cattle roundup. The ranch also houses a pioneer and cowboy museum along with the last remaining bunkhouse left from the Hashknife Outfit—the largest Arizona ranching operation in the nineteenth century. Other activities include roping lessons, pitching horseshoes, and swimming in the canyon.

McHood Park (all ages)

It's 1¾₀ miles on State Route 87 and then 4¾₀ miles on State Route 99, Winslow; (928) 289–1458. Open daily 6:00 A.M. to sunset April through October and 8:00 A.M. to sunset November through March. Free.

This park, situated on both banks of Clear Creek Reservoir, features great outdoor activities such as fishing for trout, bass, and catfish; petroglyph sites; bird-watching opportunities; picnic facilities; and a swimming area.

Homolovi Ruins State Park (all ages)

I-40, exit 257; HC 63, Box 5, Winslow 86047; (928) 289–4106; www.pr.state.az.us/Parks/park html/homolovi.html. Open daily 6:00 A.M. to 7:00 P.M. except Christmas Day. Visitor center is open daily 8:00 A.M. to 5:00 P.M. Admission is $$ per vehicle for up to four people for day use.

Six pueblo villages make up this prehistoric Native American settlement, located near present-day Winslow. These Native Americans are believed to be the ancestors of the Hopi Indians, who now live north of the area on three mesas surrounded by the Navajo Nation. The name Homolovi, which means "Place of Little Hills," applies to all of the ruins in the area. Archaeologists are currently excavating Homolovi I, an 800-room pueblo near the Colorado River. Homolovi II and Homolovi IV can be visited as well and include a first-hand glimpse at what ruins look like before extensive excavation and reconstruction. Hiking trails, picnic tables, and petroglyphs sites add to the experience. The park includes a visitor center and a campground, open from mid-April to mid-October, complete with showers and water hookups.

Old Trails Museum (ages 5 and up)

212 Kinsley, Winslow; (928) 289–5861. Open 1:00 to 5:00 P.M. Tuesday through Saturday from March through October and 1:00 to 5:00 P.M. Tuesday, Thursday, and Saturday from November through February. Free.

This funky little museum celebrates the Winslow experience with exhibits on La Posada and the Harvey Girls, Route 66, and Homolovi. Other displays include railroad memora-

An Invitation for a **Murderer**

The hamlet of Holbrook has quite a reputation in the chronicles of the Old West. Holbrook was the site of one of the most famous gunfights in the west—between Sheriff Commodore Perry Owens and the Cooper-Blevins gang. But the town's most dubious toast came as the result of a reprimand from President William McKinley to Sheriff Frank Wattron for sending out an ornate invitation to a hanging in 1899. The infamous invitation read:

George Smiley, Murderer
His soul will be swung into eternity on Dec. 8 1899 at
2 o'clock P.M., sharp.
The latest improved methods of scientific strangulation will be
employed and everything possible will be done
to make the surroundings cheerful and the execution
a success.

bilia, a moonshine still, and various antiques. Outside, check out the mural and statue commemorating the Eagles' pop song "Take It Easy," which put Winslow back on the map with the phrase " . . . standin' on a corner in Winslow, Arizona."

Navajo County Museum (ages 6 and up) 🧒

100 East Arizona Street, Holbrook; (928) 524–6558 or (800) 524–2459. Open 8:00 A.M. to 5:00 P.M. Monday through Friday. Free.

Holbrook, a ranching center that was once home to the infamous Hashknife outfit, features this museum of Wild West history. Housed in the 1898 county courthouse, this museum takes you back to Holbrook's lawless frontier days with period rooms, a restored courtroom, and the old jail.

International Petrified Forest and Museum of the Americas (all ages)
🧒 🏛 👨‍👩‍👧

Off I–40, exit 292, Holbrook; (928) 524–9178. Admission is $$ per vehicle.

Large dinosaurs attract passersby to this museum, which houses one of the largest collections of Native American artifacts in the Southwest. Exhibits include the re-created ruins of a two-room dwelling, Anasazi relics, and an extensive Meso-American collection. A playground, roaming buffalo, and hiking trails complete the experience.

Petrified Forest National Park (all ages)

North entrance, Painted Desert Visitor Center, I–40 to exit 311, 30 miles east of Holbrook. South entrance, Rainbow Forest Museum, US 180, 19 miles southeast from Holbrook; Petrified Forest; (928) 524–6228; www.nps.gov/pefo. Open daily 8:00 A.M. to 5:00 P.M. except Christmas Day, with extended summer hours. Admission is $$$ per vehicle.

A visitor center at the north entrance and the museum at the south entrance provide maps, bird and mammal checklists, and exhibits illustrating the park's geology, fossils, and ecology. The Petrified Forest was declared a national monument in 1906 and earned national park status in 1962. Today it encompasses 93,533 acres of badlands comprised of the Chinle Formation, which is more casually known as the Painted Desert. The multi-hued desert features the fossilized remains of Triassic dinosaurs and the colorful, crystallized remains of giant trees that existed more than 200 million years ago. Several easy hiking trails at the park are perfect for children of all ages. Other attractions include ancient Native American dwellings and petroglyphs at Agate House and Puerco Pueblo and the 27-mile scenic drive through the park. Be sure to watch your children while walking through the park to make sure they don't damage or collect any natural or cultural objects. Stiff fines are imposed for collecting archaeological artifacts, destroying archaeological sites, collecting rocks or fossils, and for walking or climbing on ruin walls.

On the Road **Again**

Although the famous Pony Express never actually passed through Arizona, several other mailruns traveled through the dangerous terrain of Arizona Territory. The Navajo County Hashknife Sheriff's Posse has been running mail from Holbrook to Scottsdale since 1955 to pay tribute to the mailruns of the past. The riders, dressed in authentic cowboy gear, relay the mailbags along the route, delivering more than 20,000 first-class letters for the U.S. Postal Service. To participate in the Hashknife Pony Express event, mail a letter, complete with postage and the directions VIA PONY EXPRESS, written on the envelope enclosed in a second envelope addressed to the Postmaster, Holbrook 86025.

Where to Eat

The Brown Mug. 308 East Second Street, Winslow; (928) 289–9973. Mexican and American food. A limited kids' menu. $

Captain Tony's Pizza. 2217 North Park Drive, Winslow; (928) 289–4919. An Italian eatery with a menu featuring pizzas, calzones, pasta, wings, subs, and salads. $–$$

Casa Blanca Cafe. 512 East 3rd Street, Winslow; (928) 289–4191. This family-owned restaurant serves hearty Mexican specialties. $$

Jerry's. 2600 Navajo Boulevard, Holbrook; (928) 524–2364. A family-style diner serving American food. Children's menu. $–$$

Romo's Café. 121 West Hopi Drive, Holbrook; (928) 524–2153. A popular local hangout serving Mexican specialties since the 1960s. $

Where to Stay

Best Western Adobe Inn. 1701 North Park Drive, Winslow; (928) 289–4638 or (800) 528–1234. Indoor pool, spa, and restaurant. Children under twelve stay free. $$–$$$

Comfort Inn. 2602 Navajo Boulevard, Holbrook; (928) 524–6131 or (800) 228–5150. Basic budget rooms and a swimming pool. Children under eighteen stay free. $$

Days Inn. 2035 West Highway 66, Winslow; (928) 289–1010 or (800) 329–7466. Indoor pool, spa, and complimentary continental breakfast. Children under ten stay free. $–$$

La Posada Hotel. 303 East Second Street, Winslow; (928) 289–4366; laposada.org. A Southwestern masterpiece featuring large public sitting rooms with fireplaces and gardens and dining in the Turquoise Room. $$$

Wigwam Motel. 811 West Hopi Boulevard, Holbrook; (928) 524–3048. A Historic Route 66 icon complete with a small museum of Native American artifacts and petrified wood in the lobby. $

Area Campgrounds

Cholla Lake County Park. I–40, exit 277, Holbrook; (928) 288–3717 or (928) 524–4250. Campgrounds with showers, a 360-acre lake for swimming and fishing, and picnic facilities. Hook-ups for RVs. Open mid-March to late October. $

For More Information

Holbrook Chamber of Commerce. 100 East Arizona Street, Old Court House, Holbrook 86025; (928) 524–6558; www.ci.holbrook.az.us/Chamber.htm.

Winslow Chamber of Commerce. 300 West North Road, Winslow 86047; (928) 289–2434; www.winslowarizona.org.

Annual Events

JANUARY

Hashknife Pony Express. Holbrook; (928) 524–4155. Last weekend in January. Riders carry the mail 200 miles from Holbrook to Scottsdale.

APRIL

Easter Egg Hunt. Winslow; (928) 289–1458. The Saturday before Easter Sunday. An egg hunt, visits from the Easter bunny, and children's games at Winslow City Park.

Native American Arts Auction. Ganado; (928) 755–3475. Last Saturday in April. An auction of Navajo and Hopi arts and crafts at Hubbell Trading Post.

JULY

Fourth of July. Winslow; (928) 289–2434. July 4. Performances by the Summer Stock Children's Theater, family activities, and a patriotic program complete with fireworks at the Winslow High School football field.

SEPTEMBER

Navajo Nation Fair. Window Rock; (928) 871–6478. First weekend after Labor Day in September. A five-day festival complete with parade, Native American singing and dancing, children's games, carnival, agricultural shows, ethnic foods, rodeo, arts and crafts, and the crowning of Miss Navajo.

NOVEMBER

Christmas Parade. Winslow; (928) 289–2434. Third Saturday in November. An old-fashioned parade down Route 66, arts and crafts, and a chance to sit on Santa's lap.

Festival of Lights Boat Parade. Page; (928) 645–1001. Third Saturday in November. Boaters deck their boats with lights at Lake Powell.

DECEMBER

Parade of Lights Festival. Holbrook; (928) 524–6558 or (800) 524–2459. First Saturday in December. This holiday arts and crafts festival continues into the night with a parade of lights, live entertainment, and visits with Santa.

Other Things to **See and Do**

- **Antelope Canyon Navajo Tribal Park,** Page; (928) 698–2808.
- **Blair's Dinnebito Trading Post,** Page; (928) 645–3008 or (800) 644–3008.
- **Diné Bí Keyah Trading Post,** Page; (928) 645–2404.
- **Guided Walking Tour of First Mesa,** Punsi Hall Visitor Center, First Mesa; (928) 737–2262.
- **Justin Tso's Horseback Tours,** Chinle; (928) 674–5678.
- **Lake Powell Air,** Page; (928) 645–2494 or (800) 245–8668.
- **Little Painted Desert County Park,** Winslow; (928) 289–2434.
- **Monument Valley Air Tours,** Phoenix; (888) 869–0866.
- **Navajo Country Guided Trail Rides,** Monument Valley; (435) 727–3210.
- **Navajo Museum,** Window Rock; (928) 871–6673 or (928) 871–7941.
- **Peter Toth Monument,** Winslow; (928) 289–2434.
- **Roland's Navajoland Tours,** Kayenta; (928) 697–3524 or (800) 368–2785.
- **St. Michael's Mission,** Window Rock; (928) 871–4171.
- **Window Rock Tribal Park,** Window Rock; (928) 871–6636 or (928) 871–6647.

High Reaches

W ithout a major metropolitan hub, this portion of the state primarily offers a chance to get back to nature. The diverse landscape travels from the southern desert gardens, up through rolling grasslands, and into the pine forest wonderland of the White Mountains. Although the high reaches of Arizona are incredibly beautiful, they are not especially kid friendly. Here you'll find temperatures ranging from high desert heat reaching into triple digits to the sub-zero temperatures of 11,000-foot-high Mount Baldy. When exploring this part of eastern Arizona, you need to make sure your spare tire is in good condition and that you have an emergency road kit. This is not a place

Carrie's
TopPicks for fun in the High Reaches

1. Rim County Museum, Payson

2. Tonto National Bridge State Park, Payson

3. Lyman Lake State Park, Springerville

4. Sunrise Park Ski Resort, McNary

5. Besh-Ba-Gowah Archaeological Park, Globe

6. Boyce Thompson Southwestern Arboretum State Park, Superior

7. Discovery Park, Safford

8. Black Hills Rockhound Area, Safford

9. Mount Graham Drive, Safford

10. Roper Lake State Park, Safford

HIGH REACHES

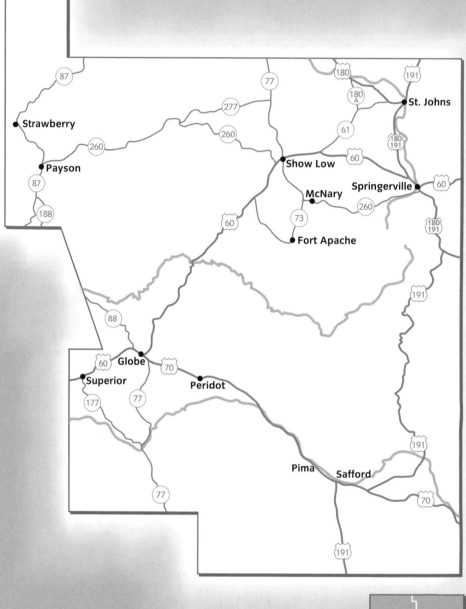

you want to get stranded without having a backup plan. Some of the back roads especially can get mucked up when it rains or snows, and light travel in the area means you could be stuck for a while.

You will find basic hotels and eateries, but your best bet is to just plan on roughing it by camping out and packing your own food. Even though the history here is about as sparse as the population, you can retrace the steps of Billy the Kid, Geronimo, and Coronado while driving the Old West Highway. Other things to do include touring cotton gins in the farming community of the Gila River Basin, fishing in the many high-country lakes in the White Mountains, and skiing at the state's largest ski resort, Sunrise Park Ski Resort.

Payson

Payson, located near the center of the state, is not only the Heart of Arizona, but is also the gateway to the forested Rim Country. The Mogollon (MUGGY-on) Rim, a ridge created from uplift, separates the Colorado Plateau in the northeastern corner of the state from the sweeping southern deserts. In the early 1880s, miners searching for gold settled the area, but when their efforts didn't pan out, settlers mined a greener gold, utilizing the forested countryside for ranching and lumbering. Payson's western charm can be seen in full force in August, when the whole town turns out to celebrate their heritage at the World's Oldest Continuous Rodeo. This country has sparked the imagination of writers and artists, the most famous being the Western author Zane Grey, whose novels brought visitors into a wildly scenic region. Today, Payson and the surrounding towns are popular retirement communities, which partly explains the lack of activities for families and young children. There are a few places worth checking out in town, but Payson is primarily used as a base for exploring the recreation wonderland of the Mogollon Rim.

Rim Country Museum (ages 5 and up)
700 Green Valley Parkway, Payson; (928) 474–3483. Open noon to 4:00 P.M. Wednesday through Sunday except all major holidays. Adults and children ages 12–17 $, under 12 free.

This museum, on historic Old Main Street, is a must-see for all lovers of the Old West. Several exhibits feature Payson's famous Western author, Zane Grey, with displays of the blueprints of his cabin, which was destroyed in a 1990 fire; books; movie posters; and even his player piano. On the main floor, the working model of a sawmill, which illustrates the importance of the lumber industry in the region, will be a hit with the kids. Upstairs you'll find period rooms ranging from a pioneer woman's kitchen to a blacksmith shop. Other buildings on the museum grounds include the first district ranger's office, a replica of the historic Herron Hotel (lost to fire in 1918), and a section of a U.S. Forest Service lookout tower.

Green Valley Park (all ages)

1000 West Country Club Drive, Payson; (928) 474–5242. Open daily. Free.

Payson's forty-five-acre park, located near the Rim Country Museum, features three man-made lakes stocked with a variety of fish. If you are older than fourteen, make sure to get an urban fishing license if you plan on casting for sunfish, bluegill, or any of the other varieties stocked in the ponds. On a nice day, the grassy slopes are strewn with people stretching out in the sun, while impromptu games of tag football and Frisbee reflect the town's easygoing charm. Picnic ramadas offer a great spot for a lunch break, and a playground keeps the kids busy. During the summer months, you can catch **free** concerts on Saturday and Sunday evenings, and miniature-sailboat regattas take over the lake in a flurry of colorful sails on Thursday mornings.

Strawberry Schoolhouse (all ages)

One and one-half miles west of the Strawberry Lodge on Fossil Creek Road, Strawberry; (928) 476–3333; www.pinestrawhs.org. Open 10:00 A.M. to 4:00 P.M. Saturday and 1:00 to 4:00 P.M. Sunday from mid-May to mid-October. Free.

This one-room log structure, tucked away in the tiny hamlet of Strawberry, will give your children a look at what school was like back in the late 1800s. Built in 1886, the Strawberry Schoolhouse is the state's oldest schoolhouse. Constructed out of hand-hewn pine logs and heated by a wood-burning stove, the schoolhouse served children in the area until 1907. One story tells of the first year of school and a mysterious thief that stole the teacher's highly prized chalk and eraser. None of the students confessed, but the mystery was finally solved during the building's restoration in 1965 when workers found the confiscated goods in a pack rat's nest in the attic. In June the town celebrates its namesake at a strawberry festival held at the schoolhouse, where you can see living-history demonstrations of such activities as butter churning, weaving, and roping.

Christopher Creek (all ages)

Payson Ranger District, 1009 East Highway 260, Payson; (928) 474–7900. Office open 8:00 A.M. to 5:00 P.M. Monday through Friday. Free.

This secluded, shady little creek offers great opportunities for children to stretch their legs while Mom and Dad kick back for some well-deserved R and R. This clear creek was named after Isador Christopher, whose homestead was raided and burned by Apaches.

Amazing Arizona Facts

Few places in the world have as diverse a set of wildlife as Arizona, which has 60 percent of all types of wildlife species found in North America.

The Search for **Fall Foliage**

If you're looking to put a little color in your life, the Forest Service can help. The toll-free fall foliage hotline provides tips on where to find peak fall color throughout the state along with general travel information. The office points visitors to the higher elevations to view the golden hues of aspen trees and directs those scouting for the brilliant reds to locales with bigtooth maple trees, scarlet sumac, squawbush shrubs, and the Virginia creeper vine. For more information call (800) 354–4595.

Christopher was away that day but had killed a bear, which was hung in one of the cabins. Army troops came across the blaze, put it out, and buried the bear, thinking it was poor old Christopher. You won't see army troops or raiding Apaches, but you might just see a bear or other wildlife in the area. Picnic facilities and great fishing holes add to the charm of a relaxing day by the clear waters.

Kohl's Ranch (ages 6 and up)

Seventeen miles east of Payson, East Highway 260, Payson; (928) 478–0030. Open daily 9:00 A.M. to 4:00 P.M. daily. Trail ride $$$$.

Kohl's Stables offers guided trail rides through the forested Rim Country year-round. Along the trail, guides narrate the countryside with tales of the region's rich history and point out local wildlife such as deer, elk, and javelina. A petting zoo at the stable introduces kids to goats, chickens, Barbados sheep, donkeys, and a pair of ostriches. And if your tots are too young for the trail ride, they can still get a cowboy experience with a pony ride in the corral. The ranch has a great restaurant and choice lodging for families.

Tonto Creek Fish Hatchery (all ages)

Twenty-one miles east of Payson on Forest Road 289, C2 Box 961, Payson; (928) 478–4200. Open daily 8:00 A.M. to 4:00 P.M. except Thanksgiving and Christmas, pending weather and construction projects. Free.

Check out the hatchery visitor center, amble around the grounds on an interpretive walk, and take a tour of the hatchery rooms. Outside, a show pond teems with monster trout ranging from eight to fifteen pounds, which the kids can feed for a quarter. If the tour gets the children itching for angling, cast a line at Tonto Creek just outside of the hatchery grounds, where rainbow, brook, and brown trout are released. The best time for trout fishing here is between May and July, and the fish usually bite well on salmon eggs—something for the squeamish to be thankful for.

Tonto National Bridge State Park (all ages)

Eleven miles north of Payson on Highway 87, P.O. Box 1245, Payson 85541; (928) 476–4202; www.pr.state.az.us/Parks/parkhtml/tonto.html. Open daily 8:00 A.M. to 6:00 P.M. April, September, and October, 8:00 A.M. to 7:00 P.M. Memorial Day through Labor Day, and 9:00 A.M. to 5:00 P.M. November through March except Christmas Day. The park closes at 2:00 P.M. Thanksgiving and Christmas Eve. Admission is $$ per vehicle for up to four adults, $ extra for each additional adult. There is no entry one hour prior to closing.

Walk across the world's largest travertine bridge and take in some of the most beautiful views at this state park. Deposits from free-flowing mineral springs continue to build this massive arch, spanning 150 feet across Pine Canyon at a width of 400 feet. Get a better look at the travertine formations under the bridge, which could easily pass over an eleven-story building, by taking one of the steep trails down into the canyon. The Apache have a story that explains the formation as the place where a water monster broke through the limestone, escaping along with all of the waters of a fabled inland sea. Now all that remains is the splendorous sight of the travertine bridge and the clear flow of Pine Creek. Intrepid explorers walking down can cool off in one of Pine Creek's swimming holes before clambering back up to enjoy a picnic lunch at one of the park's ramadas. Just be aware that the path can be slippery, and shoes with good traction are a must if you want to avoid bumps and bruises on the way down. State health law prohibits dogs on trails.

Fossil Creek LLamas (ages 8 and up)

Nineteen miles north of Payson, 10379 West Fossil Creek Road, Strawberry; (928) 476–5178; www.fossilcreekllamas.com. Hours vary. Rates $$$$; special children's rates. Reservations required.

Explore the Mogollon Rim with a llama-hiking buddy in the many programs offered by this unique operation. During your day hike, the ranch's gentle llamas will carry your family's gear and amuse you with their curiosity.-Kids will especially enjoy listening to the llamas as they hum a little tune. If you decide to extend your stay overnight, the ranch offers accommodations at the Teepee Bed and Breakfast.

Where to Eat

El Rancho. 200 South Beeline Highway, Payson; (928) 474–3111. Mexican and American food and a children's menu. $

Macky's Grill. 1111 South Beeline Highway, Payson; (928) 474–7411. American food and a complete children's menu with hot dogs, chicken strips, and fish. $–$$

Pizza Factory. 238 East Highway 260, Payson; (928) 474–1895. Pasta, pizza, and subs. $$

Tiny's Family Restaurant. 600 East Highway 260, Payson; (928) 474–5429. Pasta, subs, salads, and seafood. Children's menu. $$

Where to Stay

Best Value Inn. 811 South Beeline Highway, Payson; (928) 474–2283 or (800) 474–2283. Children under twelve stay **free.** $$–$$$

Best Western Payson Inn. 801 North Beeline Highway, Payson; (928) 474–3241 or (800) 247–9477. Pool, spa, kitchenettes, and fireplaces. $$–$$$

Days Inn and Suites. 301-A South Beeline Highway, Payson; (928) 474–9800 or (877) 474–9800. Indoor pool and spa and continental breakfast. $$–$$$

Holiday Inn Express. 206 South Beeline Highway, Payson; (928) 472–7484 or (800) 818–7484. Guest laundry, indoor pool and spa, and continental breakfast. $$$–$$$$

Area Campgrounds

Houston Mesa Campground. Two miles north of Payson on Highway 89, Payson Ranger District, 1009 East Highway 260; Payson; (928) 474–7900. RV sites. Showers, interpretive trail, and weekend programs. Open year-round. $

Ponderosa Campground. Twelve miles east of Payson, Payson Ranger District, 1009 East Highway 260, Payson; (928) 474–7900. Tent and RV sites with water hookups. Open year-round. $

For More Information

Rim Country Regional Chamber of Commerce. Mark 100, northwest corner of Beeline Highway and Main Street, P.O. Box 1380, Payson 85547; (928) 474–4515; www.rimcountrychamber.com

Springerville

None of the towns in the White Mountain Region have much in the way of amenities, but Springerville makes the most convenient stopover point while exploring this remote mountain range. This town's name comes from Henry Springer, who opened a trading post here in 1879. Since that time, the town has grown to become a major trade, lumber, and ranching center for the area. However, several other communities—Pinetop-Lakeside, Greer, and Show Low—will just as easily serve as a place to fill up on gas and groceries. Since you've made it this far, you should take the trip to Fort Apache to learn about the White Mountain Apache tribe. Most of the land you'll be traveling on up here is part of the tribe's 1.6 million acres of forests. The many mountain lakes make for great fishing and camping, and the terrain invites hiking and picnicking. While visiting the reservation, keep in mind that there are fees for most all outdoor activities, including hiking, fishing, picnicking, back-road travel, and camping. Swimming is prohibited in all Fort Apache lakes and streams. Keep in mind the Apache believe Earth is sacred. Show respect for the people and their land. Also, be aware of hunters, as this area attracts those seeking to bag elk, mountain lion, javelina, pronghorn, and smaller game during hunting season. On a positive note, the opportunities to get in touch with nature abound out here, and the region remains relatively unknown to even most Arizona residents, so you most likely won't have to share.

Big Lake Recreation Area (all ages) 🚶🏃🍁

Big Lake Visitor Center, Big Lake Recreation Complex, 20 miles southwest of Springerville on Forest Service Road 260; (928) 521–1842.

Garnet Jones and her husband, Ron, have spent more than a decade volunteering at the Big Lake Visitor Center. The center, situated in a tiny log cabin, has a plethora of information about the lake. Garnet takes children on walks along the nature trail near the center, pointing out indigo buntings, red baneberry, and mushrooms. Make sure to make it here during the lazy days of summer, though, because the center closes for the winter.

Lyman Lake State Park (all ages) 🅰️🏊🔺🎣

Seventeen miles north of Springerville, P.O. 1428, St. Johns 85936; (928) 337–4441; www.pr.state.az.us/Parks/parkhtml/lyman.html. Open daily. Day use $$.

A small dam on the Little Colorado River created this 1,500-acre lake situated at 6,000 feet. This high-plains hideaway is home to a herd of buffalo—a remnant of the Old West that children are bound to enjoy. Unrestricted water sports open up the possibilities for sailing, waterskiing, and Jet Skis. A protected swim area between two peninsulas provides yet another way to enjoy the lake. Other features include a campground, fishing pier, and hiking trails. If you're looking for a relaxed way to enjoy the Fourth of July, celebrate Independence Day with the "Fire Over Water" fireworks display. Another fun summer option is to take one of the guided petroglyphs tours to Rattlesnake Point Pueblo across the lake. One-hour tours leave on Saturday and Sunday from the visitor center at 2:00 P.M., and ninety-minute tours leave at 10:00 A.M. The tours are offered between Memorial Day and Labor Day, and reservations are recommended.

Casa Malpais Archeological Park (ages 6 and up) 🚶🏛️♿

318 East Main Street, Springerville; (928) 333–5375. Open daily 8:00 A.M. to 4:00 P.M. Adults $$, children $.

The Mogollon people, a prehistoric community dating back at this site from A.D. 1300, once inhabited this 120-room masonry pueblo. The ruins at Casa Malpais, Spanish for "house of the badlands," sits on a series of terraces at the edge of an immense lava flow. The museum orients visitors on the lives of these prehistoric peoples and provides detailed information on the site's ceremonial and burial chambers. The famous burial catacombs are off-limits to the public, but guided tours take visitors up a cliff trail and past petroglyph sites and the pueblo ruins. The tours leave daily at 9:00 and 11:00 A.M. and again at 2:00 P.M. The tours last ninety minutes and involve a 1.5-mile terraced climb up 250 feet. Be sure to wear hiking boots or sturdy shoes for this narrow, rocky hike. Hats and water are other essentials, especially during the heat of the summer months.

Show Low Lake (all ages)

Five miles south of Show Low, Show Low Lake Road, Show Low; (928) 537–4126. Open year-round. Day use $, overnight $$, attractions $$$.

Paddleboats, which are available for rent at the marina, will delight children of all ages—just make sure to keep their life jackets fastened. Armadas invite picnickers, a playground will entertain youngsters, and the lake offers great fishing for walleye, channel catfish, trout, largemouth bass, and bluegill.

Fool Hollow Lake Recreation Area (all ages)

1500 North Fool Hollow Lake Road, Show Low; (928) 537–3680; www.pr.state.az.us/Parks/parkhtml.Foolhollow.html. Open daily 5:00 A.M. to 10:00 P.M. except Christmas Day. Office hours are daily 8:00 A.M. to 5:00 P.M. Day-use fee $$ per vehicle, overnight $$$.

You can enjoy boating, trout fishing, and camping at this 800-acre recreation area centered around a small 150-acre mountain lake. The campground hosts both tents and RVs, provides several playgrounds for the kids to enjoy, and offers plenty of fresh mountain air. You can also stretch your legs on the eleven loop trails at the nearby White Mountain Trail System.

Sunrise Park Ski Resort (all ages)

Eighteen miles southeast of Pinetop-Lakeside, P.O. Box 217, McNary 85930; (928) 735–7669 or (800) 55–HOTEL; www.sunriseskipark.com. Open December to mid-April. Lift rates: Adults $$$$ for full- and half-day passes, children 12 and under $$$–$$$$.

Hugging three towering peaks in the White Mountains—Sunrise, Apache, and Cyclone Circle—Sunrise Park Ski Resort is the largest of its kind in the state. The resort features eleven lifts and sixty-five ski runs snaking though pine and aspen forests. As the resort is geared to families, you will also find a snowboard park, Nordic trails system, a tubing park, horse-drawn sleigh rides, and snowmobiling. Best of all, if not all of your children are old enough to take advantage of all the outdoor opportunities available, you can enlist the resort's child-care services. Both indoor and outdoor activities for children ages three to six and baby-sitting for infants ages two and under are available. This is also a great destination in the summer, when you can enjoy boating and fishing on the 891-acre Sunrise Lake, hiking, camping, horseback riding, mountain biking, or scenic sky rides to the forested mountaintops.

Mogollon Rim Overlook and Nature Trail (all ages)

Lakeside Ranger Station, 2022 White Mountain Boulevard, Pinetop-Lakeside; (928) 368–5111. Open 8:00 A.M. to 4:30 P.M. Monday through Friday. Free.

Situated in the Apache-Sitgreaves National Forest, this easy 1-mile walk affords views of forested valleys and ridges. All ages will enjoy the scenery, and older children will get a natural-history lesson through the interpretive signs along the way, which describe the thick stands of trees, native uses of medicinal plants, and the rich history of the region. The trailhead is located west of State Route 260, 3 miles north of the Ranger Station.

Hiking in **Circles**

High-altitude hikers of all ages can enjoy their choice of 180 miles of loop trails of varying difficulty, which meander through the woods in the White Mountains near Pinetop and Lakeside. With summer temperatures generally hovering in the seventies, the array of trails through the ponderosa pine forests of the lake-speckled Rim Country draws visitors from the overheated deserts around Phoenix and from across the country. The White Mountain Trail system currently includes eleven different loop trails. The first trails were built in 1987, and the master plan calls for connections among all eleven trails in the next several years. Pinetop-Lakeside, Show Low, the White Mountain Horseman's Association, the U.S. Forest Service, the Arizona Heritage Fund, and TRACKS developed the trails as a joint effort. Loops wander past ice caves; follow the General Crook trail, which played a key role in the Apache Wars; and pass through groves of aspen, oak, pine, and juniper.

A detailed map is available at the Pinetop-Lakeside Parks and Recreation Department, 1360 North Niels Hanson Lane, Pinetop-Lakeside ($). For more information call (928) 368–6700.

While here, make sure to stop at the station to pick up information on other nearby trails and wildlife-watching areas, including the Big Springs Environmental Study Area, Rainbow Lake, Woodland Lake, Scott Reservoir, and the White Mountain Trail System.

Porter Mountain Stables (ages 6 and up) 🐎

Porter Mountain Road, Pinetop-Lakeside; (928) 368–5306. Open May through September. One- and two-hour rides $$$$.

This small stable boasts a string of horses for all levels of riders. Trail guides are friendly and informative. This is an especially wonderful place for a child's first horseback experience, as guides will spend some time helping your child get acquainted with the rudiments of horseback riding. The scenic trails are breathtaking, making for a wonderful trip.

White Mountain Apache Cultural Center and Museum (all ages)
🏛️ 📖

127 Scout Road, Fort Apache; (928) 338–4625; www.wmat.us/wmaculture.shtml. Open daily 8:00 A.M. to 5:00 P.M. Monday through Friday year-round and 8:00 A.M. to 5:00 P.M. on Saturdays in the summer, except all major holidays. Adults and children 4 and over $, under 4 free.

The White Mountain Apache Cultural Center and Museum at Fort Apache, 5 miles south of Whiteriver, is called Nowike´ Bagowa or the "House of Our Footprints." Its climate-controlled archives safeguard the documents, photographs, tapes, and artifacts that

Permission **Slips**

Recreation on the White Mountain Apache Reservation can be a little tricky, so I would highly recommend getting a copy of the free White Mountain Apache Tribe Outdoor Recreation Regulations, which you can get by writing to P.O. Box 220, Whiteriver 85941. Arizona fishing licenses don't count for much on Apache land; if you plan on fishing the reservation's twenty-five lakes or 400 miles of mountain streams, you'll have to obtain a special fishing license from the tribal offices. Fees are adults $$ daily, children ages ten to fourteen $, and free for children under ten fishing with a license-carrying adult. Annual passes are $$$$. If you don't have a fishing license, you'll need to purchase a vehicle pass ($$) for sight-seeing and picnicking on reservation lands. While traveling in the White Mountains, be on the lookout for logging trucks, and always check on road conditions before traveling the reservation's back roads. You can pick up recreation information and permits at the Game and Fish Department (928–338–4385) or at Hon-Dah Ski and Outdoor Sport (928–369–7669).

record the history of this warrior culture that loved peace. Interpretive signing, audiotapes of folk stories, and live demonstrations accompany the main display of Apache basketry, and contemporary Apache artists are featured in changing exhibits.

Where to Eat

El Rancho. 1523 East White Mountain Boulevard, Pinetop-Lakeside; (928) 367–4557. Basic Mexican entrees. Children's menu. $

Lil' Ranglers Café. 173 West Main Street, Springerville; (928) 333–4826. Steaks, hamburgers, and salads. Children's menu. $–$$

Where to Stay

Blue Ridge Motel and Cabins. 2012 East White Mountain Boulevard, Pinetop-Lakeside; (928) 367–0758. Log-style cabins and motel units. Smaller cabins have kitchenettes, and larger cabins have kitchenettes and fireplaces. $$–$$$

Hannigan Meadow Lodge. Twenty-two miles south of Alpine off Highway 191, HC 61, Box 335, Alpine 85920; (928) 339–4370, www.hanniganmeadow.com.

Lodge units, cabins, and a restaurant. Recreational opportunities include snowmobiling, cross-country skiing, hiking, horseback riding, and fishing. $$–$$$$

Whispering Pines Resort. 237 East White Mountain Boulevard, Pinetop-Lakeside; (928) 367–4386; www. whisperingpinesaz.com. Cabins with kitchenettes and fireplaces. $$$–$$$$

Area Campgrounds

Fool Hollow Recreation Area. Three miles northwest of Show Low, Old Linden Road, Show Low; (928) 537–3680. Tent and RV sites with hookups. Lake, interpretive programs Memorial Day to Labor Day, and children's playgrounds. $

Luna Lake Campground. Alpine; (877) 444–6777; www.reserveusa.com. Birdwatching, boat launch, boat rentals, bait shop, and general store. Open from mid-May to mid-September. $

For More Information

Alpine Chamber of Commerce. P.O. Box 410, Alpine 85920; (928) 339–4330.

Pinetop-Lakeside Chamber of Commerce. 102C West White Mountain Boulevard, Pinetop-Lakeside 85935; (928) 367–4290; ci.pinetop-lakeside.az.us.

Round Valley Chamber of Commerce. 318 East Main Street, Springerville, 85938; (928) 333–2123; www.springerville-eagar.com.

Show Low Regional Chamber of Commerce. 81 East Deuce of Clubs, Show Low 85902; (928) 537–2326 or (888) SHOW LOW.

Springerville Ranger District Office. 165 South Mountain Avenue, Springerville 85938; (928) 333–4372.

White Mountain Apache Department of Game and Fish. P.O. Box 220, Whiteriver 85941; (928) 338–4385.

Head for the **Wild Blue Yonder**

A 66-mile-long loop drive on a gravel road suitable for passenger cars leads to some of the most dramatic scenery in the **Blue Range Primitive Area**, a rugged wilderness that sprawls along the Arizona–New Mexico border in prime wildlife habitat.

Blue River Road (Forest Service Road 281) begins and ends near the tiny town of Alpine and follows its namesake river for miles. Drivers not distracted by the sweeping panoramas, craggy hills, and canyons might see Rocky Mountain elk, black bear, mountain lion, or javelina. Those who want to linger a while can overnight in Alpine or set up tents in a Forest Service campground.

Blue River Road can be accessed from U.S. Route 180, 3 miles east of Alpine or from U.S. 191 about 14 miles south of the mountain hamlet.

For directions, weather, and road conditions, call the Alpine Ranger District at (928) 339–4384; for lodging call the Alpine Chamber of Commerce at (928) 339–4330.

Globe

The small community of Globe is all that is left from the nearby silver strike of 1875. At that time the area was part of the San Carlos Apache Indian Reservation, but it was officially cut off from the reservation when prospectors discovered silver in the western hills. Globe grew up as a result and was named after a globe-shaped silver nugget with the rough outlines of the continents on its surface that was found in the early mining days. After just four years the silver gave out, but copper deposits underneath prompted another boom, led by the Old Dominion Copper Company. However, like many of Arizona's mining operations, the company closed down in 1931 as a result of the Great Depression. Today this quaint community celebrates its rich history as one of the greatest copper mines in the world. Globe makes a great stopping place for those visiting nearby Native American ruins and the vegetative wonders at the Boyce Thompson Arboretum. The San Carlos Apache Reservation, the largest Apache reservation in Arizona, offers insight to the modern-day Native Americans that occupy this portion of the state. Raft down the Salt River, walk the rooms of ancient peoples, and explore the diverse landscape of high plains and rugged canyons. Even though you will have to search a little harder than in more heavily populated areas, you'll still be able to find fun activities for every member of your family.

Besh-Ba-Gowah Archaeological Park (all ages) 🏛️ 📷 🌼

150 North Pine Street (located on Jess Hayes Road; call for directions), Globe; (928) 425–0320 or (800) 804–5623. Open daily 9:00 A.M. to 5:00 P.M. except Thanksgiving, Christmas, and New Year's Day. Adults $, under 12 free.

Unlike most ruins, you can walk through the restored rooms of Besh-Ba-Gowah, a 700-year-old pueblo. Kids will especially love climbing the ladders to upper floors and looking at the pottery, utensils, and other implements of prehistoric daily life. The Salado Indians inhabited the 200-room village between A.D. 1225 and 1450. The village lay in ruins until the 1980s, when it was rebuilt from a small diorama drawn by the archaeologist Adolph Bandelier. An ethno-botanical garden outside features crops grown by these agricultural people, including wild tobacco, corn, gourds, squash, and cotton. Kids can try their hand at grinding corn at a nearby ramada with stone metates once used by these native peoples. Inside the visitor center museum, a scale model of the village shows how it appeared in A.D. 1325.

Boyce Thompson Southwestern Arboretum State Park
(all ages) 🏕️ 🚶 ♿ 🌼

37615 Highway 60, Superior; (520) 689–2811 or (520) 689–2723; www.pr.state.az.us/Parks/ parkhtml/boyce.html. Open daily 8:00 A.M. to 5:00 P.M. except Christmas Day. Adults $$, children ages 5–12 $, under 5 free.

More than 2,900 desert plants are featured in this park, which encompasses the oldest and largest botanical garden in the state. Nature trails lead through several different themed gardens, including Sonoran and Chihuahuan Desert habitats, herb and rose gardens, a riparian area, and a children's garden. A visitor center, demonstration garden, and greenhouses complete the offerings. The themed gardens can be reached off the 1½-mile main loop trail in Queen Creek Canyon. Some of the best events for kids at the park include Earth Arbor Day, held on the last Saturday in April; Bye Bye Buzzards, on the second Saturday of September; and the Fall Color Festival, on the third Saturday of November.

Gila County Historical Museum (ages 6 and up) 📷

1330 North Broad Street, Globe; (928) 425–7385. Open 10:00 A.M. to 4:00 P.M. Monday through Friday, 11:00 A.M. to 3:00 P.M. Saturday, except major holidays. Free.

As museums go, this one is tiny and not worth the stop by itself, but its location next to the Globe-Miami Chamber of Commerce makes it convenient if you plan to pick up brochures and maps of the area. The 1914 historical building was once the mine's rescue station for the Old Dominion Copper Company. Today it houses period rooms and a small collection of Apache, pioneer, and mining artifacts.

Blue Sky Expeditions (ages 5 and up) ⚠

610 East Oak Street, Globe; (800) 425–5253; www.gobluesky.com. Open daily from May to September. $$$$

Families can float away the day on this tour operator's Gila Float Trip, which leaves Winkleman City Park daily at 10:00 A.M. during the summer months. The five-hour, 10-mile trip provides opportunities to swim in the river next to the eight-person rafts or engage in a squirt-gun fight. The rafts stop on the shores of the Gila River for lunch and a chance to explore the shoreline before casting off again.

San Carlos Apache Cultural Center (all ages) 🔵

Mile marker 272 off Highway 70, P.O. Box 7760, Peridot 85542; (928) 475–2894. Open 9:00 A.M. to 5:00 P.M. Monday through Friday except holidays and during tribal events. Adults and children 12 and up $, under 12 free.

Take a trip into the past at the San Carlos Apache Cultural Center in Peridot. Historical pictures, artifacts, and a life-size diorama of the Changing Woman ceremony take visitors on a tour through the tribe's vast cultural legacy. In addition to the exhibits, educational programs and demonstrations instruct and entertain history buffs of all ages. The gift shop at the center entices lovers of Native American art with delicate beadwork, Apache violins, and intricate tribal woodcarvings.

Where to Eat

Country Kitchen. 1505 East Ash Street, Globe; (928) 425–2137. Standard American fare. Extensive children's menu. $

Irene's Real Mexican Food. 1601 East Ash Street, Globe; (928) 425–7904. Authentic Mexican specialties. Children's menu. $

R&R Pizza Express. 1100 North Broad Street, Globe; (928) 425–8575. Pizza, wings, and a spaghetti and soup buffet bar. $–$$

Where to Stay

Comfort Inn. 1515 South Street, Globe; (928) 425–7575 or (800) 228–5150. Pool and spa. Children under eighteen stay free. $$–$$$

El Rey Motel. 1201 Ash Street, Globe; (928) 425–4427. Basic budget rooms and picnic facilities. $

Motel 6. 1699 East Ash Street, Globe; (928) 425–5741. Family units, refrigerators, pool, and spa. Children under eighteen stay free. $–$$

For More Information

Globe-Miami Chamber of Commerce. 1360 North Broad Street, Globe 85501; (928) 425–4495 or (800) 804–5623; www.globemiamichamber.com.

Globe Ranger District. 7680 South Six Shooter Canyon Road, Globe 85501; (928) 402–6200; www.fs.fed.us/r3/tonto.

Safford

Deeply rooted in the rich topsoil of the rural history of the Old West, Graham County offers a great place for a relaxed weekend of family fun. Surrounded by the Pinaleno, Gila, and Peloncillo mountain ranges, this land of diversity ranges from lower Sonoran Desert to the spruce-forest heights of Mount Graham, the county's namesake and one of Arizona's tallest peaks. Cotton-gin tours, horseback riding, hiking, camping, fishing, and rockhounding top the list of things to do in this relaxed part of the country.

When visiting this area, a stop at the Graham County Chamber of Commerce is a must. The kids can stretch their legs in the park behind the building, and parents can stock up on instructive brochures and travel advice. A mini museum in the chamber center will give you a quick glimpse into the area's rich heritage with dioramas, displays of gems and minerals, and raw cotton samples for the kids to feel.

Whether visiting an old-fashioned county fair, dropping a line in a stream-fed pond, or digging for gems, you and your family will enjoy the relaxed atmosphere of this bountiful part of Arizona. By any book, history is alive and well in Graham County, where extremes and diversity mean a lingering conversation over a campfire while roasting marshmallows.

Discovery Park (ages 6 and up)

1651 Discovery Park Boulevard, Safford; (928) 428–6260; www.discoverypark.com. Open 6:00 to 10:00 P.M. Friday and 4:00 to 10:00 P.M. Saturday. Adults $$, children ages 6–11 $, children under 5 free with a paying adult; $, train ride $, simulator $$.

At the base of Mount Graham, Discovery Park provides a unique view of the mountain through the world's largest camera obscura. Other features at this educational science center include star viewing through a 20-inch reflecting telescope in the Gov Aker Observatory, a full-motion shuttle flight simulator that travels through the solar system at light speed, and educational exhibits about the universe in which we live. Outside, a train takes passengers through a restored section of the Gila River Basin in the park's wildlife watching habitat, Nature's Hideaway.

Black Hills Rockhound Area (all ages)

Bureau of Land Management, 711 Fourteenth Avenue, Safford; (928) 348–4400. Area open daily, offices open 7:45 A.M. to 4:15 P.M. Monday through Friday. Free.

Those wanting to dig down to the foundation of this region need only a bucket and shovel at the Black Hills Rockhound Area. The volcanic Black Hills in the northern end of the Peloncillo Mountains once provided a hideout for Geronimo and his followers prior to their final surrender in 1886. Arrowheads from the days when warfare ranged these hills are scattered among the region's colorful rocks. Deposits of fire agate, colored like an opal with flashing highlights of red, green, and blue, are only found in the desert regions of Arizona, southern California, and central Mexico. Safford, the Graham County seat, claims to be the Fire Agate Capital of the World, and for good reason. This relatively new gemstone, associated with volcanic deposits, was formally recognized in the 1930s and is found in

A Miner Family **Adventure**

In search of a relaxing weekend with my twin boys, I loaded up the car and set off for the broad Gila River Valley in southeastern Arizona's Graham County. The boys nodded off just out of Tucson and woke up as we neared our destination. Hayden looked out of the window, staring wide-eyed at the fluffy cotton fields. "Look," he squealed. "Snow."

Blake looked at the white countryside and then to me. "Mom," he said in his best grown-up scolding voice, "You forgot our gloves."

The "snow" was really cotton, the first bushels of which are picked by hand in October. Since we arrived at the start of ginning season, I decided to stop at one of the county's two cotton gins.

As part of the tour, we played with raw cotton, pulling it apart like taffy. They boys looked at the odd "snow" suspiciously but seemed entertained by the soft stuff. Then we followed the small group inside the noisy gin to see how the cotton is processed from the plant to 500-pound bales. Once back outside, we got the chance to get an up-close look at module trucks—huge metal monstrosities used to pick the fields. Blake and Hayden wondered when the "Tonka" trucks were going to start digging and then got distracted by the lint softly falling from the sky. So much for cotton picking.

abundance here. Children love sifting through this rich geological history, pocketing the jeweled stones, and discovering the occasional arrowhead. However, please note that it is against the law to keep artifacts, so warn the kids that they'll have to leave behind any archaeological finds.

Cotton Gin Tours (all ages)
Safford Valley Cotton Growers Co-op, 120 East Ninth Street, Safford; (928) 428–0714. Open Friday afternoons from October through December. Tours are at 2:00 P.M. Free.

If you've ever been interested in how cotton transforms from plant to fiber, a cotton-gin tour may be in order. Reminiscent of the harvests in the 1880s, the first bushels of cotton are picked by hand in October. Visitors get an opportunity to feel cotton samples as the tour operator discusses the process used to remove the seeds from the lint. The seeds, a commodity in their own right, are used as feed, cooking oil, and seed stock for the next crop. After the seed is removed, the lint is cleaned, pressed into 500-pound bales, and shipped to a warehouse for sale to textile and yarn mills. The gin rumbles noisily as it works, which might startle younger children, but back out in the yard they'll perk back up when they see the monster module trucks, which are used to pick the fields.

A Birder's **Paradise**

More than 300 species of birds can be found in Graham County's diverse habitats, which range from Sonoran and Chihuahuan lowland deserts at 2,400 feet to spruce-fir forests at 10,720 feet. You can introduce your kids to the delights of birding at the top fifty birding areas in the region featured on the Southeastern Arizona Birding Trail, a map of which is available online at www.visit grahamcounty.com/bird.asp. For more information, call the Graham County Chamber of Commerce at (928) 428–2511 or toll free at (888) 837–1841.

Cluff Ranch Wildlife Area (all ages) 🐘 🔺 🦆 🏕️

Arizona Game and Fish Department, 2002 Cluff Ranch Road, Pima; (928) 485–9430. Open daily. Free.

For a secluded outdoor destination, your family will enjoy the serene, 788-acre Cluff Ranch Wildlife Area, nestled at the base of Mount Graham. Camping, boating, and fishing in the area's three ponds top the list of things to do in this lush riparian area. While visiting this wildlife sanctuary, keep an eye out for mule deer, javelina, raccoon, badger, fox, and porcupine.

Mount Graham Drive (all ages) 🏕️ 🚶 🚐

Safford Ranger Station, 504 Fifth Avenue, Third Floor, Safford; (928) 428–4150. Open daily. Free.

On the drive up the 10,713-foot peak, you might see such birds as the great horned owl, red-naped sapsucker, and Steller's jay. Mount Graham soars 8,000 feet over Safford, the greatest vertical rise of any mountain in Arizona. The Swift Trail Parkway ascends the eastern slopes of the mountain, traveling from the lower Sonoran Desert vegetation of cactus, creosote, and mesquite to the high-forested regions of ponderosa pine, aspen, and stands of Engelman spruce. While on the 34-mile drive, keep an eye out for the Mount Graham pocket gopher, Mount Graham red squirrel, white-bellied vole, and Rusby's mountain fleabane—all of which are only found in the Pinaleno Mountains. On the way up you'll pass an apple orchard maintained by the Forest Service. Fruit stands, open in late summer and early fall, will give you a chance to sample some of the state's best. There are several developed campgrounds along the way, which you can stay in for $10.

Muleshoe Ranch Cooperative Management Area (all ages) 🐘 🚶 ⊖

The Nature Conservancy, 30 miles northwest of Willcox, RR1, Box 1542, Willcox 85643; (520) 507–5229. Open 8:00 A.M. to 5:00 P.M. Thursday through Monday except Thanksgiving and Christmas Day. Free.

Troops of black-masked coatimundis, grazing mule deer, and a variety of avian species such as green-tailed towhees, yellow-eyed juncos, and white-crowned sparrows are just a few of animals that can be seen during the guided hikes at the Muleshoe Ranch Cooperative Management Area. Muleshoe Ranch, located in the Galiuro Wilderness southwest of Safford, is part of 55,000 acres of rugged wilderness chock full of free-flowing streams and lush riparian areas. The easy ¾-mile hike, perfect for kids of all ages, is offered on Saturday from September to May and departs from the ranch at 8:00 or 9:00 A.M., depending on the weather. Accommodations (fee) at the ranch include casitas, cabins, and camping facilities from Labor Day through Memorial Day weekends.

Roper Lake State Park (all ages) 🍽️🏊🎣🏕️

101 East Roper Lake State Park, Safford; (928) 428–6760; www.pr.state.az.us/Parks/park html/roper.html. Open daily 6:00 A.M. to 10:00 P.M. Day use $. Overnight use $$$.

Families wanting to rough it can set up camp at Roper Lake State Park. A favorite getaway for locals, the park is a great place for fishing, swimming, and hiking. Adults can soak away the strains of vigorous outdoor adventures in the park's hot mineral spring while children frolic on the sandy beaches of a man-made island.

Anglers cast lines for stocked rainbow trout during the winter months in both the lake and Dankworth Ponds, 2 miles south of Roper Lake. Those in search of an easy walk through time can amble up to the Indian Village on the overlooking mesa. This 1¾-mile loop trail takes time travelers on a self-guided tour through the re-created architecture of the different peoples that once lived in the area. Buildings include a Hohokam pit house, a Salado building, and an Apache wickiup.

Amazing Arizona Facts

The North American red squirrel measures a mere 12 inches in length, making it the smallest tree squirrel in the United States. The Mount Graham red squirrel, found only on this "sky island," is slightly smaller than its cousins. The most vocal of squirrels, these chattering critters are diurnal— playing, eating, and gathering food during the daylight hours. You'll be most likely to see them during the warmest part of the day in the cold winter months and the cooler hours in the hot summer months. And if you don't see them, you might very well hear them. Territorial by nature, the Mount Graham red squirrels will chastise competitors and scold predators with a rattle call. Other sounds in their vocabulary include a variety of chirps, barks, screeches, chatter, growls, squeaks, and buzzing.

Black Hills **Backcountry Byway**

In 1872 the gold rush in nearby Clifton helped the agricultural communities blossom as the farmers raced to meet the miners' demands for wood and produce. The 21-mile Black Hills Backcountry Byway, built between 1914 and 1920 by chain gangs, connects the agricultural Gila Valley communities to the Clifton-Morenci mining communities. On this trip travelers will pass over the old Safford bridge—a perfect spot for a picnic lunch. Some of the wildlife you might spot includes diamondback rattlesnakes, mule deer, and javelinas. This road is best traveled by high-clearance vehicles and only in dry weather. For more information call (928) 348–4400.

Where to Eat

El Coronado. 409 Main Street, Safford; (928) 428–7755. A friendly restaurant featuring Mexican specialties and American mainstays. Children's menu. $–$$

Golden Corral Steak House. 2019 West Highway 70, Thatcher; (928) 428–4744. A family-oriented steak house with a buffet. $

R&R Pizza Express. 2646 West Highway 70, Safford; (928) 428–7775. Pizza, pasta, and a soup and salad buffet in a relaxed atmosphere. $–$$

Econo Lodge. 225 East Highway 70, Safford; (928) 348–0011 or (800) 553–2666. Swimming pool and **free** continental breakfast. $

Olney House Bed and Breakfast. 1104 Central Avenue, Safford; (928) 428–5118 or (800) 814–5118. A historic house with two cottages; family-style breakfast. $$$

Quality Inn. 420 East Highway 70, Safford; (928) 428–3200. Heated indoor pool, ice cream parlor, Piccadilly Circus Pizza, and a five-hole putting green. Children under eighteen stay **free.** $$$–$$$$

Where to Stay

Best Western Desert Inn. 1391 West Thatcher Boulevard, Safford; (928) 428–0521 or (800) 707–2336. Pool, kitchen suites, and restaurant. $$–$$$

For More Information

Graham County Chamber of Commerce. 1111 Thatcher Boulevard, Safford 85546; (928) 428–2511 or (888) 837–1841; www.visitgrahamcounty.com

Annual Events

APRIL

Miami Boom Town Spree. Miami; (928) 473–4403. Second weekend in April. Kids' mucking contest, mining competitions, parade, a wild bed race through the streets, cowboy shoot-out reenactments, and performances by the Apache Crown Dancers.

Herb Festival. Superior; (520) 689–2811. Second Saturday in April. Herbal cooking demonstrations, lectures by local herbalists, live entertainment, and children's games and crafts at the Boyce Thompson Arboretum.

JULY

White Mountain Native American Art Festival and Indian Market. Pinetop-Lakeside; (928) 367–4290 or (800) 573–4031. Mid-July. Native Americans from across the Southwest gather at this festival, which features indigenous dances, music, an art show, craft demonstrations, and ethnic food.

Round Valley Western July Fourth Celebration. Springerville; (928) 333–2123. July 4. Rodeo, pancake breakfast, deep-pit barbecue, parade, live entertainment, and a fireworks display.

AUGUST

World's Oldest Continuous Rodeo. Payson; (928) 474–4515. Third weekend in August. Rodeo events, children's programs, parade, and Western dance.

Eagar Daze. Eagar; (928) 333–4128. First weekend in August. A family-oriented festival complete with an ice cream social, a mud-mania event for kids, a logging competition, pancake breakfast, live entertainment, and a watermelon-eating contest.

White Mountain Bluegrass Music Festival. Pinetop-Lakeside; (928) 367–4290 or (800) 573–4031. Second weekend in August. A jam-packed entertainment schedule of good old-fashioned bluegrass and gospel, children's games, arts and crafts booths, and traditional fair food.

SEPTEMBER

Apache County Fair. St. Johns; (928) 337–2000. Mid-September. Livestock exhibitions, carnival, and food booths.

Old-Time Fiddlers' Contest. Payson; (928) 474–4515. Last weekend of September. Live entertainment, fiddle-making demonstrations, story telling, a twenty-one-fiddle salute, and arts and crafts.

OCTOBER

Graham County Fair. Safford; (928) 428–2511. Second weekend of October. An old-fashioned fair complete with animals, a parade down Main Street, gymkhana, agricultural displays, and contests.

Other Things to **See and Do**

- **Apache County Museum,** St. Johns; (928) 337–4737.
- **Aravaipa Canyon Wilderness,** Safford; (928) 348–4400.
- **Blue Sky Stables,** Greer; (928) 735–7454.
- **Butterfly Lodge Museum,** Greer; (928) 735–7514.
- **Cobre Valley Center for the Arts,** Globe; (928) 425–0884.
- **Glenbar Gin,** Safford; (928) 485–9255.
- **Hannagan Meadow,** Alpine; (928) 339–4370.
- **The J Train History and Nature Tours,** Safford; (928) 428–2820.
- **Little House Museum,** Greer; (928) 333–2286.
- **Museum of Rim Country Archeology,** Payson; (928) 468–1128.
- **OK Corral,** Payson; (928) 476–4303.
- **Payson Candle Factory,** Payson; (928) 474–2152.
- **Pinetop Lakes Equestrian Center,** Pinetop-Lakeside; (928) 369–1000.
- **Renee Cushman Art Museum,** Springerville; (928) 333–2123.
- **Shoofly Indian Ruins Archaeological Site,** Payson; (928) 474–4515.
- **Show Low Historical Society Museum,** Show Low; (928) 532–7115.
- **Thunder Raceway,** Show Low; (928) 537–1111.

Valley
of the
Sun

T he bland, red-tiled, unfurling suburbs of the understated Valley of the Sun harbor unexpected treasures for families traveling throughout Phoenix and its jostling ring of satellite communities. Kids—and parents—can stare awestruck at the massive anchor of a legendary battleship, gasp at the science-fiction glitter of glow-in-the-dark rocks, hurl foam ball pollen into a giant nose, sit in an authentic Native American pueblo and string beads, hand feed swarms of pigeons, ring the bell of a fire truck and slide down a fire pole, climb weird rock formations to reach a 100-mile view, visit the slumped and

Carrie's
TopPicks for fun in the Valley of the Sun

1. Arizona State Capitol, Phoenix

2. Arizona Mining and Mineral Museum, Phoenix

3. Arizona Science Center, Phoenix

4. Heard Museum, Phoenix

5. Pueblo Grande Museum and Archaeological Park, Phoenix

6. Phoenix Zoo, Phoenix

7. Deer Valley Rock Art Center, Phoenix

8. Rawhide Wild West Town, Scottsdale

9. Mesa Southwest Museum, Mesa

10. Casa Grande Ruins National Monument, Coolidge

VALLEY OF THE SUN

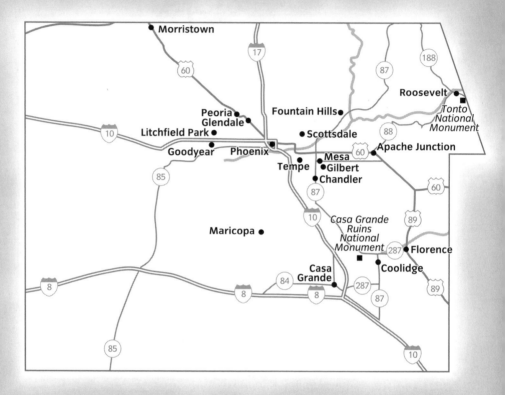

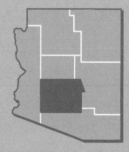

ghostly remains of a mysteriously vanished 1,000-year-old civilization, comb the mane of a pony, catch a glimpse of an endangered wolf, wander among the upside-down boojum trees that inspired Lewis Carroll's fancy, or wander through a beautiful patch of desert while attempting to decipher the enigmatic rock-art paintings of a vanished culture that once used sharpened sticks to dig hundreds of miles of canals throughout the valley. And that's just the start of the adventure.

The broad Salt River Valley, called the Valley of the Sun by locals, is the economic, cultural, and political base of Arizona. Here you'll find one of the busiest airports in the world, the Arizona State Capitol, more than half a million acres of farmland, and more than half of the entire state's population. Phoenix proper acts as the hub of the valley, with more than twenty communities lying on its outskirts—encompassing everything from the college town of Tempe to the old-fashioned charm of Glendale.

The Hohokam Indians originally inhabited the area, utilizing the Salt River for agriculture as early as A.D. 300. These prehistoric peoples created a complex and sophisticated civilization that lasted until A.D. 1450, when they mysteriously vanished. The Spanish laid claim to Arizona in 1821, and by 1850 it became a territory of the United States. Modern Phoenix started out as a small farming settlement near the Salt River, where Jack Swilling cleaned out the ancient canals and reaped his own crops of wheat and barley. More farmers followed, and by 1870 lots were being sold for $20 to $140 apiece. Today, more than 3.2 million people live in the metro area, and prime lots sell into the millions of dollars. In addition, this tourist hot spot attracts more than twelve million travelers to its sunny climes each year.

You will find that even though there are 300 days of sunshine annually, weather dictates life here. From November through April you'll find some of the best weather in the country, but from May through October most people try to beat the one-hundred-plus-degree heat by staying in air-conditioned buildings.

Outdoor recreation is best pursued in the comfortable winter months. Whether hiking the many mountain preserves ringing the valley, horseback riding, or checking out the many zoos, gardens, and parks, you and your family will have plenty to do. In the warmer summer months, many locals focus on water activities: tubing down the Salt River, lounging in the pool, or playing at a water park. And, of course, there are plenty of performing-art centers, museums, and professional sports offered year-round.

Phoenix

Darrel Duppa, one of Phoenix's early settlers, looked at the tiny agricultural community building over the ruins of the Hohokam civilization and believed that a great city would rise from the ashes of the old—just like the fabled phoenix. The phoenix—a mythical flame-colored bird the size of an eagle—is the only one of its kind in the world. Every 500 years it builds a nest, which it ignites as a pyre, and the new phoenix is reborn from the adult's ashes. The city with this fabled creature's name has since lived up to Duppa's vision of greatness. What started out as a small farming settlement is now the sixth-largest city in the nation.

Phoenix remains a quintessentially Southwestern place. The Hohokam lived here for a millennium, hacking great canals out of the dirt with sharp sticks and leaving behind places like Pueblo Grande and the rock-etched marvel of the Deer Valley Rock Art Center. They stayed put for centuries, passing down the same place names and the stories to go with them for generations. But they faltered and vanished—perhaps because some succession of flood and drought overwhelmed their monumental irrigation works. That long history and the mystery of a whole civilization that went missing provides an exciting and educational backdrop for a child-oriented exploration of the city. These days, Phoenix— the fastest growing city in the country—is about change and dreams, where three people move out for every five who move in. The city takes quick, shallow breaths, always discovering and exclaiming and packing.

Arizona State Capitol (ages 10 and up) 🏛️ 🧑‍🦽

1700 West Washington Street, Phoenix; (602) 542–4675; www.dlapr.lib.az.us/museum. Open Monday through Friday 8:00 A.M. to 5:00 P.M.; guided tours at 9:30 A.M., 11:00 A.M., and 1:00 P.M. Free.

For a lesson on history, bring the kids to the state's 1900 historic capitol building. Tours through the building's four floors take visitors into the restored House of Representatives, where kids can sit at legislative desks; past the Navajo Code Talkers exhibit, which details the involvement of the Navajo Indians during World War II; and to displays of the recovered silver service of the USS *Arizona,* which was on board when the battleship sunk in Pearl Harbor. Other things geared toward young visitors include an interactive exhibit detailing how a bill becomes a law, an exhibit on the real Uncle Sam, and a photographic

Building a Banner **for Statehood**

In 1910, two years before Arizona garnered statehood, an optimistic Capt. Charles W. Harris designed the state flag. In 1911 Nancy Hayden, wife of Arizona's Senator Carl Hayden, pieced together the bold design of blue, red, and yellow on a borrowed sewing machine. The top half of the flag displays alternating red and yellow sun rays rising from a field of blue on the bottom. The red and yellow represent the colors carried by the Spanish conquistadors that traveled to Arizona in the sixteenth century. The thirteen rays stand for the original thirteen American colonies, and the blue field is the same blue as in the U.S. flag. Inset in the center, a copper star identifies the state as the largest copper producer in the United States. On February 27, 1917, the State Legislature adopted the flag as Arizona's official state banner, and Nancy Hayden became known as the Betsy Ross of Arizona.

display of Phoenix's ostrich farming in the early 1900s. If you're at the capitol building while the legislature is in session (January through May), you can also take a tour to the visitor gallery in the modern Senate and House buildings to watch legislation in the making. Outside in the Wesley Bolin Plaza, you can see one of the anchors and the signal mast of the USS *Arizona* battleship, a Buddhist temple, and monuments dedicated to Father Kino, fallen police officers, and veterans of the Vietnam War.

Arizona Mining and Mineral Museum (ages 4 and up)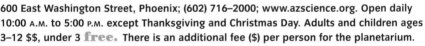

1502 West Washington Street, Phoenix; (602) 255–3795, ext. 10; www.admmr.state.az.us. Open weekdays 8:00 A.M. to 5:00 P.M. and Saturday 11:00 A.M. to 4:00 P.M. except state holidays. Adults $, children free.

This museum provides education about mining and mineral heritage to more than 20,000 kids each year. Here you'll see more than 3,000 minerals on exhibit, ranging from naturally occurring rocks that look like food (steak, potatoes, coffee, jam, and lemon meringue pie) to moon rocks. Kids especially like looking at the black-light exhibit where minerals including calcite, opal, and fluorite glow in a brilliant spectrum of fluorescent white, purple, blue, orange, pink, green, and red. Other favorite sights include a fossil dinosaur egg, dinosaur footprints, and mining exhibits. While you're here, make sure to check out the gallery housing the collection of Rose Mofford, a miner's daughter who rose to become Arizona's first woman governor.

Arizona Science Center (all ages)

600 East Washington Street, Phoenix; (602) 716–2000; www.azscience.org. Open daily 10:00 A.M. to 5:00 P.M. except Thanksgiving and Christmas Day. Adults and children ages 3–12 $$, under 3 free. There is an additional fee ($) per person for the planetarium.

This museum-style center has science down to an art. Here you'll find four floors of fun-filled activities. More than 350 interactive, hands-on exhibits explore a wide range of science—geology, applied science, biology, astronomy, chemistry, and more. Kids can watch light being divided into prisms, look at slides under microscopes, and create giant bubbles. Children especially love tossing foam balls (representing pollen and dust) into the nostrils of a giant nose, which sneezes them back out. Exhibits are constantly changing, making this a place you can visit more than once. A state-of-the-art planetarium, five-story giant screen Iwerks theater, and science store (Awesome Atom's) complete this experiment.

Heritage Square (all ages)

115 North Sixth Street, Phoenix; (602) 262–5071; www.rossonhousemuseum.org. The square's office is located in The Duplex. Office hours 9:00 A.M. to 5:00 P.M. Monday through Friday. Park hours vary. Parking is free with validation for the first hour, $ for two to eight hours.

This city block houses the last remaining group of residential structures from the original Phoenix town site. The stately Victorian buildings are now home to an assortment of museums, shops, and restaurants. Festivals are held at the Lath House Pavilion, which also has

Ghost **Stories**

With the Victorian fascination with mediums and spiritualist circles, it only seems natural that Victorian-bred Eliza Teeter haunts the tearoom that bears her name. At least that's what current owner and chef Lynne Behringer believes when spoons go missing and knickknacks change place overnight. And with the old-fashioned jewelry, silver picture frames, dainty spoons, fragrant sachets, and the like, there's plenty of things for a restless spirit to rearrange.

Eliza Teeter bought the midwestern-style bungalow from cattleman Leon Bouvier in 1911 and ran it as a boardinghouse until she peacefully passed away on her porch in 1965. After her death, the house sat vacant for several years until the city designated the block a historic landmark. The Teeter House started up once more as a Victorian tearoom, catering to the romantics of a new era.

As to Eliza Teeter's gentle presence, well, Behringer takes it all in stride. After all, why shouldn't an authentic Victorian tearoom have an authentic ghostly host?

restrooms and a drinking fountain. Events of special interest to children include the Matsuri—A Festival of Japan, held at the end of February; the Arizona Aloha Festival, the third weekend of March; the Children's Fair, the last weekend of March; the Candy Land Concert Fiesta of Lights, the Friday after Thanksgiving; and a Victorian Holiday, the second Saturday of December. Older children will enjoy the docent-guided tours through the **Rosson House,** ($), (602–262–5029). This Victorian-style home, built in 1895 for $7,525, has been fully restored complete with period rooms. Kids will also enjoy the **Arizona Doll and Toy Museum,** ($), (602–253–9337). This museum, situated in the 1901 Stevens House, features historic toys, contemporary playthings, furnished dollhouses, a replica one-room schoolhouse, and a gift shop stocked with unusual children's gifts. After shopping and checking out the buildings, stop by the **Teeter House** (602–252–4682) for an authentic Victorian tearoom experience. The tearoom offers a special Children's Tea ($) reminiscent of the teatime Victorian children would take in the nursery before bed, which includes a spot of tea with plenty of cream, finger sandwiches, fruit, lemonade, and a cookie.

Phoenix Museum of History (ages 5 and up)

105 North Fifth Street, Phoenix; (602) 253–2734; www.pmoh.org. Open 10:00 A.M. to 5:00 P.M. Tuesday through Saturday. Admission is free from 2:00 to 5:00 P.M. Wednesdays. Adults $$, children ages 7–12 $, under 7 free.

Trace Phoenix's territorial history and early statehood days, along with this area's proud multicultural heritage, at the Phoenix Museum of History. Displays include

Native American artifacts, the town's first jail, a 1920s period living room, a re-created general store, and a comprehensive look at life in Phoenix during its pioneering days. In these exhibits, kids will discover such interesting tidbits as the fact that before the advent of air-conditioning, Phoenicians slept outside with their bedposts in dishes of water to keep scorpions from climbing into bed with them—a new way of looking at the phrase, "Don't let the bed bugs bite."

George Washington Carver Museum and Cultural Center
(ages 6 and up)

415 East Grant Street, Phoenix; (602) 254–7516; www.azcama.com/museums/carver_ museum.htm. Open 9:00 A.M. to 1:00 P.M. Monday through Friday and 10:00 A.M. to 3:00 P.M. on the third Saturday of each month. Adults and children 6–12 $, under 6 free.

Before desegregation, this building housed Phoenix Union High School, which provided education for the city's black youth. Today, it is a museum and research center where you can learn about African-American history, art, and culture.

Bank One Ball Park (all ages)

401 East Jefferson Street, Phoenix; (602) 514–8400; www.arizonadiamondbacks.com. Schedule and ticket prices vary. Season runs from April through September.

Peanuts, popcorn, and Cracker Jack—you'll find it all at Bank One Ballpark, fondly referred to as BOB by locals. The 49,000-square-foot facility is the only one in the world that combines a retractable roof, air-conditioning, and a natural turf field. Phoenix fans had special reason to celebrate America's favorite family spectator sport when the Arizona Diamondbacks walked away with the World Championship in 2001, making them the first professional sports team in Arizona to win a world championship. Also, because this relatively new team first began playing in 1998, they are also the fastest baseball team to have reached and won the World Series.

Phoenix Art Museum (all ages)

1625 North Central Avenue, Phoenix; (602) 257–1222; www.phxart.org. Open 10:00 A.M. to 5:00 P.M. Tuesday, Wednesday, and Friday through Sunday, 10:00 A.M. to 9:00 P.M. Thursday. Closed all major holidays. Adults $$, children ages 6–17 $, under 6 free. Free admission each Thursday.

The Phoenix Art Museum features collections emphasizing American Art; Asian Art; European Art of the Fourteenth to Nineteenth Centuries; Western American Art; Modern and Contemporary Art; Spanish Colonial and Latin American Art; Eighteenth-to-Twentieth-Century Fashion Design; and the Thorne Miniature Rooms. However, kids will especially enjoy the interactive ArtWorks Gallery and the Children's Gallery. Check with the museum for the changing activities held on Family Sundays, which are geared to children ages five to twelve. You can also pick up a PAM KidPack at the admission desk. Each KidPack includes activity cards, puzzles, and fun challenges corresponding with the museum's collection of artworks.

Take a Spin Down **Merry-Go-Round Lane**

Nothing goes better with the romance of spring than a breezy spin on one of Phoenix's few remaining historic carousels. Painted ponies, decked with delicate garlands and sporting tails made of real horsehair; an elegant swan carriage; and a lone wooden pig grace Phoenix's finest: a fully restored, hand-painted 1912 C. W. Parker Company carousel at Schnepf Farms in Queen Creek.

The merry-go-round at Schnepf Farms is just one of three historic carousels left in the Valley. Encanto's Enchanted Island Amusement Park owns a "Little Beauty" two-row wood-and-metal model built by the Allan Herschell Company in 1948, complete with twenty-four horses and two chariots. In 1997 McCormick-Stillman Railroad Park replaced its fanciful 1929 Herschell with a newer 1950 model featuring thirty whimsical, hand-painted horses and two stationary benches—one of which has been retrofitted with wheelchair locks. Although none of these old merry-go-rounds play their original band organs, they do feature recorded carousel music from the bygone days of spring and summer.

With fewer than 200 hand-carved wooden merry-go-rounds in operation in the country, this now-dying breed once graced legions of parks, including Phoenix's Legend City and Tempe's Frontierland—both of which have long vanished from the metro-Phoenix cityscapes. The most recent loss of local childhood memories was the 1880s steam-driven Armitage-Herschell carousel at Rawhide Western Town, which was dismantled a few years ago. Modern merry-go-rounds pop up every now and then at shopping centers and carnivals, but, while they're still around, the glory of these last historic carousels wins hands-down when it comes to old-fashioned romance.

(A ride on Schnepf Farm's merry-go-round is included in the cost of attending the farm's Peach Festival, held every weekend in May; 480–987–3333. A spin on the carousel at Enchanted Island Amusement Park costs $; 602–254–2020. A ride on the carousel at McCormick-Stillman Railroad Park is $; 480–312–2312.)

America West Arena (all ages)

201 East Jefferson Street, Phoenix; (602) 379–7900 or (602) 379–2000; www.americawest arena.com. Phoenix Suns ticket office, (602) 379–7867. Phoenix Mercury ticket office, (602) 252–WNBA. Schedules and ticket prices vary.

Both the Phoenix Suns and the Phoenix Mercury play at this impressive sports facility, which can hold nearly 19,000 fans. The Phoenix Suns have had their share of acclaimed players since the team came to Phoenix in 1968. Some of the most notable are Connie Hawkins, Charles Barkley, and Kevin Johnson. The Phoenix Mercury also have a claim to fame as a charter member of the Women's National Basketball Association and began playing in 1997.

Heard Museum (all ages)

2301 North Central Avenue, Phoenix; (602) 252–8840; www.heard.org. Open daily 9:30 A.M. to 5:00 P.M. except all major holidays. Adults $$, children ages 4–12 $, children under 4 free.

Founded in 1929, this world-renowned museum displays nearly 40,000 works of Native American art and ethnographic objects in more than 130,000 square feet. A video, played on a large screen, orients visitors to the Native American cultures of the Southwest. A re-created pit house, cases of Hopi kachina dolls, and courtyards filled with interesting sculptures will entertain all ages. Children will especially enjoy exploring a re-created Zuni pueblo, working on an oversize bead loom, and hands-on craft activities. Unlike many museums filled with stuffy art, the Heard's galleries sport colorful paintings and artifacts of interest to young children. The museum store also caters to kids with a great selection of Southwestern storybooks, toys, and cactus candy. Several annual events attract Phoenix families throughout the year. Some favorites include the World Championship Hoop Dance Contest, the first weekend in February; the Heard Museum Guild Indian Fair and Market, on the first weekend of March; and Red! Hot! Alive!—A Celebration of Indigenous Cultures, on the last weekend of October.

Encanto Park (all ages)

2605 North Fifteenth Avenue, Phoenix; (602) 261–8993; www.enchantedisland.com. Open from dawn to dusk. Free.

This 222-acre urban oasis is the home to a host of outdoor activities, including canoeing, paddleboating, swimming, picnicking, and fishing. A swimming pool, golf course, tennis courts, a playground, and a children's fun park add to the options. Hours at the Enchanted Island Amusement Park vary. Rides cost $. All-day passes are available. Rides in this children's wonderland include a historic carousel, a mini Ferris wheel, bumper boats, a train, and carnival rides. Kids will also enjoy electronic games at the arcade.

Arizona Military Museum (ages 9 and up) 🖼️

Papago Park Military Reservation, 5636 East McDowell Road, Phoenix; (602) 267–2676; www.az.ngb.army.mil/Museum/museum.htm. Open 9:00 A.M. to 2:00 P.M. Tuesday and Thursday and 1:00 to 4:00 P.M. Saturday and Sunday. Free.

Older children will enjoy learning about Arizona's military history. Exhibits include displays of historic and modern uniforms, vehicles, artillery, and military artifacts dating back to the Spanish conquistadors and their travels through Arizona in the 1700s.

Hall of Flame Museum of Firefighting (all ages) 🖼️

6101 East Van Buren Street, Papago Park, Phoenix; (602) 275–3473; www.hallofflame.org. Open 9:00 A.M. to 5:00 P.M. Monday through Saturday and noon to 4:00 P.M. Sunday except Thanksgiving, Christmas, and New Year's Day. Adults $$, children ages 3–17 $, under 3 free.

What child isn't fascinated with fire engines and the firefighters who operate these shiny red machines? This museum, with more than ninety fully restored classic fire engines and fire apparatus dating from 1725 to 1961, is sure to get the attention of all ages in your group. Kids can climb aboard a 1951 fire engine, slide down a firehouse pole, and dress up in fire-fighting gear. A special kids' corner, for kids ages three and up, offers games and activities and focuses on fire safety. A quick stop at the gift shop, and your little one can take home a fire engine of his or her very own.

Mystery Castle (ages 6 and up)

800 East Mineral Road, Phoenix; (602) 268–1581. Open 11:00 A.M. to 4:00 P.M. Thursday through Sunday. Closed July through September. Adults $$, children ages 6–15 $.

Mystery Castle is an odd three-story home built out of stone, adobe, automobile parts, colored glass, and a motley assortment of odds and ends Boyce Gulley managed to salvage from different parts of the state. Here you'll even find iron bed frames from Yuma Territorial Prison. Constructed over a period of time, from the early 1930s until Gulley's death in 1945, Mystery Castle has the charm of a sand castle, which it is meant to resemble. Mary Lou Gulley adds her insight and considerable knowledge of this architectural oddity on guided tours of her father's creation.

Phoenix International Raceway (all ages) 🖼️

11901 West Baseline Road, Phoenix; (602) 252–2227; www.phoenixintlraceway.com. Open daily except all major holidays. Call for race schedule and admission fees.

NASCAR and INDY races zoom around this track, which is known as the world's fastest 1-mile oval racetrack. The raceway first opened in 1964 and since then has become one of the top facilities of its kind in the nation. The booths below the track offer a multitude of race car goodies. Make sure to bring plenty of water and sunscreen, and don't forget hats and earplugs for the little ones. However, due to increased security, no coolers or backpacks are allowed.

Squaw Peak Recreation Area (ages 6 and up) 🏕️ 🧗

2707 East Squaw Peak Drive, Phoenix; (602) 262–6696. Open daily 5:00 A.M. to 11:00 P.M. Free.

Squaw Peak is one of Phoenix's best-known landmarks with its craggy, easily identifiable pinnacle. The summit 2,608-foot rough-cut trail is one of the Valley's most popular hiking trails. Make sure to take plenty of water, wear sturdy shoes, and keep an eye out for rattlesnakes.

South Mountain Park (all ages) 🏞️ 🧗 🏕️ 🏛️

10919 South Central Avenue, Phoenix; (602) 495–0222. Open daily 5:00 A.M. to 10:00 P.M. Free.

South Mountain Park, which at 16,500 acres is the world's largest municipal park, offers a plentitude of recreational opportunities. Here you will find Hohokam ruins, hiking trails, petroglyphs, picnic areas, playgrounds, and restrooms. The park also facilitates mountain biking and horseback riding.

Pueblo Grande Museum and Archaeological Park (ages 6 and up) 🏛️ 🧗 🎒

4619 East Washington Street, Phoenix; (602) 495–0901. Open 9:00 A.M. to 4:45 P.M. Monday through Saturday and 1:00 to 4:45 P.M. Sunday. Adults and children 5 and up $, children under 5 free. Admission is free on Sunday.

The museum and Hohokam ruins sit next to a modern concrete canal built over an ancient waterway the Hohokam originally hacked out of the ground with sharpened sticks. An agricultural people, these prehistoric Native Americans farmed the valley along the Salt River as early as 1,700 years ago. The partially preserved 1,500-year-old village in this 102-acre park encompasses the ruins of an 800-year-old platform mound, old irrigation canals, and a ball court. A 2⁄3-mile walk around the site will orient you and the kids on this fascinating culture that survived in the harsh environs of the Sonoran Desert. Guided tours are offered at 11:00 A.M. and 1:00 P.M. on Saturday and Sunday, and summer camps offer an

Piestewa **Peak**

Army Pfc. Lori Piestewa, the first female Native American soldier to be killed in combat, was honored by the city of Phoenix when officials changed the name of Squaw Peak to Piestewa (py-ESS-tuh-wah) Peak. Twenty-three-year-old Piestewa, a member of the Tuba City Hopi Tribe, was killed when her unit was ambushed by Iraqi forces in April 2003. However, even though the State Board on Geographic and Historic Names has approved the mountain's new name, it could take up to five years for the U.S. Board of Geographic Names to approve the change and reprint official maps.

opportunity for kids to try their hand at being junior archaeologists. The museum's excellent exhibits, museum store, and interactive events make this a must-see.

Phoenix Zoo (all ages)

455 North Galvin Parkway, Papago Park, Phoenix; (602) 273–1341; www.phoenixzoo.org. Open daily 9:00 A.M. to 5:00 P.M. with extended summer hours. The zoo closes at 4:00 P.M. from mid-November through the first week of January and reopens for ZooLights 6:00 to 10:00 P.M., except Christmas Day (closed). Adults and children ages 3–12 $$; under 3 free.

This 125-acre zoo is internationally known for its efforts to save endangered species in its many exhibits. For an additional fee you can take the Safari train tour of the zoo grounds. Highlights include the Forest of Uco and its spectacled bears, the Arizona Trail with plants and animals of the Southwest, and the three-acre African Savanna. Kids will especially enjoy the Children's Trail, which features a butterfly garden and farm area. At Harmony Farm, children keep busy currying horses, combing cotton, and gardening as they take a turn at being a real farm hand. Other highlights at the farm include interaction with farm animals, mule rides, and historical facts on native Arizona crops such as cotton, corn, and beans. Campers eager to really experience farm life stay overnight in the schoolhouse for Harmony Farm Night Camp. Youngsters roused by the cock's crow churn butter, milk goats, and gather eggs for a homemade country breakfast before setting out to explore the barns and restored agricultural equipment. Phoenix Zoo also hosts two popular events: Boo! at the Zoo and ZooLights. Boo! at the Zoo is a Valley favorite for Halloween family fun. ZooLights ($$$), held nightly the entire month of December, features more than two million lights, live entertainment, storytelling, a nighttime stroll through the zoo, and plenty of hot chocolate. Be sure to bring mittens and coats. Temperatures drop fast at night in the desert.

Desert Botanical Garden (all ages)

1201 North Galvin Parkway, Phoenix; (480) 941–1225; www.dbg.org. Open daily 7:00 A.M. to 8:00 P.M. May through September and 8:00 A.M. to 8:00 P.M. October through April except July 4 and Christmas Day. Adults $$, students with ID $, children ages 3–12 $, under 3 free.

A showcase for Sonoran Desert plants, this garden will give children a chance to learn about such funky cacti as the jumping cholla, saguaro, and the boojum tree (which is named after the mythical creature in Lewis Carroll's poem "The Hunting of the Snark"). There are four trails, marked with informative signs, winding through 145 acres of themed gardens—Sonoran Desert Trail, Desert Discovery Trail, Cactus House and Succulent House, and the Center for Desert Living Trail. A visitor center, cafe, and plant shop round out the organic orientation. The gardens also host guided tours, concerts, and special events, which you can check out on their hotline at (480) 481–8134.

Every Day Is April Fool's Day **in the Desert**

With the profusion of prickly plants inhabiting Arizona's deserts, telling the difference between real cacti and other spiny desert plants can be vexing even for Arizona natives. Both cacti and most cactuslike members of the agave family have some resemblance due to the common adaptations needed to survive drought—including succulent tissues to store water, thick skins to prevent evaporation, and prickles to discourage thirsty desert denizens. Some of the most common imposters confused for cacti include the white flowering Joshua trees, the spiny-tipped agave "century plant," the prickly white flowering "desert spoons"—all of which are related to the lily and amaryllis—and the long-armed, red-flower-tipped ocotillo.

Valley Youth Theatre (ages 4 and up)

525 North First Street, Phoenix; (602) 253–8188; www.vyt.com. Tickets $$. Call for show times and season schedule.

This award-winning theater focuses entirely on youth, both in production and audiences. Situated in downtown Phoenix, the theater offers a rich season with such shows as *Grease, A Winnie-the-Pooh Christmas Tail,* and *Cinderella.*

COFCO Chinese Cultural Center (all ages)

668 North Forty-fourth Street, Phoenix; (602) 275–8578. Open daily 7:00 A.M. to 7:00 P.M. Free.

Deep in the heart of Phoenix lie mystical springs, grand statues, and replicas from five ancient cities. Built as a place of quiet meditation and beauty and offering a glimpse of treasures from China's ancient emperors, the Chinese gardens surrounding the Chinese Cultural Center take visitors on a cultural journey through time. Designed by the famous garden architect Madame Ye, the gardens adhere to Feng Shui principles and are attended by Pi Xie, mythical animal guardians from 523 B.C. Some of the featured struc-

Buckle **Up**

In Arizona it's the law. The Governor's Office of Community and Highway Safety says: "In the back. In the belt. Every time." All children under five years of age must always ride securely fastened in a safety seat built for their size. This is a primary law, which means that you can be stopped and ticketed if an officer sees a child riding in a vehicle unrestrained. For more information call (602) 255–3216.

tures in the gardens include a Li Ting pavilion circa A.D. 1500 and a Li Xing gate dating back more than 4,000 years. After relaxing in the gardens, visitors can browse in the center's specialty retail stores, shop in the upscale Asian supermarket, and sample a wide variety of cuisines from different regions in China and Asia in the center's restaurants.

Castles-n-Coasters (ages 4 and up)

9445 North Metro Parkway East, Phoenix; (602) 997–7575; castlesncoasters.com. Open daily. Hours vary. Unlimited ride pass and ride pass with one round of golf $$$, golf $$.

This family fun park features a double-loop roller coaster, log ride, carousel, Sea Dragon, NasKart Racers, kiddie rides, miniature golf, and a two-level arcade. Your best bet is to purchase an all-day pass, but you can purchase rides separately. Kids under five years old golf free with an adult. There were problems with gang activity years ago, but security has pretty much nullified this problem.

Pioneer Arizona Living History Museum (all ages)

3901 West Pioneer Road, Phoenix; (623) 465–1052; www.pioneer-arizona.com. Adults and children ages 6–18 $$, children ages 3–5 $, under 3 free. Open 9:00 A.M. to 5:00 P.M. Wednesday through Sunday mid-September through May and 9:00 A.M. to 2:00 P.M. Friday through Sunday June through mid-September.

Walk through the opera house where Lily Langtry sang, visit with a working blacksmith, and enjoy a medicine show at Pioneer Arizona Living History Museum. Just 30 miles north of downtown Phoenix, this Western village provides the perfect setting to relive Arizona's territorial days. The museum features original buildings and artifacts from a time long past. A wagon rests outside the bank, and old-fashioned tools fill the walls of the carpenter shop. The tiny town also includes a school, church, sheriff's office, cabins, and wood frame houses. Kids will especially enjoy the gunfights, scavenger hunt, and critter corral.

Deer Valley Rock Art Center (all ages)

3711 West Deer Valley Road, Phoenix; (623) 582–8007; www.asu.edu/clas/anthropology/ dvrac. Adults $$, children ages 6 to 12 $, under 6 free. Open 9:00 A.M. to 2:00 P.M. Tuesday through Friday, 7:00 A.M. to 5:00 P.M. Saturday and noon to 5:00 P.M. Sunday May through September; 9:00 A.M. to 5:00 P.M. Tuesday through Saturday and noon to 5:00 P.M. Sunday October through April.

Prehistoric Native Americans chipped more than 1,500 petroglyphs into the boulders and rocks at the site preserved by the center. Here you and kids will see this rock art, some of which dates as far back as 5000 B.C., in its natural setting at the Hedgpath Hills petroglyph site. Interpretive displays add to the discovery along the ¼-mile trail leading through the surrounding desert preserve. Back at the center, kids will learn how to interpret the petroglyphs, go on a scavenger hunt, and make their own rock-art masterpieces. Binoculars are available at the center for viewing distant rock art. Guided tours, which leave at 10:00 A.M. on Saturday October to April, offer additional insight and information about rock studies.

Turf Paradise (ages 5 and up)

1501 West Bell Road, Phoenix; (602) 942–1101. Races run 12:30 to 5:00 P.M. Friday through Tuesday September to May. $, under 16 free.

Everyone will enjoy watching world-class thoroughbreds race this track. Kids will have fun picking out their favorite horses, and adults can indulge in a little side betting of their own. Facilities include a restaurant and a family picnic area.

Waterworld Safari (ages 4 and up)

4243 West Pinnacle Peak Road, Phoenix; (623) 581–8446; www.golfland-sunsplash.com. Open daily in the summer only. $$$. Additional fees for tube and locker rentals.

You'll have a blast at this north Phoenix water park. Take a ride on the wild side on the six-story, high-speed Kilimanjaro water slide. Other family favorites on this twenty-five-acre surf and swim park include the Serengeti surf wave pool, the Black Mamba and Togo water slides, and Congo River Rapids. Little ones get in on the fun at Jungle Jim's children's wading pool and the long, easy Zambezi River ride.

Where to Eat

Farm at South Mountain. 6106 South Thirty-second Street, Phoenix; (602) 276-6360. Pack up the kids and come for an utterly relaxing lunch in the great out-doors. Have a picnic at a converted cottage that sits on the grounds of a small working farm. $$

5 & Diner. 5220 North Sixteenth Street, Phoenix; (602) 264–5220. Serves breakfast, lunch, and dinner all day. Thick shakes and malts, extensive children's menu, and jukebox music 1950s style. $$

Fry Bread House. 4140 North Seventh Avenue, Phoenix; (602) 351–2345. If you've never had fry bread, this is the place to stop for lunch or dinner. Try the delectable Navajo tacos or a piece of fry bread drizzled in honey. $

Houlihans. 11011 North Tatum, Paradise Valley; (602) 996–8118. Steaks, sandwiches, and salads in a relaxed atmosphere. Special children's menu. $$

Jerry Tucci's Brick Oven Pizzeria. 4602 East Cactus Road, Phoenix; (602) 996–1023. Pizza, pasta, seafood, steak, veal, and salads. Tuesday kids eat free. $$

Red Devil Italian Restaurant. 3102 East McDowell Road, Phoenix; (602) 267–1036. Touted as the best pizza joint in Arizona. $$

Rustler's Rooste. 7777 South Pointe Parkway, Phoenix; (602) 431–6474. Ribs, chicken, pork chops, prime rib, and steaks in a Western atmosphere. Kids will love sliding down the chute to the dining room. Children's menu. $$$

Souper Salad. 10005 North Metro Parkway East, Phoenix; (602) 678–5466. All-you-can-eat buffet with soups, salads, pastas, breads, and desserts. Children under five eat **free.** $

Where to Stay

Arizona Biltmore Resort and Spa.
2400 East Missouri Road, Phoenix; (602) 955–6600 or (800) 805–8210; www.arizona biltmore.com. Special recreational opportunities for children ages four to twelve at the Kids Korral, including bike rides, arts and crafts, contests, pastry-shop tour, swimming, and visits to the resort playground. $$$$

Comfort Inn. 1344 North Twenty-seventh Avenue, Phoenix; (602) 415–1623. Microwave and refrigerator, continental breakfast, and pool. Kids under eighteen stay **free.** $$$

Embassy Suites Phoenix-Scottsdale.
4415 East Paradise Village Parkway South, Phoenix; (602) 765–5800 or (800) EMBASSY; www.embassysuitesscottsdale. com. **Free** breakfast, heated outdoor pool and spa. Children seventeen and under stay **free.** $$$

Legacy Golf Resort. 6808 South Thirty-second Street, Phoenix; (602) 305–5500; www.legacygolfresort.com. Children's pool, activities, and playground. Children under twelve stay **free.** $$$$

Pointe Hilton Tapatio Cliffs Resort. 11111 North Seventh Street, Phoenix; (602) 866–7500 or (800) 947–9784; www.pointehilton.com. More than three areas of pools, water slide, and daily activities for children at the Kid's Corral. $$$$

Pointe South Mountain Resort. 7777 South Pointe Parkway, Phoenix; (602) 438–9000 or (877) 800–4888; www.pointe southmtn.com. This luxury resort boasts a multitude of recreational opportunities for the entire family. Kids will especially enjoy the Cactus Kids Club's activities, which are geared for ages five to twelve, and the Oasis water park's four-level Slide Canyon tower, 10,000-square-foot Oasis Wave pool, Zuni Active River, Lil' Pony Lagoon, and Caliente Springs hot tub. $$$$

Sunshine Hotel and Suites. 3600 North Second Avenue, Phoenix; (602) 248–0222. Features four pools, spa, and resort-style water park. Rooms include Nintendo. $$–$$$$

For More Information

Greater Phoenix Convention and Visitors Bureau.
One Arizona Center, 400 East Van Buren Street, Suite 600, Phoenix 85004, (602) 252–5588; www.phoenix cvb.com.

West Valley

The sprawling West Valley offers a wide variety of activities as it contains the rapidly evolving borderland between the modern city, the farm towns from which Phoenix originated, and the open desert beyond the irrigated edges of civilization. Glendale and Peoria form the urbanized heart of the area, which spreads outward to include beautiful desert parks and even a huge desert lake, sustained now with water imported hundreds of miles from the Colorado River. Adventurous families can enjoy a host of activities, including a chocolate-factory tour, a bug museum, a science center, horseback riding on a desert mountain preserve, and a museum dedicated to beads.

The West Valley has key advantages for families, including modestly priced hotel rooms and a relaxed country charm. But maximizing an exploration of this area requires a certain amount of planning, as the kid-friendly attractions are scattered throughout this area—where cities tend to blur into one another.

Bead Museum (ages 5 and up)

5754 West Glenn Drive, Glendale; (623) 931–2737; www.thebeadmuseum.com. Open 10:00 A.M. to 5:00 P.M. Monday through Saturday (open until 8:00 P.M. Thursday), and 11:00 A.M. to 4:00 P.M. Sunday. $. Free admission on Sunday.

The human fascination with round objects is traced back 40,000 years in this small museum dedicated to the history of the bead. Beads have been used throughout human history as currency, sacred objects, for adornment, and as brightly colored bits on children's toys. These baubles of glass and gleam might not seem that important, but they all have a story to tell. Although children will pass through the museum fairly quickly, the gift shop will especially appeal to young children interested in making a necklace of their very own.

Cerreta Candy Company (all ages)

5345 West Glendale Avenue, Glendale; (623) 930–1000; www.cerreta.com. Open 8:00 A.M. to 6:00 P.M. Monday through Saturday. Free.

Located in historic downtown Glendale, this family-owned and -operated candy factory specializes in chocolates of every kind imaginable. Children and adults alike will especially enjoy the free samples. As you nibble fudge truffles, chocolate-covered cherries, and walnut caramels, you can watch workers in their crisp white uniforms create confections in large copper kettles. Free thirty-minute guided tours are given at 10:00 A.M. and 1:00 P.M. Monday through Thursday.

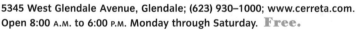

Historic Sahuaro Ranch (ages 4 and up) 🔲🚗🏛🏕

9802 North Fifty-ninth Avenue, Glendale; (623) 939–5782; www.sahuaroranch.org. Grounds open daily 6:00 A.M. to sunset. Museum Store open 10:00 A.M. to 2:00 P.M. Wednesday through Friday, 10:00 A.M. to 4:00 P.M. Saturday, and noon to 4:00 P.M. Sunday. Free.

During the territorial days of the 1880s and 1890s, Sahuaro Ranch gained praise as a model fruit farm with picture-perfect crops of white Adriatic figs, Le Conte pears, navel oranges, peaches, apricots, and olives. After a series of droughts killed many of the fruit trees in the last years of the nineteenth century, the ranch turned to raising cattle, grains, and other crops. Today this historic homestead is a city park. While touring the grounds, check out the lush rose garden and gazebo, roam the orchards, look for the colorful peacocks wandering the grounds, and show the children the park's antique tractors. The Fruit Packing Shed often acts as a gallery and hosts historic exhibits. Tours of the restored Main House are scheduled at various times Wednesday though Sunday for a small fee. The ranch hosts Sahuaro Ranch Days mid-November, an event featuring an antique tractor and engine show, hay wagon rides, and demonstrations of butter churning, plowing, and other activities related to early ranch life.

Katydid Insect Museum (all ages) 🔲

5060 West Bethany Home Road, Glendale; (623) 931–8718; www.insectmuseum.com. Open 11:00 A.M. to 4:00 P.M. Monday through Friday and noon to 4:00 P.M. Saturday. Adults, students, and children ages 5–11 $, under 4 free.

With more than 26,000 species of insects in Arizona, it seems only natural for the state to host an insect museum. Although the collection contains some exotic arthropods, including a live Goliath tarantula named Poochie, most of the insects displayed are Arizona natives. Here kids will get an up-close look at termites, live mealworms, and wasp nests. The ladybug-themed bathroom is a favorite, and kids and several school groups have posed for photos in the red-and-black polka-dot room.

Cactus **League**

The Cactus League brings twelve major-league baseball teams to Arizona each year for spring training, which is a great way to introduce children to America's favorite pastime. The first Cactus League baseball game was the Indians against the Giants in March 1947. Today, you can see the Arizona Diamondbacks, Colorado Rockies, and the Chicago White Sox play in Tucson; the San Diego Padres and the Seattle Mariners play in Peoria; the Milwaukee Brewers in Maryvale; the Oakland A's in Phoenix; the San Francisco Giants in Scottsdale; the Anaheim Angels in Tempe; and the Chicago Cubs in Mesa. For more information log onto www.cactus-league.com.

Peoria Arizona Historical Society Museum (ages 6 and up)

Eighty-third and Madison Avenues, P.O. Box 186, Peoria 85380–0186; (623) 972–3587. Open 10:00 A.M. to noon Wednesday through Friday and 10:00 A.M. to 2:00 P.M. Saturday. **Free.**

The society's museum houses relics from Peoria's cotton days, including scales, hooks, and even a mini cotton bale. Curator Priscilla Cook takes visitors on guided tours through the old two-room schoolhouse built in 1906, illustrating the exhibits with her memories and experiences she's gathered since she moved to Peoria in 1929. Exhibits include a schoolroom complete with scarred wooden desks, a kitchen with a cast-iron stove, and the displays of Peoria's founding families.

Peoria Sports Complex (all ages)

16101 North Eighty-third Avenue, Peoria; (623) 412–4211; www.peoriaaz.com/sports complex. Days and hours vary. Tickets range from $ to $$$$.

Peoria Sports Complex was the first major-league baseball spring training and player development facility in the country to be shared by two professional ball teams: the San Diego Padres and the Seattle Mariners. Spring training games provide a great opportunity to introduce youngsters to America's favorite sport without having to fight crowds and pay premium prices. So in Peoria it's all about peanuts and popcorn and Cracker Jacks—at least during the spring season. The complex also hosts festivals, arts and crafts shows, and concerts throughout the rest of the year. Call for a complete schedule.

Polar Ice (all ages) ⚫

15829 North Eighty-third Avenue, Peoria; (623) 334–1200 or (888) 691–1214; www.polariceent.com. Open daily. Public skating sessions vary. Call for hours. Adults and children ages 3–12 $$, under 3 **free;** skate rental $.

You might wonder at ice-skating in the desert, but this fairly new ice-skating center will wow your kids on even the hottest day of summer. During the evening weekend sessions a DJ spins funky tunes and turns on a kaleidoscopic light display to add to the family fun. In addition to the two ice rinks, this state-of-the-art ice center offers a pizzeria, coffee shop, pro shop, private and public skating lessons, hockey clinics, and a game zone with more than forty video and interactive arcade games. Come dressed warmly; even when Phoenix hits those triple digits it stays pretty chilly inside.

The Challenger Center (all ages)

21170 North Eighty-third Avenue, Peoria; (623) 322–2001; www.azchallenger.org. Open 9:00 A.M. to 4:00 P.M. Monday through Friday and 10:00 A.M. to 4:00 P.M. Saturday except all major holidays. Adults $$, students $.

This Peoria center is one of only forty such centers in the United States and of those is the most technologically advanced. Created as education centers in honor of the fateful *Challenger* mission in 1986, the center allows visitors to experience space travel in simulated mini missions. Participants play the roles of the flight crew, mission controllers, and scientists on a mock rendezvous with a comet. The mission-control panel in Peoria's center is modeled after the Johnson Space Center in Houston. Children will enjoy a visit to the center for stargazing, mission participation, or just touring through the center. Reservations are required for the simulated space flight, so be sure to call ahead.

Lake Pleasant Regional Park (all ages)

41835 North Castle Hot Springs Road, Peoria; (928) 501–1710 or (602) 372–7460; www.maricopa.gov/parks/lake_pleasant. Open daily. Park entrance fee is $$ per vehicle and $ per watercraft.

Located just 30 miles north of Phoenix, Lake Pleasant and the surrounding park encompass nearly 24,000 acres of high desert countryside. This recreation area is great for picnicking and fishing from the shore, and if you're really lucky, you might catch sight of one of the wild burros roaming these protected lands. The park is also an ideal place for camping and boating. If you don't have a boat of your own, you can always rent one from the **Pleasant Harbor Marina** (623–566–3100). The marina's Jet Skis, fishing boats, pontoon boats, and sports boats rent by the hour ($$$$), with special half- and full-day rates.

White Tank Mountain Regional Park (all ages)

13025 North White Mountain Road, Waddell; (623) 935–2505; www.maricopa.gov/parks/white_tank. Open 6:00 A.M. to 8:00 P.M. Sunday through Thursday and 6:00 A.M. to 10:00 P.M. Friday and Saturday. Fees $ per vehicle.

With more than 29,000 acres, this West Valley desert park in the White Tank Mountains attracts quite a crowd of families looking for outdoor recreation opportunities. Some favorite activities include camping, hiking on the park's 50 miles of trails, and mountain biking. There are also camping facilities, picnic areas, and a playground for the kids.

White Tank Riding Stables (all ages)

Entrance of White Tank County Park, where Olive Avenue dead-ends west of State Route 303, Maricopa; (623) 935–7455. Open daily. Closed May 1 to October 31. Call for hours. Reservations recommended. One- and two-hour rides $$$$, pony ride $$$.

Check out the largest county park in Maricopa from the vantage and comfort of one of the stable's horses. Guided tours will take you and the kids on a journey through the desert terrain and past the remains of prehistoric Native Americans. Have the kids on the lookout for mule deer, coyotes, foxes, and hawks. Children have to be eight to take a trail ride, but younger kids will still enjoy the chance to play cowboy on a half-hour pony ride along the trail, with a guide holding the reins. Other family favorites here include the small petting zoo, hayrides, and picnic tables.

Wildlife World Zoo (all ages)

16501 West Northern Avenue, Litchfield Park; (623) 935–9453; www.wildlifeworld.com. Open daily 9:00 A.M. to 5:00 P.M. Adults $$$, children ages 3–12 $$, under 3

Nestled between farmland, an air force base, and suburban development, a paradise awaits exploration. Visitors encounter more than 400 different species while strolling down the zoo's paths. Endangered hoofed animals roam their grassy pastures, rare birds fly freely in the lush walk-through aviaries, and exotic fish swim through the large aquarium. Those who want to get closer to the wildlife can travel through African habitats occupied by free-roaming ostrich, antelope, and water buffalo on the zoo's Safari Train. A petting zoo and Wildlife Encounters shows entertain and educate children. But the family favorites are the towering feeding platform, which puts you face to face with the zoo's long-legged giraffes, and the Lory feeding exhibit, where you venture into an aviary to feed apples to these brilliantly colored exotic birds. If you visit in December, make sure to check out the zoo's Christmas light displays at Wild Winter Nights.

Where to Eat

Aunt Pittypat's Kitchen. 7123 North Fifty-eighth Avenue, Glendale; (623) 931–0838. Sandwiches, hamburgers, grilled cheese, and chicken. $

Chevy's Mexican Restaurant. 7700 West Arrowhead Towne Center, Glendale; (623) 979–0055. California-style Mexican cuisine. Special kids' meals, which include ice cream. $$

Claim Jumper. 3063 West Agua Fria Freeway; Thirty-first Avenue and Beardsley Road, Glendale; (623) 581–8595. Pizzas, sandwiches, ribs, steaks, and salads. Children's menu. $$$

Fuddruckers. 7704 West Bell Road, Glendale; (623) 979–8826. Hamburgers, ostrich, chicken, turkey burgers, steaks, and salads in a casual atmosphere. Traditional children's menu. $$

Pete's Fish & Chips. 5516 West Glendale Avenue, Glendale; (623) 937–6001. Fried fish, chicken, and shrimp. $$

Where to Stay

Best Western Phoenix-Glendale. 5940 Northwest Grand Avenue, Glendale; (623) 939–9431 or (800) 333–7172; www.best

western.com. Two pools, laundry facilities, and continental breakfast. Children stay **free.** $

The Quality Inn at Talavi. 5511 West Bell Road, Glendale; (602) 896–8900; quality inn.com. Pool, spa, and continental breakfast. Children under twelve stay **free.** $$–$$$

Ramada Limited. 7885 West Arrowhead Towne Center, Glendale; (623) 412–2000; www.ramada.com. Outdoor pool, continental breakfast, and refrigerators. Kids stay **free.** $$$

Spring Hill Marriott Suites. 7810 West Bell Road, Glendale; (623) 878–6666; www.marriott.com. Suites, refrigerator, microwave, continental breakfast, heated pool, and spa. Kids stay **free.** $$$

For More Information

Glendale, Arizona Convention and Visitor Bureau. 5800 West Glenn Drive, Suite 140, Glendale 85301; (623) 930–4500 or (877) 800–2601; www.visitglendale.com.

Northwest Valley Chamber of Commerce. 12801 West Bell Road, Suite 14, Surprise 85374; (623) 583–0692; www.northwestvalley.com.

Peoria Chamber of Commerce. 8355 West Peoria Avenue, P.O. Box 70, Peoria 85380; (623) 979–3601; www.peoria chamber.com.

Scottsdale

Scottsdale, which bills itself as the West's Most Western Town, is the Valley's high-end tourist destination—with prices and activities more oriented toward older, richer visitors who want to cruise galleries, stay in golf-oriented resorts, and soak up the Western resort lifestyle. Nonetheless, the area offers some first-rate parks and public facilities; a border with some splendid, boulder-strewn reaches of the Sonoran Desert; and an array of other family-oriented attractions and facilities. Even if you're traveling on a kid-dominated budget, you can have a great time wandering around Scottsdale—especially if you head to the northern reaches where the city is assembling parcels for one of the most extensive and scenic city-owned, open desert parks in the country, which is mostly centered on the sun-bronzed McDowell Mountains. Families exploring the Scottsdale area will encounter a world-class park-playground featuring a half-size steam-engine train chugging and whistling up and down a mile-long track, a first-class wild-animal park with an impressive tiger who swims and a snake so big it takes a couple of kids to lift it, simulated Wild West shootouts on the dusty streets of an authentic-looking cow-town street, and the largest sundial in the Northern Hemisphere—where kids can arrange themselves around the circle and perhaps brush up against the awesome realization that they're living on a huge rock spinning through space.

McCormick-Stillman Railroad Park (all ages) 🚂 🍴 🏛 🎡

7301 East Indian Bend Road, Scottsdale; (480) 312–2312. Open daily 10:00 A.M. to 5:30 P.M. Free. Train and carousel rides $.

Encompassing thirty centrally located acres at the southeast corner of Scottsdale and Indian Bend Roads, this railroad park offers a wonderful experience for train lovers of all ages. Take a mile-long train ride behind a ⅝-scale steam locomotive, check out historic exhibits, and take a spin on a historic merry-go-round. Children will especially enjoy the Western fort, complete with a wrought-iron stagecoach, and the playground, which features misters and digging equipment. An ice cream stand, gift shop, and picnic facilities add to the fun.

Out of Africa Wildlife Park (all ages) ▢▢▢

9736 North Fort McDowell Road, Scottsdale; (480) 837–7779; www.outofafricapark.com. Open 9:30 A.M. to 5:00 P.M. Tuesday through Sunday October through May except Thanksgiving and Christmas. Summer hours vary. Adults $$$, children ages 3–12 $$, under 3 **free.**

Pet a python, feed a tiger, and learn about lions at Out of Africa Wildlife Park's specialized shows. Geared to entertain and educate, the action-packed adventures at this one-of-a-kind animal park in Fountain Hills keep visitors on their toes. Tiger Splash, one of the favorite shows, features tigers jumping, playing, and swimming with their toys and trainers. In between shows, habitats bring visitors up close with the park's inhabitants. Playgrounds provide a perfect place for kids to romp while parents take it easy at the many misted picnic areas.

Crackerjax Family Fun and Sports Park (all ages) ▢▢

16001 North Scottsdale Road, Scottsdale; (480) 998–2800; www.crackerjax.com. Open daily 10:00 A.M. to 10:00 P.M. Jax Pass $$$.

With twenty-eight acres filled with family fun, this amusement park offers an automated driving range, golf school, miniature golf, go-karts, batting cages, bumper boats, volleyball, an arcade, and a restaurant and clubhouse.

Ice Den (all ages) ▢

9375 East Bell Road, Scottsdale; (480) 585–7465; www.coyotesice.com. Call for public skating sessions; (480) 473–5881. Admission $$, skate rental $.

Families can skate on the same ice as the Phoenix Coyotes during public

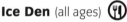

Sunny **Days**

If you want to check the accuracy of your watch with the sun, a visit to the **Great Carefree Sundial** on Easy Street in Carefree will set you straight. The great gold structure, the largest sundial in the Western Hemisphere, competes in size only with the remarkable astrological observatories erected in India two and a half centuries ago. The gnomon, or shadow-casting portion of the sundial, is 62 feet long, with the tip rising 35 feet above the solar plaza, which itself is 90 feet in diameter. The gnomon points to the North Star and coincides with Mountain Standard Time. The sunburst, a wrought-iron globe 7 feet in diameter, hangs below the gnomon. Decorated with simulated solar flares wrought with multicolored glass, the sunburst glistens in the sunlight, and at night it gleams from the illumination of the lights lining the reflecting pool below. For more information call (480) 488–3381.

skating sessions at the 120,000-square-foot, state-of-the-art Alltel Ice Den. Friday night is teen night and includes a live DJ, free skate rental, a laser light show, and door prizes. Saturday night is family night, with Radio Disney music, free skate rental, and door prizes.

Rawhide Wild West Town (all ages) 🍴 🏚 🚫 🔒

23023 North Scottsdale Road, Scottsdale; (480) 502–1880; www.rawhide.com. Open 5:00 P.M. to 10:00 P.M. Monday through Thursday and 11:00 A.M. to 10:00 P.M. Friday through Sunday. Admission free. Rides $–$$$.

Step back to the Old West in this re-created 1880s Western town. All family members will enjoy Native American powwows, gun fights in the street, stagecoach rides, gold panning, a petting ranch, train rides, rock climbing, cowboy cookouts, and burro rides. Western shops offer everything from old-fashioned photography to children's leather jackets. After touring the town, stop by the Golden Belle Steakhouse for hearty Western fare of steaks, ribs, and barbecue chicken.

Taliesin West (ages 4 and up) 🏛

Located at Frank Lloyd Wright Boulevard and 114th Street and Cactus Road, Scottsdale; (480) 860–2700; www.franklloydwright.org. Open daily 9:00 A.M. to 4:00 P.M. except Easter, Thanksgiving, Christmas Day, and New Year's Day. Adults $$$, children 4–12 $$.

Frank Lloyd Wright, considered by many as the premier architect of the twentieth century, created Taliesin West in 1939 to be his winter headquarters. Located on 600 acres near the McDowell Mountains, Taliesin West now serves as a school for a new generation of aspiring architects. "Our new desert camp belonged to the Arizona desert as though it had stood there during creation," said Wright. Several tours of the facility and grounds are offered. Children will especially enjoy the tour of the temporary shelters, which first-year students must build as a study of desert architecture.

Where to Eat

Arcadia Farms Café. 7014 East First Avenue, Scottsdale; (480) 941–5665. Gourmet sandwiches, lunch, and dinner. Reservations suggested. $$$

Buca di Beppo. 3828 North Scottsdale Road, Scottsdale; (480) 949–6622. Chicken, pasta, and veal served family-style. Children's portions available. $$$

Jillian's. 21001 North Tatum Boulevard (in the Desert Ridge shopping center), Phoenix; (480) 538–8956. This two-story complex boasts video games and virtual-reality bowling alleys to keep the kids occupied while you wait for your burgers. $$

Pinnacle Peak Patio. 10426 East Jomax, Scottsdale; (480) 585–1599. Western cowboy fare and live entertainment. Dads get their ties shorn off and tacked to the wall, and kids earn badges as junior deputies. Open for dinner only. $$$

Satisfied Frog. 6245 East Cave Creek Road, Cave Creek; (480) 488–3317. Kids will love this funky little restaurant, which offers hearty Western fare. $$

Where to Stay

Camelback Inn Resort Golf Club and Spa. 5402 East Lincoln Drive, Scottsdale; (480) 948–1700; www.camelbackinn.com. Children's Hopalong College features arts and crafts, water games, tennis clinics, bicycling, playground activities, nature walks, and pizza parties. $$$$

Comfort Suites. 3275 North Civic Center Boulevard, Scottsdale; (480) 946–1111. Complimentary continental breakfast, refrigerators, and microwaves. $$

Four Seasons Resort Scottsdale at Troon North. 10600 East Crescent Moon Drive, Scottsdale; (480) 515–5700; www.fourseasons.com. In-room kids' amenities include stuffed animals, complimentary milk and cookies, special kid-size toiletries, videos, nightlights, and kid-size terrycloth robes. Children's activities in the Kids for All Seasons program include horseback riding, desert jeep tours, treasure hunts, and Southwestern-style arts and crafts. Children under 18 stay **free.** $$$$

Holiday Inn Express. 3131 North Scottsdale Road, Scottsdale; (480) 675–7665. **Free** breakfast, area shuttle, pool, gift shop, and video games. $$$

Hyatt Regency Scottsdale Resort. 7500 East Doubletree Ranch Road, Scottsdale; (480) 991–3388; www.scottsdale hyatt.com. Offering a 2½-acre water playground complete with water slide and sand beach. Camp Hyatt Kachina entertains kids with activities such as Navajo bead working, cookie decorating, T-shirt design, sand painting, and "Kids in the Kitchen." $$$$

The Phoenician. 6000 East Camelback Road, Scottsdale; (480) 941–8200 or (800) 888–8234; www.thephoenician.com. Featuring nine pools and eleven restaurants. The Funician's Kids Club offers a year-round kids' camp filled with daily activities such as nature walks, ranger presentations, and jungle-gym fun. $$$$

Sunburst Resort. 4925 North Scottsdale Road, Scottsdale; (480) 945–7666 or (800) 528–7867; www.sunburstresort.com. Lagoon-style pool and beach area, dining room serving American cuisine. Check out the resort's special family packages. $$$

For More Information

Carefree/Cave Creek Chamber of Commerce. 748 Easy Street, P.O. Box 734, Carefree 85377; (480) 488–3381; www.carefree-cavecreek.com.

Scottsdale Area Chamber of Commerce. 7343 Scottsdale Mall, Scottsdale 85251-4498; (480) 945–8481; www.scottsdalecvb.com.

Tempe

Although this charming city is known primarily as a college town, you'll still find a few places to entertain the kids. Home to Arizona State University, with a student population of more than 50,000, Tempe invites all ages to explore the shops lining Mill Avenue. Kids will enjoy clambering on the giant bunnies tucked away at Centerpoint just off Sixth Street. As you explore Tempe, you'll discover a lake teeming with colorful sailboats, a theater with a six-story screen, water parks, a cool ice skating rink, and a children's theater.

Childsplay (all ages)

Tempe Performing Arts Center, 132 East Sixth Street, Tempe; (480) 350–8101 or (800) 583–7831; www.tempe.gov/childsplay. Office open 9:00 A.M. to 5:00 P.M. Monday through Friday. Show times and prices vary.

This award-winning professional theater produces shows geared specifically for families. Each season's show includes a suggested age range appropriate for the production. Some shows offered in the past have included *Schoolhouse Rock Live!*, *The Velveteen Rabbit*, and *The Reluctant Dragon*.

Kiwanis Park Recreation Center and Indoor Wave Pool (all ages)

6111 South All America Way, Tempe; (480) 350–5201; www.tempe.gov/pkrec/krc. Open 7:00 A.M. to 10:00 P.M. Monday through Thursday, 7:00 A.M. to 7:00 P.M. Friday, 8:00 A.M. to 6:00 P.M. Saturday, and 8:00 A.M. to 9:00 P.M. Sunday. Call for prices.

This 125-acre park provides a great place for year-round family fun. Featured activities include an indoor heated wave pool and water slide, tennis courts, a batting range, gymnasium, picnic armadas, sand volleyball courts, soccer fields, and playgrounds. If water sports are more what you had in mind, you can rent a boat or go fishing on the twelve-acre lake.

Arizona Cardinals (all ages)

8701 South Hardy Drive, Tempe; (602) 379–0101 or (800) 999–1402; www.azcardinals.com. Football games are held in Sun Devil Stadium. Season runs August through January. Tickets $$$$ per game. Flex Packs are available as well as alcohol-free sections.

Watch the Arizona Cardinals play in ASU's Sun Devil Stadium on autumn Sundays. This football team was founded in 1898 and is a charter member of the National Football League. Unlike most NFL football teams, the Cardinals don't have their own facility—although there is one in the works, scheduled to open in 2006. Because they play in a college stadium, be advised that parking is a nightmare, and the facilities are spartan at best.

IMAX Theatre (ages 5 and up)

5000 Arizona Mills Circle, Arizona Mills Mall, Tempe; (480) 897–IMAX; www.imax.com/tempe. Call for shows and show times. $$

Children will love experiencing the world through film on a six-story, 82-foot-wide screen. Some featured flicks in the past have included *T-Rex: Back to the Cretaceous, Journey Into Amazing Caves,* and *Everest.*

Fiddlesticks Family Fun Park (all ages)

1155 West Elliot Road, Tempe; (480) 961–0800. 8800 East Indian Bend, Scottsdale; (480) 951–6060; www.fiddlesticksaz.com. Open daily. Hours vary. $$$

Both locations offer go-karts, bumper boats, batting cages, and miniature golf. In addition, the Tempe Fun Park features a driving range, and the Scottsdale location has Atlantis laser tag and a Kiddie Land with several rides for younger children.

Big Surf (ages 4 and up) 🌊

1500 North McClintock Drive, Tempe; (480) 947–7873 or (480) 947–2477; www.golfland.com. Open 10:00 A.M. to 6:00 P.M. Monday through Saturday and 11:00 A.M. to 7:00 P.M. Sunday from Memorial Day to Labor Day. $$$

This twenty-acre wet and wild water park features a beach, water slides, play areas, volleyball courts, and a surf pool. Make sure to lather the kids up with sunscreen as the summer sun can quickly burn exposed skin.

Oceanside Ice Arena (all ages) 🏒

1520 North McClintock Drive, Tempe; (480) 941–0944; www.iskateaz.com. Open daily 10:00 A.M. to 9:00 P.M. except Thanksgiving and Christmas Day. Call for open skating sessions. $

This ice arena, open year-round, offers public skating, skating lessons, hockey lessons, open hockey, and rink rental. Check out the Web site for special discounts and coupons. Also, if you forget gloves for the little ones, you can pick up a pair in the completely outfitted pro shop.

Tempe Town Lake (all ages) 🍴 ⛺

80 West Rio Salado Parkway, Tempe; (480) 350–8625; www.tempe.gov/rio. Lake open daily 5:00 A.M. to 10:00 P.M. Free.

Created in the Salt River bed, this little lake is open for public boating from sunrise to sunset, unless you have proper lighting, and then you can boat until 10:00 P.M. Along the lake waterfront, near Mill Avenue, you'll find rows of shops and restaurants. Kids will enjoy walking along the beach, but it might be hard keeping them out of the water as there is no public swimming available. However, a new one-acre splash playground and kiddie train rides should keep even the tiniest tots entertained. For thirty-minute narrated boat tours of Tempe Town Lake or boat rentals, stop by Rio Lago Cruise (990 West Rio Salado Parkway; 480–517–4050).

Where to Eat

Billy Joe's BBQ. 1730 East Elliot Road, Suite 11, Tempe; (480) 831–0822. Southern style barbecue in a relaxed atmosphere. Limited children's menu. $$$

Joe's Crab Shack. 1606 West Baseline Road, Tempe; (480) 345–0972. 1604 East Southern Avenue, Tempe; (480) 730–0303; www.joescrabshack.com. Crab, shrimp, chicken, soups, salads, and sandwiches. Rug Rat menu includes chicken fingers, popcorn shrimp, corn dogs, macaroni and cheese, pizza, and hamburgers. $–$$

Monti's La Casa Vieja. 3 West First Street, Tempe; (480) 967–7594. Steak, pork, seafood, sandwiches, salads, and soups are served at this local landmark hangout. Monti's claim to fame, other than its fabulous steaks, is that it happens to have been the birthplace of the late Senator Carl Hayden. Children's menu. $$–$$$

Rainforest Café. 5000 South Arizona Mills Circle, Tempe; (480) 752–9100. A lush jungle features calls of the wild, impromptu thunderstorms, and great burgers. Specialty children's menu. $$$$

Where to Stay

Embassy Suites Hotel. 4400 South Rural Road, Tempe; (480) 897–7444. Full cooked-to-order breakfast, refrigerator and microwave, pool, hot tub, and game room. Children under twelve stay **free.** $$$–$$$$

Hampton Inn & Suites. 1429 North Scottsdale Road, Tempe; (480) 675–9799. Continental breakfast, family suites, two swimming pools, and tennis courts. Children stay **free.** $$–$$$

Holiday Inn. 915 East Apache Boulevard, Tempe; (480) 968–3451. Restaurant, family suites, shuttle to the Phoenix Zoo, and pool. Children under twelve stay and eat **free.** $$$

Spring Hill Suites by Marriott. 5211 South Priest Drive, Tempe; (480) 752–7979. Studio suites with kitchenettes, continental breakfast, swimming pool, and hot tub. Children stay **free.** $$$

Tempe Mission Palms Hotel. 60 East Fifth Street, Tempe; (480) 894–1400 or (800) 547–8705; www.missionpalms.com. This upscale hotel in downtown Tempe features comfortable rooms, a beautiful courtyard, and a rooftop pool and spa. $$$–$$$$

For More Information

Tempe Convention and Visitor Bureau. 51 West Third Street, Suite 105, Tempe 85281; (480) 894–8158; www.tempecvb.com.

East Valley

Out here you'll find the sweeping fields of some of Maricopa County's remaining agricultural communities; the small suburbs of Chandler, Queen Creek, and Apache Junction; and the bustling city of Mesa, Arizona's third-largest city. While visiting this sprawling area east of Phoenix, you and the kids will find several museums oriented toward youth, ancient ruins of the Salado Indians, and a family fun park. Explore the many mountain preserves by foot, on horseback, or by mountain bike. Walk through the old Mesa prison, search for gold in the Superstition Mountains, and take a steamboat tour of one of the desert lakes. Whatever your fancy, you're sure to find it in the eastern reaches of the Valley of the Sun.

Arizona Museum for Youth (all ages)

35 North Robson Street, Mesa; (480) 644–2467; www.arizonamuseumforyouth.com. Open 1:00 to 5:00 P.M. Tuesday through Friday and Sunday and 9:00 A.M. to 5:00 P.M. Saturday except major holidays. $

Located in downtown Mesa, this is an art museum you can kid around in. A visit to this innovative, nationally recognized fine-arts museum will illustrate why *USA Today* named it one of the best children's museums in the country. Art-based activities, taken from cultures worldwide, create a comprehensive hands-on environment for kids to discover the beauty of paint and pigment, sculpture and style.

Park of the Canals (all ages)

1710 North Horne, Mesa; (480) 644–2351. Open daily 8:00 A.M. to 10:00 P.M. Free.

This thirty-one-acre park features the ancient canal systems of the prehistoric Hohokam Indians. Children will enjoy the large playground and the desert botanical garden that features trees, shrubs, and more than twenty-five varieties of prickly pear cacti.

Firebird International Raceway (ages 6 and up)

20000 Maricopa Road, Box 5023, Chandler 85226; (602) 268–0200; www.firebirdraceway.com. Call for events and prices.

View cars tearing down the ¼-mile track at speeds exceeding 320 miles per hour, boats shattering world records on the lake, and monster trucks pounding a little iron. Most events are loud, so you should bring protective hearing devices to protect little eardrums.

Sirrine House Historic Museum (ages 5 and up)

160 North Center, Mesa; (480) 644–2760. Open 10:00 A.M. to 5:00 P.M. Saturday and 1:00 to 5:00 P.M. Sunday October through March. Free.

If you're in the neighborhood, take a quick jaunt over to Mesa's only fully restored historic house museum. Joel Sirrine built this distinctive Queen Anne–style home for his new bride, Caroline, in 1896. Your best bet is to tour the home and its period rooms during one of the museum's kid-friendly special events, which in the past have included A Victorian Christmas in Candlelight and Fun and Games of Long Ago.

Golfland/Sunsplash (ages 3 and up)

155 West Hampton Drive, Mesa; (480) 834–8319; www.golfland-sunsplash.com. Golfland is open year-round and Sunsplash is open during the summer months. Admission $$$. Golf $.

At this amusement park the kids can horse around in a giant playground, play miniature golf, or get wet on any of the park's seventeen water-related rides. Other features include a 15,000-square-foot arcade castle, a pizza parlor, motorized Li'l Indy racecars, laser tag, and bumper boats.

Mesa Southwest Museum (ages 4 and up)

53 North Macdonald Street, Mesa; (480) 644–2230; www.mesasouthwestmuseum.com. Open 10:00 A.M. to 5:00 P.M. Tuesday through Saturday and 1:00 to 5:00 P.M. Sunday except all major holidays. Adults $$, children ages 3–12 $, under 3 free.

Explore Southwestern night skies in the Hall of Astronomy, check out Arizona's stony wealth in the Hall of Minerals, and get a glimpse of a time when dinosaurs roamed Earth in the Prehistoric Wing. Children will ohh and ahh at the animatronic dinosaurs on the three-story Dinosaur Mountain. The Discovery Resource Center is especially kid-friendly with its hands-on approach to learning with bug displays, computer programs, chunks of minerals and petrified wood, casts of dinosaur bones and teeth, and coloring areas. In this massive museum you'll also experience the life of ancient cultures from the mammoth-hunting Paleo-Indians to the Hohokam peoples, walk through an adobe representation of the first Spanish mission built in Arizona, and take an adventure through a tunnel to discover the legend of the Lost Dutchman's Mine. The rocky tunnel exits into territorial jail cells, which were used until the 1970s. The final two permanent exhibits include a re-creation of Mesa's Main Street in the 1900s and a display chronicling Arizona's movie history. Make sure to wear good shoes, and plan on spending several hours at this gem of a museum.

Mesa Youththeatre (all ages)

155 North Center Street, Mesa; (480) 644–2681. Show schedule varies. $$

This award-winning children's theater produces a variety of programs for children and teenagers. The small theater has a season schedule of three plays a year. Offerings in the past have included such theatrical works as *Really Rosie* and *Wetlands*.

Salt River Tubing and Recreation (ages 8 and up)

Fifteen miles north of Highway 60 on Power Road, Mesa; (480) 984–3305; www.saltriver tubing.com. Open daily at 9:00 A.M. May through September. Trips range from ninety minutes to five hours. Tube rental and shuttle $.

Hop on your own personal rubber yacht for a leisurely float down the Salt River. Inner-tube rental and shuttle service are provided. Families need to be aware that this is often a huge party activity for college students and would be best advised to take the trip during the week. Unfortunately, not all river runners keep it clean and pack their garbage, which oftentimes include glass bottles and cans—so make sure to keep shoes on for the float.

Mike's Bike Chalet (ages 7 and up)

5753 East Brown Road, Suite 102, Mesa; (480) 807–2944. Store hours vary. Bike rentals $$$$.

If you and the kids want to enjoy some of Phoenix's mountain preserves or numerous bike routes but find yourself without wheels, Bike Chalet is your answer. Here you can rent everything from mountain bikes and road bikes to tandems and kid's BMX bikes. Other amenities include car racks and maps of bike paths in the area. Delivery is available.

Desert Dog Hummer Adventures (all ages)

17212 East Shea Boulevard, Fountain Hills; (480) 837–3966; www.azadventures.com. Open daily 6:00 A.M. to 10:00 P.M. $$$$; special discount for children under 10.

Kids of all ages will enjoy these narrated tours from the comfort of a Hummer. See petroglyphs, explore Native American ruins, and enjoy wildlife watching as you travel through the legend-riddled Sonoran Desert.

Fort McDowell Adventures (ages 6 and up)

Three miles north of Shea Boulevard on Beeline Highway, 16302 East Vaughn, Gilbert; (480) 816–1513; www.fortmcdowelladventures.com. Open 8:00 A.M. to 4:00 P.M. Monday through Saturday. Call for summer hours. $$$$

The kids will love the scenic trail rides winding through the Yavapai–Fort McDowell Indian Reservation, located on the fringe of Phoenix. Standard one-hour rides through the wilderness are available for kids age six and up, and the longer rides are geared for ages eight and up. Other features include overnight pack trips, pony rides, hayrides, cattle drives, private rodeos, and dinner rides.

Usery Mountain Recreation Area (all ages)

3939 North Usery Pass Road #190, Mesa; (480) 984–0032. Open 6:00 A.M. to 8:00 P.M. Sunday through Thursday and 6:00 A.M. to 10:00 P.M. Friday and Saturday. Entry fee $ per vehicle.

Located 12 miles northeast of downtown Mesa, this 3,600-acre desert park features the best of desert recreation, including family camping, picnicking, horseback riding, mountain biking, and hiking. The area takes its name from Usery Mountain, which was a hideout for the desperado and horse thief King Usery. You'll find hiking trails suitable for a variety of ages and skill levels. Families will want to explore the 1-mile Merkl Memorial Trail, which loops around interesting rock formations near the picnic facilities. Interpretive signs point out the desert plants encountered along the way. Kids can also frolic away an afternoon in the playground while parents sit back and enjoy the scenic vistas.

McDowell Mountain Regional Park (all ages)

Four miles north of Fountain Hills on McDowell Mountain Road, P.O. Box 18415, Fountain Hills 85219; (480) 471–0173. Open 6:00 A.M. to 8:00 P.M. Sunday through Thursday and 6:00 A.M. to 10:00 P.M. Friday and Saturday. Entry fee $ per vehicle.

This 21,000-acre park features 35 miles of trails suitable for hikers and horseback riders of all levels. Near the family campground, you'll find several easy loop trails marked with interpretive signs. Parts of the park range in elevation from 1,600 to 3,000 feet, which provides several panoramic vistas of the mountain ranges surrounding the East Valley, including the McDowells, the Mazatals, Four Peaks, and the Superstitions. Other amenities include picnic areas, playgrounds, and special events.

Goldfield Ghost Town (all ages)

Four miles north of Apache Junction on State Route 88, Apache Junction; (480) 983–0333; www.goldfieldghosttown.com. Open daily 10:00 A.M. to 5:00 P.M. except Christmas Day. **Free.**

This authentic ghost town, located at the base of the legendary Superstition Mountains, was voted as the Best Place to Take the Kids by the *Phoenix New Times* newspaper. The town boomed in 1893, and even though the gold is gone, Goldfield provides a look back in time to the 1890s Old West. There's plenty to keep the kids busy here—horseback riding, narrow-gauge train rides, mine tours, jeep tours, helicopter tours, hiking trails, gunfight reenactments, gold panning, and a museum filled with mining artifacts. A bed-and-breakfast, the Mammoth Steakhouse, and live Old West entertainment in the saloon add to the old-fashioned experience.

Lost Dutchman State Park (all ages)

6109 North Apache Trail, Apache Junction; (602) 982–4485; www.pr.state.az.us/Parks/ parkhtml/dutchman.html. Office open daily 8:00 A.M. to 5:00 P.M. Day use $$ per vehicle.

The park is situated at the foot of the Superstition Mountains, where German immigrant Jacob Walz reputedly discovered a huge cache of gold. The legendary Lost Dutchman Mine is still sought by prospectors today. The kids can join in the search for gold from several trails that lead from the park into the wilderness of the Tonto National Forest. Park amenities include picnic tables, grills, a primitive campground, showers, and restrooms. Forest rangers lead guided hikes every Saturday at 9:00 A.M.

Saguaro Lake (all ages)

2324 East McDowell Road, Phoenix. Marina, (480) 986–5546. Marina open daily 9:00 A.M. to 5:00 P.M. Monday through Saturday.

This desert lake offers a great variety of outdoor activities, including boating, camping, fishing, picnicking, and water sports. The Lakeshore Restaurant (928–984–5311) provides a nice place to have lunch if you didn't pack your own, and **Precision Marine** (480–986–0969) offers boat rentals. However, if you don't want to rent a boat, the **Desert Bell Excursion** (480–984–2425) will take you and the kids on a ninety-minute paddleboat cruise around the lake.

Dolly Steamboat Excursion (all ages)

Canyon Lake, P.O. Box 977, Apache Junction 85217; (480) 827–9144; www.DollySteam Boat.com. Leaves daily at noon and 2:00 P.M. except Thanksgiving and Christmas Day. $$$$

These ninety-minute narrated tours are a great way for you and your family to explore this desert lake. On the tour you'll see plants and wildlife indigenous to the Sonoran Desert as the captain recounts legends of the looming Superstition Mountains. If you have a pair of binoculars, bring them. Have the kids on the lookout for bighorn sheep roaming the steep canyon walls.

Tonto National Monument (ages 4 and up) 🚗 🧗 🏛️
Highway 188, south of Roosevelt Lake, HC02 Box 4602, Roosevelt 85545; (928) 467–2241; www.nps.gov/tont. Open daily 8:00 A.M. to 5:00 P.M. except Christmas Day. The trail closes at 4:00 P.M. Admission is $ per person or $$ for a family.

This monument features two sets of cliff dwellings, built around A.D. 1300 by the Salado Indians. A 1-mile round-trip paved trail take visitors up about 350 feet to the lower cliff dwelling. Along the way, you'll discover interpretive signs detailing the area's rich history and information on local plants and wildlife. The upper cliff dwelling is only accessible on guided tours. This 3-mile, moderately strenuous hike is only appropriate for older children who can make it up the steep trail. The guided hike is available November through April by reservation only. Back at the visitor center you can watch an eighteen-minute video on the dwellings, and the kids can check out artifacts left behind by these prehistoric peoples in the monument's small museum.

Where to Eat

Barleen Family Country Music Dinner Theatre. 2275 Old West Highway, Apache Junction; (480) 982–7991. Southwestern cuisine, home cooking, and live family entertainment. Closed June through October. $$$

Bill Johnson's Big Apple. 3110 North Arizona Avenue, Chandler; (480) 892–2542. Ribs, steak, sandwiches, and salads. Extensive children's menu. Dress is casual. $$

The Landmark Restaurant. 809 West Main Street, Mesa; (480) 962–4652. This historic dining room has photos of Arizona's history on its walls. The restaurant is known for its prime rib but also serves pork, steak, chicken, and seafood. Children's menu. $$$

Organ Stop Pizza. 1149 East Southern Avenue, Mesa; (480) 813–5700. This unique parlor serves up pizza with style to the tune of the xylophones, chimes, pianos, drums, and cymbals of a mighty Wurlitzer organ. $$

Rockin' R Ranch. 6136 East Baseline Road, Mesa; (480) 832–1539. A dinner theater with Western shows and an all-you-can-eat cowboy-style barbecue dinner. Reservations required. $$$

Romano's Macaroni Grill. 5035 East Ray Road, Phoenix; (480) 705–5661. Specialty and traditional pasta dishes, chicken, seafood, and salads. Children's menu with Italian and American favorites. $$

Ruby Tuesday. 6555 East Southern Avenue #1542, Mesa; (480) 641–8188. Hamburgers, sandwiches, and salad bar. Children's menu. $$

Where to Stay

Holiday Inn Mesa Hotel & Suites. 1600 South Country Club Drive, Mesa; (480) 964–7000. Family suites, heated outdoor pool with waterfall, spa, and a full-service restaurant. $$$

Residence Inn by Marriott. 941 West Grove, Mesa; (480) 610–0100; www. marriott.com/residenceinn. One- and two-bedroom suites, continental breakfast, and heated pool. Children under twelve stay free. $$$–$$$$

For More Information

Apache Junction Area Chamber of Commerce. 567 West Apache Junction Trail, Apache Junction 85220; (480) 982–3141; www.apachejunctioncoc.com.

Chandler Chamber of Commerce. 218 North Arizona Avenue, Chandler 85224; (480) 963–4571.

Fountain Hills Chamber of Commerce. 16838 East Palisades, P.O. Box 17598, Fountain Hills 85269; (480) 837–1654; www.fountainhillschamber.com.

Mesa Chamber of Commerce. 120 North Center, P.O. Box 5820, Mesa 85201-5820; (480) 969–1307; www.mesachamber.org.

Casa Grande

This small agricultural town might not seem like a hot spot for visitors at first, but it is home to one of the most impressive examples of Hohokam ruins in Arizona. More than 200,000 visitors stop to see Casa Grande Ruins National Monument, but this sleepy little town also offers the chance to shop in an outlet mall and discover the pioneering spirit of a hamlet that was once just a spot in the road where the railroad stopped over.

Casa Grande Ruins National Monument (all ages)

1100 Ruins Drive, Coolidge; (520) 723–3172; www.nps.gov/cagr. Open daily 8:00 A.M. to 5:00 P.M. except Christmas Day. Adults $, children under 16 free.

The weatherworn mud walls of this mysterious Hohokam ruin, built between A.D. 1100 and 1400, is the single most impressive remains of this prehistoric culture. Archaeologists are still puzzled on the building's purpose but guess it may have been a temple, palace, or even an astrological observatory. The four-story building sits under a pagoda-like pavilion, put up to help stabilize the mud structure, which has been succumbing to the elements over the years—melting back into the earth from which it was formed. After taking the walking trail to see Casa Grande (Spanish for "big house"), check out the exhibits of Hohokam pottery, jewelry, and other artifacts at the museum. Children will especially find it interesting that Hohokam children played a ball game, much like modern-day soccer, in ball courts near the ruins.

A Miner Family **Adventure**

For our first excursion to a family farm, my sons Hayden and Blake decided to cowboy it up in their new duds sent by Grandma. After all, they explained in their little boy voices, farms had horses, and horses need cowboys.

Once we arrived at Schnepf Farms for the annual Pumpkin and Chili Party, we were off and running past the pumpkin patch straight to the animal pens. Here we found goats, chickens, and one stunted mule that seemed to take amusement from tugging on passersby's clothing. Hayden walked up to the mule with a frown on his face. It wasn't quite what he expected, I think. The mule and boy regarded each other for a moment, and then the curious animal plucked Hayden's red cowboy hat right off his head. Hayden squealed, and I ran forward just as the mule dropped it in the mud. I cleaned it up as best I could and gave it back to Hayden, who scowled at the animal. "Bad horse," he said.

We set off to explore the rest of the farm, took a spooky train ride through the orchard, and made our very own scarecrow. "Horses eat hay," Blake piped up. We rode the carousel, picked pumpkins, and took a tumble down the slide at Witch Mountain.

One of the last attractions we visited was Hillbilly Bob's Pig Races. Before the show, Bob's cousin Eleanor brings out laughter with a spooky Southwestern rendition of "The Three Little Pigs." Children clambered up front, lining the fence as though they were pickets themselves, riveted to the charming story. Then the races were about to begin, so Bob moved them all back to give the pigs room to run. Bob and audience members from earlier shows taught us how to beckon pigs with a loud "Suuuey," which young and old gleefully called out into the clear night air. Hayden was chosen to compete in the race after I hoisted him over my head in a valiant attempt to get noticed among the crowd. I joined him in the front as his twin brother, Blake, glared at us from our seat. We rooted noisily as the rare pigs raced around the track to obtain their Oreo cookie treats. Hayden squealed with delight when his pig finished first, earning him a coveted rubber pig nose. Blake scowled because he didn't get to race. "Why does Hayden get a nose and I don't," he complained rather loudly. To keep the peace I bought Blake his very own plastic pig nose, and we headed toward the car. They raced along—two horseless little cowboys with pig profiles—and I followed with a pumpkin tucked under one arm and a lumpy scarecrow precariously balanced over my shoulder.

McFarland State Historical Park (ages 6 and up)

On the corner of Main and Ruggles Streets, P.O. Box 109, Florence 85232; (520) 868–5216; www.pr.state.az.us/Parks/parkhtml/mcfarland.html. Open 8:00 A.M. to 5:00 P.M. Thursday through Monday except Christmas Day. Adults and children ages 7–13 $, under 7 free.

This park illustrates Pinal County's frontier days, when the adobe building once housed the county courthouse, sheriff's office, and jail. You'll also learn about Ernest McFarland, a chief justice of the Supreme Court, who began his political career here in 1925 as a Pinal County attorney. A picnic area and a playground will entertain the youngsters.

Where to Eat

A&M Pizza. 1264 East Florence Boulevard, Casa Grande; (520) 316–0656. Pizza, pasta, and salads in a casual atmosphere. $$

Barney's. 665 North Pinal Avenue, Casa Grande; (520) 426–1377. Steaks, seafood, and prime rib. Diverse children's menu. $$$

BeDillon's Restaurant & Cactus Garden. 800 North Park Avenue, Casa Grande; (520) 836–2045. Southwestern-style entrees, grilled steaks, seafood, and chicken served in a historic 1917 house. Cactus garden provides educational opportunities, and a small museum houses Native American artifacts. Children's menu. $$

Where to Stay

Best Western Casa Grande Suites. 665 Via del Cielo, Casa Grande; (520) 836–1600. Suites and kitchenettes, deluxe continental breakfast, swimming pool, spa, and exercise room. Children stay free. $$

Holiday Inn Casa Grande. 777 North Pinal Avenue, Casa Grande; (520) 426–3500. Heated pool, restaurant, and spa. Children stay free. $$

Inn at Rancho Sonora. 9198 North Highway 79, Florence; (520) 868–8000. Bed-and-breakfast in an adobe inn, outdoor grills, heated pool, spa, and RV park. $$–$$$

For More Information

Greater Casa Grande Chamber of Commerce. 575 North Marshall Street, Casa Grande 85222-5246; (520) 836–2125 or (800) 916–1515; www.casagrande chamber.org.

Annual Events

FEBRUARY

Renaissance Festival and Artisan Marketplace. Apache Junction; (520) 463–2700. February through March. Jousting tournaments, visit with King Henry and his court, food, a marketplace, period crafts, live entertainment, and festival games.

MARCH

Open House at Adobe Mountain Wildlife Rehabilitation Center. Phoenix; (623) 582–9806. First weekend in March. An annual wildlife fair with educational exhibits, presentations, and lectures.

Civil War Battle Reenactment. Picacho Peak; (520) 466–3183. Second weekend of March. Reenactment of the Civil War's westernmost battle, the battle of Picacho Peak.

Ostrich Festival. Chandler; (480) 782–2220. Second weekend in March. Ostrich races, international foods, and arts and crafts.

Dons of Arizona Lost Dutchman Gold Mine Superstition Mountain Trek. Apache Junction; (602) 258–6016. Second weekend in March. Search for Jacob Waltz's fabled lost mine, pan for gold, and watch a firefall tumble down the mountainside.

Worldport—Glendale's Celebration of the Nations. Glendale; (623) 930–2299. Last weekend in March. Live ethnic entertainment, a parade of nations, Discovery Pavilion, and an international bazaar.

APRIL

Maricopa County Fair. Phoenix; (602) 252–0717. Mid-April. Livestock exhibits, a carnival, and kids' activities.

Mesa, Arizona Easter Pageant. Mesa; (480) 964–7164. Mid-April. This pageant, which has been held every Easter since 1928 with the exception of the World War II years, features a volunteer cast of more than 400 actors on a 9,600-square-foot stage.

Arizona Asian Festival. Phoenix; (602) 788–8899. Third weekend in April. Live entertainment, cuisine, and hands-on activities related to India, China, Korea, Thailand, the Philippines, Laos, Vietnam, and Japan.

Arizona **Warfare**

The battle of Picacho Peak was really a mistake—a surprise collision between the advance guard of a 2,350-man Union army from California and a Confederate patrol out of Tucson, then occupied by 300 troops. The Union patrol, commanded by Lt. James Barrett, initially captured two of the enemy and was questioning them when more Confederates attacked, killing Lieutenant Barrett and two privates. The Federals rejoined their main force, and the Confederates abandoned Tucson. The confrontation was a confusing skirmish of dusty death, but it exudes an allure to this day, and now more people show up to watch it being replayed each year than those who lived in the Southwest at the time of the battle.

Heard Museum Guild Native American Student Arts and Crafts Show. Phoenix; (602) 252–8840. Early April. Exhibits of more than 1,200 works of art by Native American youth across the country, at the Heard Museum.

Maricopa County Fair. Phoenix; (602) 252-0717. Mid-April. Educational exhibits, 4-H competitions, horse shows, games, and rides at the state fairgrounds.

JULY

Fabulous Phoenix Fourth. Phoenix; (602) 262–4633. Fourth of July. Live entertainment, games, and the largest fireworks display in the Southwest.

Tempe's Kiwanis Fourth of July Celebration. Tempe; (480) 350–5180. Fourth of July. Children's games and activities, food, live entertainment, and fireworks displays.

Downtown Cooldown. Tempe; (480) 921–2300. Mid-July. Featuring twenty tons of snow, a parade, kids' activities, water games, hands-on arts and crafts, games, and food.

OCTOBER

Pumpkin and Chili Party. Queen Creek; (480) 987–3333. Every weekend in October. Hillbilly Bob's Pig Races, a two-acre corn maze, live bluegrass and country music, melodrama theater, carousel rides, trick-or-treating, a spooky train ride, you-pick pumpkins, scarecrow making, and a chili dinner at Schnepf Farms.

Arizona State Fair. Phoenix; (602) 252–6771. Mid-October. Carnival, games, rides, live entertainment, farm animals, arts and crafts, and food.

NOVEMBER

The Metris Thunderbird Classic. Scottsdale; (602) 840–9005. First weekend in November. Live entertainment, hot-air balloons, and a desert glow.

Glendale Glitters Holiday Light Extravaganza. Glendale; (623) 930–4500. The weekend after Thanksgiving through mid-January. A holiday celebration featuring 500,000 lights, arts and crafts, visits from Santa Claus, live entertainment, and horse-drawn carriage rides.

APS Fantasy of Lights. Tempe; (480) 967–4877. The weekend after Thanksgiving through the first week of January. Electric light parade, boat parade, live entertainment, Fantasy on Ice, and fireworks.

DECEMBER

Tumbleweed Christmas Tree Lighting Ceremony. Chandler; (480) 782–2727. First Saturday in December. Arts and crafts, visit with Santa, and holiday activities at A. J. Chandler Park.

Holidays at the Heard Museum. Phoenix; (602) 252–8848. End of December. Take a Native American perspective of this season of cheer with art exhibits and demonstrations, live Native American song and dance presentations, and native foods.

Fiesta Bowl Parade. Tempe; (480) 350–0900. Last weekend in December. Live entertainment, arts and crafts booth, kids' games and activities, and a college football parade.

Other Things to **See and Do**

- **ABC/Desert Biking Adventures,** Scottsdale; (888) 249–BIKE or (602) 320–4602.
- **Adventures Out West,** Phoenix; (602) 996–6100 or (800) 755–0935.
- **Ak-Chin Him-Dak Eco Museum,** Maricopa; (520) 568–9480.
- **Arcosanti,** Mayer; (602) 254–5309.
- **Arizona Railway Museum,** Chandler; (480) 821–1108.
- **Arizona White-Knuckle Adventures,** Scottsdale; (866) 342–9669.
- **Arrowhead Desert Tours,** Phoenix; (602) 942–3361.
- **Buckeye Valley Museum,** Buckeye; (623) 386–4333.
- **Build-A-Bear Workshop,** Scottsdale; (480) 946–2327.
- **Casa Grande Art Museum,** Casa Grande; (520) 836–3377.
- **Cave Creek Outfitters,** Scottsdale; (480) 471–4635.
- **Chandler Museum,** Chandler; (480) 782–2717.
- **Desert Mountain Jeep Tours,** Scottsdale; (480) 860–1777 or (800) 567–3619.
- **Desert Storm Hummer Tours,** Scottsdale; (480) 922–0020.
- **Don Donnelly Stables,** Gold Canyon; (480) 982–7822.
- **Estrella Mountain Regional Park,** Goodyear; (623) 932–3811.
- **Fort McDowell Adventures,** Fountain Hills; (480) 816–1513.
- **Hoo-Hoogam Ki Museum,** Scottsdale; (480) 850–8190.
- **Korean Cultural Center,** Mesa; (602) 813–4255.
- **Manistee Ranch,** Glendale; (623) 435–0072.
- **Mesa Arts Center,** Mesa; (480) 644–2242.
- **Mesa Historical Museum,** Mesa; (480) 835–7358.
- **Museo Chicano,** Phoenix; (602) 257–5536.
- **Mystic Saddle Ranch and Trail Rides,** Cave Creek; (623) 742–6700 or (877) 942–6700.
- **OK Corral Riding Stable,** Apache Junction; (480) 982–4040.
- **The Outback Safari Co.,** Scottsdale; (480) 987–8335.
- **Petersen House Museum,** Tempe; (480) 350–5151.
- **Phoenix Police Museum,** Phoenix; (602) 534–7278.

- **Roosevelt Lake,** Apache Junction; (520) 467–2245.
- **Salt River Project History Center,** Tempe; (602) 236–2723.
- **Scottsdale Museum of Contemporary Art,** Scottsdale; (480) 994–2787.
- **Stuffington Bear Factory,** Phoenix; (602) 225–9513.
- **Telephone Pioneer Museum,** Phoenix; (602) 630–2060.
- **Tempe Historical Museum,** Tempe; (480) 350–5100.
- **Tortilla Flat;** (480) 984–1776.
- **Unicorn Balloon Company,** Scottsdale; (480) 991–3666 or (800) 755–0935.
- **Vision Art Gallery,** Chandler; (480) 917–6859.
- **West Valley Art Museum,** Surprise; (623) 972–0635.
- **Windwalker Expeditions Inc.,** Cave Creek; (480) 585–3382 or (888) 785–3382.

Old West Territory

Southern Arizona remains the state's most diverse region, with vivid "sky island" mountains looming above sweeping grasslands, the greatest variety of birds in North America, staged gunfights in the streets of the "town too tough to die," eerie limestone caves with bizarre rock formations, and weird forests of rock hoodoos. Here the Sonoran Desert gives way to the desolate wilderness of the Chihuahuan Desert, yet this region also hosts the sky islands, a world-renowned birding paradise. Mount Lemmon, home to the country's southernmost ski resort, best illustrates this dramatic diversity as the thirty-minute drive up the mountain will take you through as many different Merriam zones that you would encounter if you took the 2,000-mile drive from Arizona to Canada.

Carrie's
TopPicks for fun in the Old West Territory

1. Arizona-Sonora Desert Museum, Tucson

2. Arizona State Museum, Tucson

3. Old Tucson Studios, Tucson

4. Organ Pipe Cactus National Monument, Ajo

5. Tumacacori National Historical Park, Tumacacori

6. Coronado National Memorial, Hereford

7. Kartchner Caverns State Park, Benson

8. Ramsey Canyon Preserve, Sierra Vista

9. Bisbee

10. Tombstone

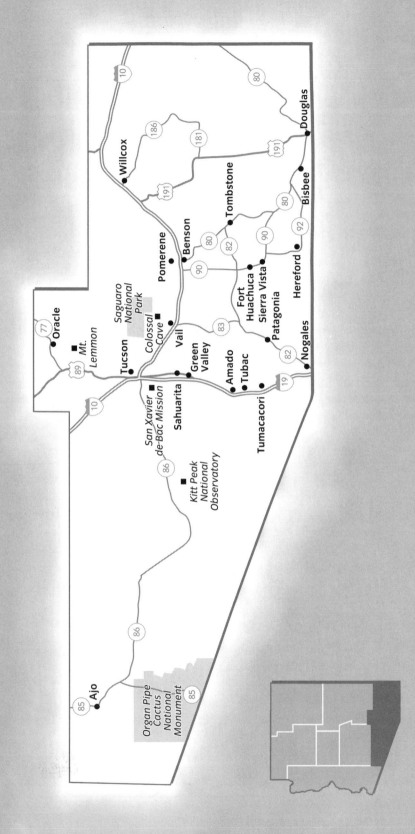

OLD WEST TERRITORY

The climate varies as much as the landscape—from the sweltering summer heat of the desert grasslands to the chilly winters on 9,000-foot mountain peaks in the Santa Catalina, Santa Rita, Huachuca, and Chiricahua mountain ranges. The combination of high mountain elevations and the clear, dry air has made this region a haven for astronomers working out of Whipple and Kitt Peak Observatories. Plants, birds, and animals also have a strong presence as a result of the varied topography. Birders especially love all of the opportunities to see rare and endangered birds that can be found only in this portion of the country as a result of migratory pathways up the San Pedro River. Birding hot spots in the Sonita Creek area and the Huachuca Mountains boast the greatest variety of hummingbirds in North America, with hundreds drawn to feeders at places like the Nature Conservancy's Ramsey Canyon—to the delight of kids and adults alike.

The region offers a wonderful opportunity to get kids interested in history, with attractions that include a look back at the days of the Spanish explorers, the desperate wars with the Apache Indians, gold mining, gunfights, and ranching—a 300-year swath of some of the nation's most famous incidents and conflicts. Here visitors can find traces of Coronado, Father Kino, Cochise, Geronimo, Wyatt Earp, Johnny Ringo, and a host of infamous characters. The first people to use the area were Ice Age big game-hunters, who stalked mammoth and camels and giant ground sloths through the then-forested lowlands. They were succeeded by a diverse group of people who built stone pueblos and farmed the bands of scattered desert streams. The first non–Native Americans to explore this region were the Spanish explorers and missionaries that settled near present-day Tubac in the 1500s. They left behind the spectacular living mission of San Xavier in Tucson and the haunting ruins of Tumacacori north of Nogales. The fierce resistance of the Apache Indians who lived in the mountains that run north and south all along the border halted the northern expansion of the Spanish and stalled the settlement of the Americans until Geronimo's surrender in 1886.

Here one can also brush up against the vivid history of the Old West, especially in Tombstone, where the gunfight at the OK Corral between the Earps and the Clantons is reenacted. The region boomed in the 1800s with the silver strike in Tombstone and the copper lodes in Bisbee. You'll find a few mining operations still working down south, but for the most part the mines have closed down, leaving a host of ghost towns in their wake. The southeastern corner is now mainly composed of ranching and agricultural communities; however, the towns of Bisbee and Tombstone keep memories of the Old West alive with their museums, historical buildings, and special tributes. Tucson also retains a hint of its earlier days, but the town gets most of its flavor from its Hispanic and Native American cultural influences. All in all, this region offers the perfect combination of history and adventure for a family looking for a vacation that teaches as well as entertains.

Tucson

Tucson offers an array of urban pleasures befitting a key border city with a diverse history stretching back to the first Spanish explorers. Here you'll find a variety of fun and informative museums where kids can ride a fiberglass horse, sit in the *Air Force One* jet used by President John F. Kennedy, marvel at the gigantic bones of mammoths stone-age hunters stalked 12,000 years ago, and visit a Hohokam village.

Known as the Old Pueblo by locals, Tucson is set in a desert valley at an elevation of 2,400 feet and is the state's second largest city. Despite its urban atmosphere, Tuscon's outdoor recreation is a favorite activity of residents and visitors alike. Stretch your legs at one of the state or national parks in town or take a quick jaunt into one of the mountain ranges ringing Tucson for a refreshing look at the desert and its diverse wildlife and vegetation. The desert is especially beautiful when it flowers in bright splashes of red, pink, yellow, white, and orange in April and May. Back in town, you and your family can also watch extravagantly staged gunfights in the streets of a movie set, visit a fort that played a key role in the Apache Wars, and stop by a ranch that breeds itty-bitty horses the size of a Saint Bernard.

Arizona Historical Society Museum (ages 5 and up) 🖼️

949 East Second Street, Tucson; (520) 628–5774; www.arizonahistoricalsociety.org. Open 10:00 A.M. to 4:00 P.M. Monday through Saturday except major holidays. Adults $$, children ages 12–18 $, under 11 free.

Here kids can weigh different bulk items on a scale, ride a fiberglass horse, and walk through a replica 1900s copper mine. The exhibit "Exploring 1870s Tucson" offers many hands-on activities for children. Other exhibits enable you to trace Arizona's history from the Spanish conquistadors to Arizona's statehood. Period rooms introduce visitors to prehistoric Native Americans, Mexican immigrants, mountain men, and territorial pioneers. Check for special exhibits and special events.

Pima Air and Space Museum (ages 7 and up) 🖼️

6000 East Valencia Road, Tucson; (520) 574–0462; www.pimaair.org. Open daily 9:00 A.M. to 5:00 P.M. except Thanksgiving and Christmas Day. Adults and children ages 7 and up $$, under 7 free.

The low humidity in the Tucson area made this the perfect spot to store and preserve aircraft, and this museum does just that. Housing the largest private collection of airplanes in the world, this facility boasts more than 250 historic aircraft. Here you'll find a replica of the Wright brothers' 1903 *Wright Flyer* as well as military jets and bombers, ultralights, and civilian aircraft. Space exhibits, an aviation hall of fame, and a tour of the presidential plane used by Kennedy and Johnson add to the exhilarating experience.

Reid Park Zoo (all ages) 🐘

1100 South Randolph Way, Tucson; (520) 791–4022 or (520) 791–5064; www.tucsonzoo.org. Open daily 9:00 A.M. to 4:00 P.M. except Christmas Day. Closed at noon on Thanksgiving. Adults $$, children ages 2–14 $, under 2 free.

Not only will you find the standard lions, tigers, and bears, but you'll also discover a variety of animals from around the world at the zoo. Make sure to check out the South American loop trail, featuring twelve lush exhibits and a walk-in aviary. The zoo is small but still offers a satisfying menagerie of local and exotic wildlife. If you're in the area in December, make sure to visit the zoo at night for the annual Festival of Lights.

Picacho Peak State Park (all ages) 🔺 🏕 🍁

Exit 219 off I–10, P.O. Box 275, Picacho 85241; (520) 466–3183; www.pr.state.az.us/Parks/ parkhtml/picacho.html. Open for day use 8:00 A.M. to 10:00 P.M. Day use $$. Overnight $$$.

The only Civil War battle held in Arizona occurred near Picacho Peak on April 15, 1862. This historic skirmish, which lasted only 90 minutes and resulted in just three Union casualties, is re-created by living history groups at the Civil War Reenactment held on the second weekend of March.

Picacho Peak features several hiking trails, ranging from easy to difficult. Children will especially enjoy the 0.5-mile interpretive Nature Trail and the 0.2-mile interpretive Children's Cave Trail. This state park features camping, picnic areas, restrooms, and a playground.

Arizona-Sonora Desert Museum (all ages) 🐘 🍴 🍁

Speedway Boulevard, Tucson; (520) 883–2702; www.desertmuseum.org. Open daily 8:30 A.M. to 5:00 P.M. October through February and 7:30 A.M. to 5:00 P.M. March through September. Extended hours on summer Saturdays. Adults $$, children ages 6–12 $. Under 6 free.

This living museum ranks as one of the best of its kind in the world. Here you'll find plants and animals indigenous to the Sonoran Desert, which extends from Arizona down to the Gulf of California in Mexico. More than your ordinary zoo experience, the zoo has nearly 400 different desert denizens, including javelinas, scorpions, bighorn sheep, beavers, rattlesnakes, Gila monsters, and mountain lions. The natural surroundings are also home to more than 1,400 different plants, making this a trip to a botanical garden as well. Kids will enjoy exploring the homes of burrowing animals in an underground exhibit. A limestone cave and a Pollination Garden are other family favorites. Wear a hat and sturdy shoes to best explore this attraction and plan on spending the better part of the day wandering the grounds, doing hands-on activities, and perusing the many exhibits and displays. Kids can also become more involved with the museum by joining Los Coatis Kids Club (ages 6–12) by calling (520) 883–3025.

Saguaro National Park—Rincon Mountain District (all ages)
(⚇) (⊞) (⛺) (❀)

Sixteen miles east of downtown off the Old Spanish Trail, 3693 South Old Spanish Trail, Tucson; (520) 733–5153; www.nps.gov/sagu. Park open 7:00 A.M. to sunset. Visitor center open daily 8:30 A.M. to 5:00 P.M. $$ per vehicle.

The Saguaro National Park offers a great outdoor location for all the kids. Start at the visitor center to watch the ten-minute slide show about the park, and then meander through the Cactus Garden. The monument's 8-mile Cactus Forest Drive offers scenic vistas through the foothills of the Rincon Mountains. A few more miles will take you to a picnic area with a portable restroom. There is no water, so make sure to take plenty for you and the kids.

Saguaro National Park—Tucson Mountain District (all ages) (⚇) (❀)
2700 North Kinney Road, Tucson; (520) 733–5158; www.nps.gov/sagu. Visitor center open daily 8:30 A.M. to 5:00 P.M. Park open 7:00 A.M. to sunset. Free.

The Red Hiss Visitor Center is a great place to start when exploring this side of the split park. The center offers a trail map (for a small fee), exhibits, and a video that describes the Sonoran Desert. Special programs and nature walks are offered from December through April. Call for dates and times. The short Cactus Garden Trail will familiarize you and the kids with the towering saguaro, which is only found in Mexico and some portions of the

Amazing Arizona Facts

Estimated Maximum Ages of Sonoran Desert Plants

- **Engelmann prickly pear**—30-plus years
- **Golden agave**—40 years
- **Triangle-leaf bursage**—50 years
- **Teddy bear cholla**—60-plus years
- **Fishhook barrel cactus**—130-plus years
- **Catclaw acacia**—130-plus years
- **Ocotillo**—200 years
- **Saguaro**—200-plus years
- **Foothill paloverde**—200-plus years
- **Ironwood**—800-plus years

Cultural **Tourism**

Cultural Corridors of Pima County, a companion guidebook and audio CD, takes visitors to Pima Country for a look at the area's unique, lesser-known attractions. The guidebook (fee) offers an insider's look at the natural and cultural heritage of this rich region through the arts, tales, and daily celebrations of local people. Information: Tucson Pima Arts Council, 10 East Broadway Boulevard, Suite 106, Tucson 85701; (520) 624–0595; www.tucsonpimaarts council.org/CommArts/cultural corridors.htm.

southwestern United States, and a variety of other plants indigenous to the desert. Many other short loops and trails crisscross through the park, offering access to panoramic vistas, overlooks, petroglyph sites, and picnic areas.

Arizona State Museum (ages 5 and up)

University of Arizona, 1013 East University Boulevard, Tucson; (520) 621–6302; www.state museum.arizona.edu. Open 10:00 A.M. to 5:00 P.M. Monday through Saturday and noon to 5:00 P.M. Sunday except all major holidays. Free. Donation requested.

Founded in 1893, this museum houses an extensive collection of Native American artifacts from prehistoric, historic, and contemporary tribes. As the oldest and largest anthropology museum in the Southwest, this is the place to take the family for a good look at the archaeology and anthropology of Arizona. Kids will see a replica of a life-size Mogollon cliff dwelling, bones of giant mammoths hunted by Paleo-Indians 12,000 years ago, and exhibits on the cultures of ten different Arizona tribes. The museum offers frequent special family-oriented events, which often include hands-on activities geared for children.

Flandrau Science Center and Planetarium (ages 3 and up)

University of Arizona Campus, University Boulevard and North Cherry Avenue, Tucson; (520) 621–STAR (7827); www.flandrau.org. Center open daily 9:00 A.M. to 5:00 P.M. and 7:00 to 9:00 P.M. Thursday through Saturday; Sunday 1:00 to 5:00 P.M. $–$$

This science center has hands-on experiments with electricity, light, and astronomy. The theater entertains audiences with shows on astronomy and the workings of the universe. A favorite with the kids is a human sundial. Kids stand on the line corresponding to the date to discover the time. New restrictions subject all bags to a search, and the center advises visitors to keep all backpacks and nonessential baggage in the car. While you're here, check out the **Mineral Museum** (520–621–4227) on the lower level, which houses one of the largest public rock and mineral collections in the country. Here you'll see nearly 2,000 of the collection's 15,000 minerals, gems, and meteorites.

Old Pueblo Trolley, Inc. (all ages)

360 East Eighth Street, Tucson; (520) 792–1802; www.oldpueblotrolley.org. Runs 6:00 to 10:00 P.M. Friday, noon to midnight Saturday, and noon to 6:00 P.M. Sunday. One-way and all-day passes available. $

Ride historic electric trolleys through Tucson along University Avenue and Fourth Street past a variety of shops and restaurants housed in restored historic buildings. The route terminates near the Marriott Hotel, the Arizona Historical Society, and the main gate of the University of Arizona.

Catalina State Park (all ages)

Fourteen miles north of downtown Tucson on Oracle Road, P.O. Box 36986, Tucson 85740; (520) 628–5798; www.pr.state.az.us/Parks/parkhtml/catalina.html. Open daily 5:00 A.M. to 10:00 P.M. Visitor center open daily 7:00 A.M. to 5:00 P.M. Day use $$ per vehicle. Overnight use $$$.

Easy trails and short loops provide excellent hiking opportunities for families with small children who are exploring this 5,500-acre state park. A ½-mile trail (Romero Ruins Interpretive Trail) leads you through a Hohokam village and a nineteenth-century ranch. The 1-mile Nature Trail loop and Birding Trail provide scenic wonders and great critter spotting. The 2³⁄₁₀-mile Canyon Loop Trail is open for hikers, equestrians, and bikers. The campground fills up frequently during the spring, so get there early to get a spot.

Pusch Ridge Stables (all ages)

13700 North Oracle Road, Tucson; (520) 825–1664. Open daily except Christmas Day. One- and two-hour trail rides $$$$.

Horse and nature lovers can experience the best of both worlds on trail rides through the desert beauty of the Catalina Mountains. If you have younger children, check out the stables' walk and lead rides ($$) for tots under six.

Amazing
Arizona Facts

The origin of the name Arizona has been traced to a Tohono O'odham village called Ali-Shonak, which means "little spring." The Spanish settlers, who couldn't quite pronounce the name, began calling it Arissona or Arizonac. By the time the Mexican War ended in 1848, the name had transformed into Arizona and the name stuck.

DeGrazia Gallery in the Sun (ages 7 and up) 🎨

6300 North Swan Road, Tucson; (520) 299–9191 or (800) 545–2185; www.degrazia.org. Open daily 10:00 A.M. to 4:00 P.M. except Thanksgiving, Easter, and Christmas Day. Free.

Housed in a building designed and constructed by the late, world-renowned Tucson artist Ettore "Ted" DeGrazia, the gallery showcases his recognizable work portraying the Sonoran Desert and its people. Connected to the gallery is a rustic chapel covered with the artist's whimsical, colorful art illuminated by nature's light—the sun. Children will love DeGrazia's brilliant hues and his favorite subject matter—kids.

Oracle State Park (all ages) 🧗 🏛 🎏

Center for Environmental Education, 3820 Wildlife Drive, Oracle; (520) 896–2425; www.pr.state.az.us/Parks/parkhtml/oracle.html. Open daily 7:00 A.M. to 5:00 P.M. except Christmas Day.

This 4,000-acre park features environmental educational experiences for children and wide-open spaces for everyone in the family to enjoy. Tours of the historic Kannally Ranch House, homesteaded in 1902 by Illinois transplant Neil Kannally, are held at 10:00 A.M. and 2:00 P.M. Saturday and Sunday. Hiking trails and a picnic area add to the relaxed natural environment of this former ranch. The park offers two annual events worth taking the time to enjoy—Earth Day in April and a Pumpkin Festival in October.

Fort Lowell Museum (all ages) 🏛 🎨

2900 North Craycroft Road, Tucson; (520) 885–3832. Open 10:00 A.M. to 4:00 P.M. Wednesday through Saturday except all major holidays. Adults $, children under 12 free. First Saturday each month free.

As part of the Apache War campaign, the Sixth U.S. Cavalry patrolled the desert and protected supply wagons, stagecoach travelers, and the town of Tucson. Fort Lowell sits on an ancient Hohokam site, making it one the most continuously inhabited places in Arizona. The U.S. Army base became a fort in 1879 and kept busy during the Geronimo campaigns until the Apache chief finally surrendered in 1886. With the last of the Native American wars in 1891, the army abandoned the fort to the elements. Today, a few of the original buildings have been restored and turned into galleries chronicling the fort's military history.

Old Tucson Studios (all ages) 🎪

201 South Kinney Road, Tucson; (520) 883–0100; www.oldtucson.com. Hours vary. Adults $$$, children ages 4–11 $$, under 4 free.

Built as the set for the 1939 movie Arizona, this old movie studio has been transformed into a re-creation 1880s frontier town. The set has been used as the location for more than 250 films, including Clint Eastwood's *The Outlaw Josey Wales,* Paul Newman's *The Life and Times of Judge Roy Bean,* and Kirk Douglas's *Gunfight at the O.K. Corral,* as well as the more recent *Young Guns II, Geronimo,* and *Tombstone.* Fans of TV shows *Little House on the Prairie* and *Gunsmoke* might also recognize it as the backdrop for scenes in these shows. In 1995 a fire devastated a good portion of the set, but it has since been mostly rebuilt. Featured activities include a train ride, stage shows, staged gunfights in the streets, and gold panning.

Gateway Ice Center (all ages) 🏒

7333 East Rosewood Street, Tucson; (520) 290–8800, ext. 221. Open daily. Call for session times. Admission $$. Figure-skate and hockey-skate rental $.

Daily skating, pick-up hockey, and public and private lessons are offered here. A light and music show picks up the pace on Friday and Saturday nights. Amenities include a full-service restaurant, a fully equipped pro shop, and a video arcade.

Golf N' Stuff Family Fun Center (all ages) 🎡

6503 East Tanque Verde Road, Tucson; (520) 296–2366; www.golfnstuff.com. Open 10:00 A.M. to 10:00 P.M. Sunday through Thursday and 10:00 A.M. to 1:00 A.M. Friday and Saturday. Golf is $$, under 5 free. Bumper boats and laser tag are $, and go-karts are $$. All Park Pass $$$.

This family-oriented entertainment center features miniature golf, laser tag, a rock-climbing simulator, batting cages, a kiddie carousel, snack bar, and castle arcade.

Gaslight Theatre (all ages) 🎵

7010 East Broadway Boulevard, Tucson; (520) 886–9428. Open Tuesday through Sunday. Show times vary. Adults $$$, under 12 $$.

This popular theater produces musical-comedy melodrama for family entertainment. Shows in the past have included the comic *Lady Liberty, The Count of Monte Cristo,* and *The Mummy's Curse.*

Picture Rocks Miniature Horse Ranch (all ages) 🐂 🚙 🛏️

6611 North Taylor Lane, Tucson; (520) 682–8009. Open by appointment. $$

This miniature ranch's itty-bitty horses, donkeys, and goats will delight your youngsters. Hugging these pint-size pets is not only allowed, it's expected. You are also encouraged to bring whole-wheat bread so the kids can feed the 300 free-range chickens wandering the grounds. Other features include picnic tables, a gift shop, and a bed-and-breakfast.

Sabino Canyon Tours, Inc. (all ages) 🚶

5900 North Sabino Canyon Road, Tucson; (520) 749–2861 or (520) 749–2327; www.sabinocanyon.com. Open 9:00 A.M. to 4:00 P.M. Monday through Friday and 9:00 A.M. to 4:30 P.M. Saturday and Sunday. Shuttle is $$ adults, $ children ages 3–12. Moonlight shuttle is $$ adults, $ children ages 3–12. Reservations required for moonlight shuttle rides.

For a scenic outdoor adventure, take a forty-five-minute narrated tram ride through Sabino Canyon, a desert oasis in the foothills of the Santa Catalina Mountains. The tram begins its journey on the slopes of Mount Lemmon and winds through lush greenery to Seven Falls. You can get off the tram at any of its stops and explore the canyon's waterfalls and wildlife (or hitch a ride mid-hike if you're bushed). The tram leaves the visitor center every hour on the hour on the weekdays and every half hour on weekends. In addition to being the loading site, the visitor center orients tourists to the canyon's attractions, including its hiking trails, naturalist-led walks, and butterfly and hummingbird sanctuaries. For a spectacular nighttime adventure, take a moonlight tram ride April through December during the full moon. The moonlight shuttle runs three times a month, so reservations are required.

International Wildlife Museum (all ages)

4800 West Gates Pass Road, Tucson; (520) 617–1439; www.thewildlifemuseum.org. Open 9:00 A.M. to 5:00 P.M. Monday through Friday and 9:00 A.M. to 6:00 P.M. Saturday and Sunday except Thanksgiving and Christmas. Adults and students ages 13–17 $$, children ages 6–12 $, under 6 free.

This interactive natural-history museum features more than 400 stuffed mammals, insects, and birds exhibited in naturalistic dioramas. There are also guided group tours, interactive computers, wildlife films, and a restaurant. Younger kids will enjoy the woolly mammoths roaming prehistoric plains but might be frightened by the stillness of more recognizable animals such as tigers and bears.

Mission San Xavier del Bac (ages 5 and up) 🏛

1950 West San Xavier Road, Tucson; (520) 294–2624; www.sanxaviermission.org. Open daily 8:00 A.M. to 5:00 P.M. Free.

Attend mass in Arizona's oldest church. Built in the 1700s by Spanish missionaries and the Tohono O'odham Indian converts, Mission San Xavier is one of the finest examples of mission architecture in the country. Called the White Dove of the Desert, the mission boasts a folksy yet reverent atmosphere and continues to serve the peoples on the Tohono O'odham Reservation. Have the kids look in swirls of the facade for a cat on one side and a mouse on the other. One story says that if the cat ever catches the mouse, the world will end. The wife of a cavalry officer wrote in the 1870s, "I could hardly tear myself from the spot, and returned again and again to ascend the belfry stairs and wonder and speculate upon the strange mystery called San Xavier del Bac." Visitors still experience this wonder today.

Mount Lemmon Ski Valley (ages 3 and up)

10300 Ski Run Road, Mount Lemmon; (520) 576–1400 or (520) 576–1321; www.fs.fed.us/r3/coronado/scrd/rec/skiing/skivalley.htm. Open daily mid-December through April. Lift tickets are $$$$ for adults and $$$ for children under 12. Summer lift tickets are $$ adults, $ children ages 3–12.

For an up-close look at the varied terrain on the ascent of 9,157-foot Mount Lemmon, take the forty-minute scenic drive up a paved road to the summit. The scenic highway travels from the harsh desert landscape of the lower Sonoran Desert to a Canadian Zone mature forest complete with juniper, piñon, and pine. In the winter months, skiers shush down the snowy slopes at Mount Lemmon Ski Valley, the southernmost ski area in the United

States. The double chairlift takes skiers to sixteen different runs, which includes a bunny slope. Stop by the shop for ski rentals, snowboards, and information on group and private ski lessons. During the spring and summer months, the chairlifts take visitors up the mountain to enjoy the cool weather and breathtaking views. If you take the skyride to the top during the Lady Bug Elevation Celebration during June, you'll be able to scoop up ladybugs, by the tens of thousands, as they emerge from hibernation "houses."

Moons over **the Desert**

Those visiting the Sonoran Desert quickly discover that Mother Nature's seasons—winter, spring, summer, and fall—don't quite apply here as they do in most parts of the country. Perhaps the Tohono O'odham Indians of southern Arizona know the best way to describe the desert seasons, which are named after the moon each month. These moons best describe the desert cycle, with such titles as Saguaro Moon, the month the Tohono O'odham gather the fruit of the stately saguaro cactus; No More Fat Moon, when the animals lose their extra layers of stored fat; Green Moon, describing the month plants get their foliage; Yellow Moon, a poetic expression of the desert in bloom; and Painful Moon, the harsh month when food becomes scarce.

The Tohono O'odham Calendar of Seasons:

- **Saguaro Moon**—June
- **Rainy Moon**—July
- **Short Planting Moon**—August
- **Dry Grass Moon**—September
- **Small Rains Moon**—October
- **Pleasant Cold Moon**—November
- **Big Cold Moon**—December
- **No More Fat Moon**—January
- **Gray Moon**—February
- **Green Moon**—March
- **Yellow Moon**—April
- **Painful Moon**—May

Biosphere 2 Center (ages 5 and up)

Highway 77, Oracle; (520) 838–6200; www.bio2.edu. Open daily 8:30 A.M. to 5:00 P.M. except Christmas Day. Adults $$$, children ages 6–17 $$, under 6 free.

Take a peek into life on Mars—well, almost. What began as an experiment on colonizing neighboring planets is now an ongoing research facility studying the relationship between ecosystems and the effect of global warming. Tours take visitors through the quarantine rooms and the Demonstration Laboratories, a smaller-scale version of Biosphere 2. The facility also hosts a guided tour (additional fee) that will take visitors older than six years of age under the glass to see the Biosphere's ocean, the living quarters of the original Biospherians, and the technology behind this experimental center. Amenities include the Lions Den Café, Desert Dick's Gift Shop, and stroller rentals.

Colossal Cave Mountain Park (ages 5 and up)

16711 East Colossal Cave Road, P.O. Box 70, Vail 85641; (520) 647–7275; www.colossal-cave.com. Open 9:00 A.M. to 5:00 P.M. Monday through Saturday and 9:00 A.M. to 6:00 P.M. Sunday and holidays. Extended hours mid-March through mid-September. Entry fee $ per vehicle, with an additional $ per person over six people. Adults $$, children ages 6–12 $, under 6 free. Trail rides $$$$; (520) 647–3450.

Guided tours teach visitors about underground formations and the history of the cave but leave out the location of a rumored stash of $60,000 in outlaw gold. Children must be able to climb 363 steep steps during the forty-five-minute tour. Other features include a campground, a cafe, picnic facilities, a small museum of Hohokam artifacts, a gift shop, and trail rides.

Organ Pipe Cactus National Monument (ages 5 and up)

Visitor Center, 10 Organ Pipe Drive, Ajo; (520) 387–6849; www.nps.gov/orpi. Visitor center open daily 8:00 A.M. to 5:00 P.M. except Christmas Day. Entry fee $$ per vehicle for seven days.

Although you can visit Organ Pipe Cactus National Monument year-round, if you want to see the desert bloom, you'll have to do it in the summer. The rising temperatures make the monument's longer hikes arduous, but the scenic drives offer a perfect way for visitors to enjoy the creamy blossoms set on top of the magnificent saguaro and organ pipe cactus. Other flowering perennials that can be enjoyed during the summer months include cholla, prickly pear, hedgehog, palo verde, ironwood, and ocotillo.

The monument's visitor center offers a comprehensive look at the plants and animals in this remote part of southern Arizona, with slide shows, nature trails, and exhibits. Children will especially enjoy the Junior Ranger program and kids' activities. The graded dirt road is a little slow going, so allow about a half day for the drive. Picnic tables along the way make for a good stopping point. The desert here is harsh and unforgiving, so make sure to wear sunscreen and pack plenty of water. The Tohono O'odham Indians live in the area and often host special events for the public. Check the visitor center for a schedule of upcoming events.

Kitt Peak Observatory (all ages)

58 miles southwest of Tucson off Highway 86/Ajo Way, Tucson; (520) 318–8726; www.noao. edu/kpno. Open daily 9:00 A.M. to 3:45 P.M., except Thanksgiving, Christmas, and New Year's Day. Free. Stargazing program $$$$ by reservation only (includes boxed dinner).

One of the world's leading observatories, Kitt Peak boasts the world's largest collection of telescopes and the world's largest solar telescope. The visitor center offers astronomy exhibits and the history of the complex. Docent-led tours take visitors to different tele-scopes at 10:00 A.M., 11:30 A.M., and 1:30 P.M. Visitors can take a self-guided tour of the grounds and, after dark, peer into the awesome telescopes with the observatory's stargazing program, a three-and-a-half-hour session offered nightly, weather permitting. The night viewing sessions are recommended for children ages eight and up.

Amazing
Arizona Facts

If you've ever wondered what in the world a haboob is, ponder no more. A haboob is a giant dust storm or wall of dirt reaching up to 3,000 feet high and traveling up to 30 miles per hour. Haboobs travel along the ground and are so thick that you can't see sunlight through them. These tremendous dust storms occur only in the Sahara Desert of Africa and the deserts of the southwestern United States. However, astronomers have discovered similar storms on Mars, which might leave you wondering what else we have in common with the Red Planet.

The Tohono O'odam tribe in southern Arizona traces its heritage to the ancient Hohokam Indians, farmers that built extensive canal systems to irrigate their fields. The O'odham, called the Papagos by the Spanish in the 1700s, were master desert farmers. They harvested a wide variety of wild crops, including saguaro fruit, mesquite bean pods, and cholla buds and also diverted runoff with such skill they could also grow corn, squash, and beans. They are also known for their intricately designed coil basketry, which they traded across the Southwest and into the deep reaches of Mex-ico. Today the O'odham peoples keep their traditions close and continue to thrive in this arid landscape of sand and stone.

Sonoran Desert **Kids**

Pima County sponsors a Web site just for kids. Learn about
Sonoran plants and wildlife, read an online picture book, and
play the new Sonoran Desert Endangered Species Card Game at
www.co.pima.az.us/cmo/sdcp/kids.

Tohono Chul Park (all ages) 🍴 🪑 🍁

7366 North Paseo del Norte, Tucson; (520) 742–6455; www.tohonochulpark.org.
Park open daily 8:00 A.M. to sunset. Exhibit house open daily 9:00 A.M. to 5:00 P.M. Free
admission on the first Tuesday of each month. Adults $$, children ages 5–12 and students
with ID $, under 5 free.

The forty-nine-acre Tohono Chul Park, which means "desert corner," is home to more than
500 species of plants and animals. Here you might encounter javelina, desert tortoise,
black-tailed jackrabbit, and a myriad of birds. The Alice C. Herman Garden for Children is
especially delightful. Make sure to pick up a booklet filled with information and activities.
While you're here, make sure to visit the Demonstration Garden's rock wall, which shows
the geologic formations of the Santa Rita Mountains. The Exhibit House rotates exhibits
every few weeks, and there are lectures, tours, and interpretive programs. The park is a
great place to enjoy a picnic lunch, but if you didn't pack one, stop by the Tea Room,
which serves breakfast, lunch, and afternoon tea.

Trail Dust Town (all ages) 🍴 🏠

6541 East Tanque Verde Road, Tucson; (520) 296–4551. Shops open daily 1:00 to 10:00 P.M.
Free.

This reconstructed frontier town offers shops, a century-old carousel, stockades, steam-
engine rides, gold panning with "Prospector Al," dining at the original Pinnacle Peak steak-
house, and a mock Wild West shootout. Be prepared, though: Most of the entertainment
begins in the evening.

Tucson Botanical Gardens (ages 6 and up) 🍁

2150 North Alvernon Way, Tucson; (520) 326–9686; www.tucsonbotanical.org. Open daily
8:30 A.M. to 4:30 P.M. except July 4, Thanksgiving, Christmas Day, and New Year's Day.
Adults $$, children ages 6–12 $; under 6 free.

The gardens offer summer classes for kids with fun, hands-on activities on desert plants,
insects, and environmental issues. The Children's Discovery Garden will delight your kids
as they learn about the life of a plant. However, the giant insects—a bee, a butterfly, and a
bat—might intimidate toddlers. Other featured gardens include the Butterfly Garden,
Xeriscape Desert Garden, Plants of the Tohono O'odham Path, the Backyard Bird Garden,
and the Native American Crops Garden.

Tucson Children's Museum (all ages)

200 South Sixth Avenue, P.O. Box 2609, Tucson 85702; (520) 792–9985; www.tucson childrensmuseum.org. Open 10:00 A.M. to 5:00 P.M. Tuesday through Saturday and noon to 5:00 P.M. Sunday except Thanksgiving, Christmas Day, and New Year's Day. Adults $$, children ages 16 and under $.

This museum, designed especially for kids ages two to eleven, introduces children to new cultures and lets them explore careers, play games, and conduct science experiments in fun, interactive hands-on programs. Kids can see a Tyrannosaurus Rex up close in Dinosaur Canyon, pretend to broadcast the news, and ride in a submarine. A gift shop sells mementos and souvenirs.

Bedroxx (ages 6 and up)

4385 West Ina Road, Tucson; (520) 744–7655; www.bedroxx.com. Open 9:00 A.M. to midnight Sunday through Thursday, 9:00 A.M. to 2:00 A.M. Friday and Saturday. Open Bowl $, Retro Glow Bowl $$$, shoe rental $.

Kids will especially love the Retro Glow Bowl (includes shoe rental) on Friday and Saturday nights at this family-oriented entertainment center, which also features more than 120 arcade games, a pizzeria, and pool tables.

Funtasticks Family Fun Park (all ages)

221 East Wetmore Road, Tucson; (520) 888–4653; www.funtasticks.com. Hours vary. Closed Christmas Day. Fees for attractions vary. Value packages $$$. Family Package (includes one round of miniature golf and three attractions, excluding laser tag, with a minimum of four people) $$.

This five-acre entertainment park offers miniature golf, go-karts, bumper boats, batting cages, a video arcade, laser tag, and a seven-ride Kiddie Land.

Tucson Museum of Art and Historic Block (ages 6 and up)

140 North Main Avenue, Tucson; (520) 624–2333; www.tucsonarts.com. Open 10:00 A.M. to 4:00 P.M. Monday through Saturday and noon to 4:00 P.M. Sunday. Closed Monday during the summer. Adults $$, students $, children under 13 free.

The museum houses a permanent collection that boasts contemporary art as well as pre-Columbian, Western, and Asian. Situated on the site of Tucson's Spanish Presidio, the Historic Block features five distinctive homes built between 1850 and 1907. Check out the schedule of family events and activities under Family Arts Day online.

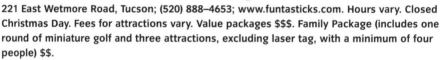

Where to Eat

Caruso's. 434 North Fourth Avenue, Tucson; (520) 624–5765. Open daily at 4:30 P.M. For more than fifty years, three generations of the Zagona family have served lasagna, homemade ravioli, spaghetti, and other Italian favorites. Children's portions available for spaghetti and ravioli. $

El Charro Mexican Café. 311 North Court Avenue, Tucson; (520) 622–1922. The oldest Mexican restaurant in the United States serves traditional Sonoran-style entrees. Diverse children's menu. $$–$$$

Jonathan's Tucson Cork. 6320 East Tanque Verde Road, Tucson; (520) 296–1631. Ostrich, buffalo, prime rib, steak, chicken, and seafood. Children's menu. $$–$$$

Little Anthony's Diner. 7010 East Broadway Boulevard, Tucson; (520) 296–0456. All-American entrees in a 1950s-style diner. $

Peter Piper Pizza. 6049 East Grant Road, Tucson; (520) 296–9396. Pizza and video games in a family atmosphere. Call for other locations in the Tucson area. $

Red Robin Restaurant. Tucson Mall, 4500 North Oracle Road, Suite 155, Tucson; (520) 292–0888. Gourmet burgers, sandwiches, salads, and pasta dishes. Standard children's menu. $

Triple C Chuckwagon Suppers. 8900 West Bopp Road, Tucson; (520) 883–2333 or (800) 446–1798. Great Western fare complete with Western stage show and the world-famous Sons of the Pioneers. Open late December through April. Reservations required. $$$

Where to Stay

AmeriSuites. 6885 South Tucson Boulevard, Tucson; (520) 295–0405 or (800) 74–SUITE. Family suites with kitchenettes, continental breakfast, outdoor heated pool. $$$

Arizona Inn. 2200 East Elm Street, Tucson; (520) 325–1541 or (800) 933–1093; www.arizonainn.com. Historic hotel with tennis courts, heated pool, spa, exercise room, restaurants, croquet, and Ping Pong. Children under ten stay **free.** $$$$

Clarion Randolph Park Hotel. 102 North Alvernon Way, Tucson; (520) 795–0330 or (800) 227–6086. Family suites with kitchenettes, hot breakfast buffet, exercise room, and outdoor heated pool. $$$–$$$$

Lazy K Bar Guest Ranch. 8401 North Scenic Drive, Tucson; (520) 744–3050 or (800) 321–7018. This family-oriented ranch offers horseback riding, swimming, tennis, volleyball, basketball, hiking, and family-style meals. Located about 16 miles northwest of downtown Tucson at the foot of the Tucson Mountains. A three-day minimum stay is required. The ranch is closed during the summer months. $$$$

Tanque Verde Guest Ranch. 14301 East Speedway, Tucson; (520) 296–6275 or (800) 234–DUDE. This magnificent ranch offers many activities to keep kids (ages four to eleven) occupied. Featured activities include horseback riding, swimming, arts and crafts, tennis, and nature walks. This family resort also offers cookouts and buffets. $$$$

Westin La Paloma. 3800 East Sunrise Drive, Tucson; (520) 742–6000 or (800) 876–3683. This luxurious resort has a twenty-seven-hole golf course, fitness center, tennis and racquetball courts, three restaurants, two huge pools, and a water slide. Westin Kids Club for children under twelve. Children under twelve stay and eat for **free.** $$$$

White Stallion Ranch. 9251 West Twin Peaks Road, Tucson; (520) 297–0252 or (800) 782–5564. This family-owned and - operated ranch stretches across 3,000 acres of grazing land. All children get the opportunity to be on horseback—ages five and up get their own horses, and toddlers can double up with their parents. Children especially love the ranch's petting zoo of pygmy goats, deer, and sheep. Closed May through October. $$$$

For More Information

Marana Chamber of Commerce. 13881 North Casa Grande Highway, Marana 85653; (520) 682–4314; www.maranachamber.com.

Metropolitan Tucson Convention & Visitor Bureau. 100 South Church Avenue, Tucson 85701; (520) 624–1817 or (800) 638–8350; www.visittucson.org.

Northern Pima County Chamber of Commerce. 200 West Magee Road, Suite 120, Tucson 85704; (520) 297–2191; www.the-chamber.com

Green Valley

This rambling area between Tucson and the Mexican border offers a bit of that, a dash of this, and a smidgen of everything else—history, birding, hiking, shopping, and culture. Highlights include the crumbling ruins of a once grand mission at Tumacacori, the artist colony of Tubac, the booming border town of Nogales, and the chance to get out of the car at Madera Canyon, where the kids can scramble over the rocks and down grassy trails with the greatest diversity of birds and butterflies in North America. Native Americans have been taking advantage of the mild climate, diverse wildlife, abundance of plant types, and range of elevations for thousands of years. Here, the first Spanish missionaries entered North America and began a stubborn, centuries-long struggle with the Apache— who regularly raided settlements throughout this area—sometimes forcing the temporary abandonment of ancient settlements like Tubac. In this region you'll find a kid-friendly tour of a 2-mile-wide open pit mine where you can watch humongous shovels loading 320-ton trucks, a serene preserve that offers a glimpse of Southwestern grasslands before cattle grazing altered them dramatically, a hummingbird ranch, a kid-friendly observatory, and the fascinating border-town shopping possibilities offered by Nogales—where price haggling is part of the fun.

ASARCO Mineral Discovery Center and Mine Tours (ages 5 and up)

1421 West Pima Mine Road, Sahuarita; (520) 625–7513; www.mineraldiscovery.com. Open 9:00 A.M. to 5:00 P.M. Tuesday through Saturday except major holidays. Admission to the Center **free.** Mine tours, adults $$, children ages 5–12 $, under 5 **free.** Reservations for tours suggested.

The award-winning, kid-friendly Discovery Center offers a self-guided tour, short videos, and outdoor exhibits of the massive equipment needed to extract copper from the ground. Bring a camera for photo opportunities as your children climb in a giant tire and stand next to monster mining machines. The Mine Tours take you close to the 2-mile-wide, ½-mile-deep pit and will give you and the kids a great view of the enormous shovels loading the 320-ton trucks. On weekdays at 4:00 P.M., visitors get the chance to watch a mine blast. Picnic tables dot the cactus garden and landscaped area surrounding the Discovery Center.

Las Cienegas National Conservation Area (all ages) 🐘🚶🏕️🚲
Highway 83 southeast of Sonoita, BLM, 12661 East Broadway, Tucson; (520) 258–7200; www.az.blm.gov/ncarea.htm. Open daily. Free.

This 42,000-acre preserve gives modern visitors the chance to see the area before overgrazing destroyed the native grasses. Six-foot grasses now sweep through the 66-square-mile riparian woodland. Bird-watching, hiking, primitive camping, picnicking, and horseback riding are a few of the outdoor opportunities that await visitors to this area. Cienega Creek, a perennial water resource, runs through the preserve and supports a riparian cottonwood forest. Juniper, oak, and mesquite trees are also scattered throughout the park. Camping is restricted to fourteen days.

Jesse Hendrix Hummingbird Ranch (ages 5 and up) 🐘
56 Comoro Canyon Lane, HCR Box 85, Nogales 85621; (520) 287–8615. Open March through September. Free.

Jesse Hendrix saw a hummingbird one morning and put out a feeder. The next day he saw two. A few weeks later he added a few more hummingbird feeders, and today, during peak season more than 15,000 hummingbirds pass through his ranch to imbibe of the

Watchable **Wildlife Tip**

The vibrantly colored, neotropical elegant trogon can be found only in one spot in the United States—the southernmost part of Arizona along a migratory path reaching down into Mexico and Central America. The elegant trogon visits southeastern Arizona to nest in the summer months. According to biologists at the Arizona Game and Fish Department, the best place to catch a glimpse of this stunning bird is in the Santa Rita Mountains at Madera Canyon and along Sonoita Creek upstream of Patagonia Lake. Other good places to seek out the elusive elegant trogon are at Ramsey Canyon in the Huachuca Mountains and along Cave Creek in the Chiricahua Mountains.

nectar in his 150 feeders. According to the Audubon Society and the American Birding Association, visitors can see more hummers at one time here than anywhere else in the United States.

Madera Canyon (ages 4 and up) ⊛ ⊛ ⓐ

Sixteen miles east of I–19 at exit 63, Nogales Ranger Station, 303 Old Tucson Road, Nogales; (520) 281–2296; www.santaritalodge.com. Open daily 6:00 A.M. to 10:00 P.M. Parking fee $$ per vehicle.

Wildlife watching, birding, picnicking, hiking, and camping top the to-do list when visiting this tropical canyon nestled in the Santa Rita Mountains. Bird-watching is the favorite activity here, with the colorful elegant trogon as the star attraction. The elegant trogon and many of the other 200 bird species found here migrate to the canyon from Mexico. Here you also might see bear, deer, javelina, coatimundi, and mountain lion.

Patagonia Lake State Park (all ages) ⓐ ⊛ ⓐ ⓣ

400 Lake Patagonia Road, Nogales; (520) 287–6965; www.pr.state.az.us/Parks/parkhtml/ patagonia.html. Open daily 4:00 A.M. to 10:00 P.M. Day use hours 8:00 A.M. to 10:00 P.M. Day use $$.

This state park offers great fishing, camping, hiking, and bird-watching opportunities. The 265-acre reservoir provides a great place to cast a line for bass, crappie, sunfish, catfish, and bluegill. The marina rents fishing boats as well as paddleboats and canoes. A portion

Amazing
Arizona Facts

Nearly 400 species of butterflies—more than half of the total number found in the entire continent—live in Arizona. The best time to search out butterflies in the Southwest is in the rainy season between the months of July and September; this is when the adults are breeding and laying their eggs. The highest concentration of species in Arizona reside in the southeastern portion of the state—specifically in Santa Cruz, Cochise, and Pima Counties. Chances of finding butterflies increase when two habitats overlap. Some of the best, easily accessible butterfly-watching areas include Sabino Canyon in the Santa Catalina Mountains, Madera and Florida Canyons in the Santa Rita Mountains, and Ramsey and Garden Canyons in the diverse Huachuca Mountain range. Along with discovering them near their favorite flowers, you might also find butterflies congregating in "puddle parties," depressed wet spots where the insects gather to replace vital trace elements.

of the lake is cordoned off for water recreational sports, and you can swim at Boulder Beach. For an additional fee ($) you can join rangers on bird-watching boat tours Wednesday, Saturday, and Sunday mornings at 9:00 A.M. Hiking trails, a campground, and picnic facilities add to the charm of this family favorite.

Patagonia-Sonoita Creek Preserve (all ages) 🕊

379 Roadrunner Lane, P.O. Box 815, Patagonia 85624; (520) 394–2400; www.nature.org. Open 6:30 A.M. to 4:00 P.M. Wednesday through Sunday April through September, 7:30 A.M. to 4:00 P.M. October through March. Free. Donation ($$) suggested.

This nature preserve supports a whole host of plants, birds, and wildlife. While walking the 2 miles of trail loops you might see a few examples of more than 260 species of birds; such animals as coati mundi, javelina, white-tailed deer, and bobcat; and diverse plants, including towering Fremont cottonwoods, Arizona black walnut, and canyon hackberry. Guided nature walks are held every Saturday at 9:00 A.M. The preserve does not allow picnicking, camping, or pets. Summer months get downright sticky here, so make sure to lather up the kids with sunscreen and insect repellent.

Titan II Missile Museum (ages 6 and up) 🈂

1580 West Duval Mine Road, Sahuarita; (520) 625–7736; www.pimaair.org/TitanMM/titan home.shtml. Open Wednesday through Sunday 9:00 A.M. to 5:00 P.M. May through October, daily 9:00 A.M. to 5:00 P.M. November through April, except Thanksgiving and Christmas Day. Adults $$, children ages 7–12 $, under 7 free.

Straight from the Cold War, this once-secret military facility would impress even James Bond. After descending past security and blast doors, visitors watch as tour guides demonstrate the launch sequence. After descending another 200 feet, you'll see the hidden missile—a monument to a time of tense global relations. Children enjoy the museum more when they participate in the Junior Missiler Program, in which they receive an educational treasure hunt of a booklet with puzzles and questions that relate to the Cold War. Once the kids find all the answers on the tour, they receive a special missiler badge. Tours leave every half hour, with the last tour departing at 4:00 P.M. Reservations are suggested, but walk-ins are accepted.

Tubac Presidio State Historic Park (ages 5 and up) 🕊 🏛 🈂 🚂

Burrel Street One, P.O. Box 1296, Tubac 85646; (520) 398–2252; www.pr.state.az.us/Parks/parkhtml/tubac.html. Open daily 8:00 A.M. to 5:00 P.M. except Christmas Day. Adults and children ages 7–12 $, under 7 free.

The ruins of the presidio, a Spanish garrison that became Arizona's first state park, testify to this cozy hamlet's violent history. Here you can see the foundation walls of the presidio, and an adjacent underground museum takes visitors on a trip through Tubac's past with exhibits that include remnants of military occupation, cases filled with Spanish armor, Apache weapons, and Mexican saddles. On Sunday afternoons in October, the park hosts a Living History Program from 1:00 to 4:00 P.M., which portrays the Spanish colonial period. Also in October (the weekend closest to the nineteenth), the park hosts the Anza

Days Cultural Celebration, marking the 1775 departure of Juan Bautista de Anza's colonists as they traveled north to start a settlement in what is now San Francisco. While you're here, take a walk down the **Juan Bautista de Anza National Historic Trail.** This historic 4½-mile trail is one of two sections of the original 600-mile trail leading to present-day San Francisco, California. The trail connects Tubac Presidio State Historic Park to Tumacacori National Historic Park and crosses the Santa Cruz River. Hikers may start the trail at either park. The birding on this trail is excellent, and the visitor center has a bird list.

Tumacacori National Historic Park (ages 5 and up) 🏛️ 🧑‍🤝‍🧑

1891 East Frontage Road, P.O. Box 67, Tumacacori 85640; (520) 398–2341; www.nps.gov/tuma. Open daily 8:00 A.M. to 5:00 P.M. except Thanksgiving and Christmas Day. Adults $, children under 16 Free.

The museum introduces visitors to mission life, the Native Americans who inhabited the Tumacacori mission, Father Eusebio Kino, and the mission's tumultuous history. A self-guided tour includes the church, the mortuary chapel, graveyard, and other buildings in the park. Faded drawings of the Twelve Apostles can still be seen on the chapel walls. During September through June, Mexican or Native American crafts are demonstrated. On the first weekend in December, Native American dances, crafts, and food are highlighted during the Tumacacori Fiesta. On some January through April nights, guides take visitors through the mission by moonlight. Bring a flashlight and dress for cool desert nights.

Whipple Observatory (ages 6 and up)

Santa Rita Mountains, P.O. Box 97, Amado 85645; (520) 670–5707; linmax.sao.arizona.edu/help/FLWO/whipple.html. Visitor center open 8:30 A.M. to 4:30 P.M. Monday through Friday except federal holidays. Tours, adults $$, children ages 6–12 $.

Bring your budding astronomers along with their telescopes to the "Astronomy Vista," a knoll equipped with special concrete pads and benches. The road to the site is paved and the climb to the telescope pads is on a short, steep dirt trail. The visitor center offers special tours Monday, Wednesday, and Friday from March through November, which feature lectures and telescopic viewing. Tours leave for Mount Hopkins at 9:30 A.M. and return around 3:00 P.M. Don't forget to pack a picnic lunch for the midday break. Be prepared for chilly temperatures, possible rain showers, and thin air. Reservations are required.

Coronado National Memorial (all ages) 🧑‍🤝‍🧑 🚗

4101 East Montezuma Canyon, Hereford; (520) 366–5515; www.nps.gov/coro. Visitor center open daily 9:00 A.M. to 5:00 P.M. except Thanksgiving and Christmas Day. Free.

This memorial commemorates Francesco Vásquez de Coronado's journey through this area in 1540 during his search for the mythical Seven Cities of Cíbola. Nestled in the Huachuca Mountains on the United States–Mexico border, the memorial has a wonderful forest drive with panoramic lookouts, an extensive network of hiking trails, and a scenic setting for a picnic lunch. A visitor center provides historical information on Coronado as well as information on the area's flora and fauna. A family favorite is a visit to the nearby cave. The easy hike to the cave takes about thirty to forty-five minutes. Once thought to be a hideout for Apache war parties, the 20-foot-high and 70-foot-wide cave provides a great look at cave rock formations, including stalagmites and stalactites. The cave only reaches 600 feet, so you don't have to worry about losing the kids—who will love the little nooks, crannies, and crawl spaces. Make sure to bring flashlights and plenty of water.

Where to Eat

Cow Palace. 28802 South Nogales Highway, Amado; (520) 398–2201. Hamburgers, steak, fish, and chicken. Children's menu. A piano player sings tunes Thursday, Friday, and Saturday evenings. $

Home Plate Restaurant. 277 McKeown Avenue, Patagonia; (520) 394–2344. Standard American fare. Children's menu. $

Stage Stop Inn Restaurant. 303 McKeown Avenue, Patagonia; (520) 394–2211. Mexican entrees, steak, and hamburgers. Children's menu. $

Tosh's Hacienda Restaurant. 14 Camino Otero, Tubac; (520) 398–3008. Mexican entrees and Sonoran specialties. Children's menu. $$

Wisdom Café. 1931 East Frontage Road, Tumacacori; (520) 398–2397. Mexican dishes and specialties. A favorite stopover of celebrities, including Diane Keaton, Kareem Abdul-Jabbar, and Johnny Bench. $–$$

Where to Stay

Circle Z Ranch. P.O. Box 194, Patagonia 85624; (520) 394–2525 or (888) 854–2525; www.circlez.com. Arizona's oldest guest ranch offers horses, birding, a pool, and tennis courts. Open November though May. $$$

Santa Rita Lodge Nature Resort. Thirteen miles southeast of Green Valley, Coronado National Forest, HC 70, Box 5444, Sahuarita 85629; (520) 625–8746; www.santaritalodge.com. Nestled in Madera Canyon in the Coronado Forest, the Santa Rita Lodge offers nature programs and birding walks. Bird feeders hang outside the doors, and pictures grace the room's walls to help visitors identify the many birds in the area. $$$

The Sonoita Inn. 3243 Highway 82, Sonoita; (520) 455–5935; www.sonoitainn. com. Continental breakfast. Children under eight stay **free.** $$$$

Stage Stop Inn Motel. 303 McKeown Avenue, Patagonia; (520) 394–2211. Family suites with kitchenettes, outdoor heated pool, and a restaurant. $$

Tubac Country Inn. 13 Burrell Road, Tubac; (520) 398–3178. A country-style bed-and-breakfast in the village. No children under five. $$$

Tubac Golf Resort. 65 Avenida del Otero, P.O. Box 1297, Tubac 85646; (520) 398–2211, ext. 166 or (800) 848–7893; www.tubacgolfresort.com. A historic forty-acre ranch featuring a golf course, tennis courts, swimming pool, spa, and a restaurant. Under 12 stay **free.** $$$$

For More Information

Green Valley Chamber of Commerce. 270 West Continental #100, Green Valley 85614; (520) 625–7575; www.green valleyazchamber.com.

Nogales–Santa Cruz Chamber of Commerce. 123 West Kino Park, Nogales 85621; (520) 287–3685; www.nogales chamber.com.

Tubac Chamber of Commerce. P.O. Box 1866, Tubac 85646; (520) 398–2704; www.tubacaz.com.

Benson

The Benson area, which includes Sierra Vista, Chiricahua National Monument, and the San Pedro River, offers a more rambling, nature-oriented, and scenic range of options than other areas in this region. Kartchner Caverns has perhaps the most spectacular attraction, one of the ten most accessible and impressive caves in the world according to some lists—festooned with bizarre crystal, rock, and limestone formations. Another spectacular geologic spectacle here are the Chiricahua Mountains, created in a titanic volcanic explosion and outpouring of ash and lava millions of years ago. Deep layers of welded volcanic ash were buried, fused, then lifted to the surface again—where eons of ice and rain have sculpted them into extravagant pillars and bizarre formations. The mountains, named for the Apache Indians who defended the Chiricahua Mountains fiercely against white settlers until Geronimo's final surrender in 1886, offer a wealth of possibilities for exploration, including the ruins of Fort Bowie—a site of one of the most infamous battles in the Apache Wars.

Both Benson and Sierra Vista provide a good base of operations to explore the area. Besides exploring Kartchner Caverns and the Chiricahuas, you and the kids can search for beaver along the meandering San Pedro River, try to distinguish the fourteen different kinds of hummingbirds that visit Ramsey Canyon Preserve, visit historic Fort Huachuca in Sierra Vista, and wander the back canyons, seeking a glimpse of the fabled elegant trogon—a semitropical bird so rare and colorful that die-hard birders travel here from all over the world to catch a glimpse.

Kartchner Caverns State Park (all ages)

P.O. Box 1849, Benson 85602; (520) 586–4100 or (520) 586–CAVE; www.pr.state.az.us/Parks/parkhtml/kartchner.html. Open daily 7:00 A.M. to 6:00 P.M., except Christmas Day. Park fees $$$ per car. Throne Room cave tour, adults $$$, children ages 7–13 $$, under 7 free. Big Room cave tour, adults $$$$, children ages 7–13 $$$, under 7 not allowed. The Big Room is open mid-October through mid-April. Reservations recommended for the Throne Room and required for the Big Room.

The famous Kartchner Caverns, hailed as one of the top ten caves in the world, are usually booked months in advance, although there are some first-come, first-served spots available for walk-up visitors to the Rotunda/Throne Room. The tram will shuttle you to the cave's entrance, where you will have to go through an air lock. Yellow and red limestone formations decorate the 2⁵⁄₁₀-mile-long cave system. Magnificent columns reach up to 53 feet. One soda straw formation is only ¼ inch in diameter and 21 feet high. Nearly every type of cave formation can be seen in this pristine, living cave. The Big Room, which opened to the public in November 2003, features the world's most extensive formation of brushite moonmilk and the first reported occurrence of turnip shields. A campground with hookups is available at the park ($$$$ a night) with a fourteen-day limit. The 550-acre park is located in the Chihuahuan Desert and offers beautiful views of the low rolling hills of the Whetstone Mountains and plenty of hiking and outdoor exploration for you and your family.

Fort Huachuca Museum (all ages)

U.S. Army Garrison, Fort Huachuca; (520) 533–5736. Open 9:00 A.M. to 4:00 P.M. Monday through Friday and 1:00 to 4:00 P.M. Saturday and Sunday except major holidays. Free. Donation ($) suggested.

Dioramas, historic photographs, Native American artifacts, and period rooms highlight the history of this active military base north of the Mexican border. One exhibit, the "Black Experience," portrays the life of the Buffalo Soldiers, a famous, fearless army company comprised completely of African-American soldiers. Barracks and other buildings line the parade grounds, which will give you and the kids a good look at the merger of the old and the new. When driving onto the base, be prepared to show your driver's license, vehicle registration, and proof of insurance. While you are here be sure to check out the adjoining U.S. Army Intelligence Museum.

Gammons Gulch Ghost Town Movie Set (ages 5 and up)

59 East Rockspring Road, P.O. Box 76, Pomerene 85627; (520) 212–2831; www.gammons gulch.com. Open 9:00 A.M. to 4:00 P.M. Wednesday through Sunday September through May. Summer hours by appointment only. Adults $$, children under 12 $.

Here's an 1880s Old West town with a twist—owner Jay Gammon built it from authentic pieces of old buildings and then furnished it with antiques. It's worked so well, Hollywood has used it numerous times. This ten-acre town boasts a telegraph office, hotel, blacksmith shop, assay office, a mine, and saloon. Gammon often takes visitors on guided tours and tells stories about his father, a one-time bodyguard for the famous Western actor John Wayne. If you have some extra time, you can get a good look at the desert on the nearby nature loop trail.

Ramsey Canyon Preserve (all ages)

Ramsey Canyon Road, Sierra Vista; (520) 378–2785; www.nature.org. Open daily 9:00 A.M. to 4:00 P.M. November through February, 8:00 A.M. to 5:00 P.M. March through October. Closed Thanksgiving, Christmas, and New Year's Day. Adults $$, children under 16 free.

Learn about **Arizona Folklore**

Everyone knows that Dolan Ellis knows how to spin a yarn. Holding the role as Arizona's Official Balladeer since 1966, Ellis pays homage to the songs, legends, myths, and poems of Arizona at 2:00 P.M. on Saturday and Sunday at the **Arizona Folklore Preserve** near Sierra Vista in Ramsey Canyon. The preserve also hosts guest artists throughout the year and carries a complete line of books, music, and videos of Arizona folk artists. Adults $$, children under twelve $. For reservations call (520) 378–6165.

Up to fourteen different species of hummingbirds call Ramsey Canyon home, at least for a migratory stopover from spring to early autumn. Butterflies, fellow pollinators, also appear during the warmer months. Ramsey Canyon and Ramsey Creek, which flows year-round, are part of the San Pedro River Ecosystem—the most extensive and ecologically valuable riparian ecosystem remaining in the region. Smoking and pets are not permitted in the preserve. A bird observatory and the Hamburg Trail offer families an afternoon of delightful activities.

San Pedro Riparian National Conservation Area (all ages) (A) (🚗) (🚶)
BLM's San Pedro Project Office, 1763 Paseo San Luis, Sierra Vista; (520) 458–3559; www.az. blm.gov/ncarea.htm. Office open daily 8:00 A.M. to 4:00 P.M. Monday through Friday. San Pedro House open daily 9:30 A.M. to 4:30 P.M. Free.

After paying your fees at the San Pedro House, you and the kids can wander the conservation's many hiking trails. This protected 36-mile stretch of river supports a rich array of wildlife. As many as 350 different species of birds, 82 mammals, and 45 reptiles and amphibians can be found in this cottonwood-willow riparian habitat. Several hikes start at the San Pedro House and loop to the river and ponds. The San Pedro Trail is a more lengthy walk—eventually it will be a 40-mile trek running the length of the national conservation area. You can also camp at the conservation area ($). While visiting the preserve,

Amazing
Arizona Facts

Ira H. Hayes, a Pima Indian, is the Native American war hero of World War II who is in the famous photograph of Iwo Jima.

take a few minutes to check out Fairbank, an 1881 ghost town that will be sure to spark your children's interest. They will especially enjoy peeking into remaining buildings and taking the 1½-mile trek up to the ruins of the Grand Central Mill.

Fort Bowie National Historic Site (all ages) 🏛 ⛹ 🏕

3203 Old Fort Bowie Road, HCR 2, Box 6500, Willcox 85643; (520) 847–2500; www.nps.gov/fobo. Visitor center open daily 8:00 A.M. to 5:00 P.M. except Christmas Day. **Free.**

The U.S. Army built this fort to protect Apache Springs, a vital water hole used by bands of nomadic Apache Indians. But even this almost didn't end the thirty-year war waged by the Apache Chief Geronimo and his band. After the Indian Wars, the soldiers departed the post in 1894. Visitors to this historic site have to make a 1½-mile trek from the parking lot to the fort, which was intended in order to preserve the site and buildings. Make sure to take plenty of water and pack a picnic lunch for your return.

Rex Allen Arizona Cowboy Museum (all ages) 🎠

150 North Railroad Avenue, Willcox; (520) 384–4583. Open daily 10:00 A.M. to 4:00 P.M. except Thanksgiving, Christmas, and New Year's Day. Singles and couples $, families $$.

This museum houses the Willcox Cowboy Hall of Fame, movie posters of this famous singing cowboy, and a plethora of cowboy and movie memorabilia. Tucson resident Rex Allen and his son, Rex Allen Jr., provided the recorded music that you'll hear in the background while visiting this nostalgic little museum. A large mural painted outside will keep kids entertained as they look for several animals hidden in the painting. If they find them all, the museum awards a special prize.

Chiricahua National Monument (all ages) 🐾 🏛 ⛹ ⛺

13063 East Bonita Canyon Road, Willcox; (520) 824–3560; www.nps.gov/chir. Open daily 8:00 A.M. to 5:00 P.M. except Christmas Day. Adults $$, under 16 free.

The monument protects some of the most spectacular rock formations found in the Chiricahua Mountains. Volcanic rock, fractured by uplift and weathered by the elements, creates a veritable forest of fantastic stone sculptures. You'll find plenty of hiking trails, picnic areas, and a primitive campground at the monument. The ranger station also offers guided tours of Far Away Ranch, an 1880s building that now acts as a museum chronicling the life of one of the area's first families. Of special interest is the fireplace on the ranch's back porch. Stones used to construct the fireplace were carted from a three-tier, 110-foot-tall monument built by the Buffalo Soldiers when they were stationed in the region in 1885–86. If you look closely, you can see the inscription IN MEMORY OF JAS. A. GARFIELD, a free-thinking pioneer who proposed equal pay for black soldiers.

Apple Annie's Orchard (all ages) 🏕

2081 West Hardy Road, Willcox; (520) 384–2084. Open daily 8:00 A.M. to 5:30 P.M. mid-July through October. **Free.**

Even though Arizona is far from Washington climes, you can partake of America's favorite fruit and even pick a few if the whim catches you. Children love wandering through the orchard in search of the perfect fruit to pick. Apple Annie's provides picking equipment and bags for your fruity loot. After a hard afternoon of apple picking, you and the kids can purchase a sweet treat from the bakery or enjoy an applewood-smoked burger at one of the orchard's picnic tables.

Where to Eat

Golden China Restaurant. 220 West Fry Boulevard, Sierra Vista; (520) 458–8588. Menu items and a Chinese buffet. Kids' specials. $

Horseshoe Café. 154 East Fourth Street, Benson; (520) 586–3303. Mexican entrees, steak, prime rib, sandwiches, hamburgers, and salads. Children's menu. $–$$

La Casita Mexican Restaurant. 465 East Fry Boulevard, Sierra Vista; (520) 458–2376. Mexican and American favorites. Children's menu. $

Rip Griffin's. 1501 Fort Grant Road, Willcox; (520) 384–5311. Mexican entrees, steak, fish, barbecue, chicken, and salads. Children's menu. $–$$

Toy's Egg Roll Buffet. 100 East Fry Boulevard, Sierra Vista; (520) 459–7648. Chinese-food buffet and a salad bar. Kids' specials. $

Where to Stay

Days Inn. 621 Commerce Drive, Benson; (520) 586–3000. Mini suites, continental breakfast, and outdoor heated pool. Children under twelve stay **free.** $–$$

Holiday Inn Express. 630 South Village Loop, Benson; (520) 586–8800. Family suites with kitchenettes, breakfast buffet, and outdoor heated pool. Children under eighteen stay **free.** $$–$$$

Sierra Suites. 391 East Fry Boulevard, Sierra Vista; (520) 459–4221. Suites with a refrigerator and microwave, deluxe continental breakfast, laundry room, exercise room, outdoor heated pool, and spa. $$–$$$

Skywatchers Inn. 1311 Astronomers Road, Benson; (520) 586–7906. This inn is an astronomer's paradise, with eight telescopes and experts available to answer questions about southern Arizona's night skies. Full breakfast. Children are welcome. $$–$$$

Windemere Hotel. 2047 South Highway 92, Sierra Vista; (520) 459–5900 or (800) 825–4656. Suites, American breakfast buffet, restaurant, outdoor heated pool, and spa. Children under eighteen stay **free.** $$–$$$

For More Information

Benson–San Pedro Valley Chamber of Commerce. 249 East Fourth Street, Benson 85602; (520) 586–2842; www.benson chamberaz.com.

Greater Sierra Vista Area Chamber of Commerce. 21 East Wilcox Drive, Sierra Vista, 85635; (520) 458–6940 or (800) 288–3861; www.sierravistachamber.org.

Willcox Chamber of Commerce. 1500 North Circle I Road, Willcox 85643; (520) 384–2272 or (800) 200–2272; www.willcox chamber.com.

Bisbee and Tombstone

These historic mining towns nearly died out when the rich veins of gold, silver, and copper played out, but somehow they staggered along on the edge of ghost-town status until they were reinvented as places where visitors could savor the real relics of one of the nation's most fascinating, myth-laden historical periods—the violent and extravagant days of the Old West.

Legendary Tombstone was the backdrop for the famous feud between the Earp brothers and the Clanton gang at the OK Corral. The town's Western storefronts, the staged drama in the actual OK Corral, and the headstone epitaphs in Boot Hill all offer a chance to get kids interested in the history of the Old West. The spectacular, boulder-strewn Dragoon Mountains loom to the northeast of Tombstone and offered first Cochise and then Geronimo a secure refuge from their enemies. Now they offer an enjoyable outing when the kids absolutely have to run off some accumulated energy from behaving themselves for too long a stretch. Bisbee might not be as famous as Tombstone today, but back in the late 1880s and early 1900s, Bisbee surpassed Tombstone in riches and grandeur. Here you'll see beautiful Victorian architecture, including the reputedly haunted Copper Queen Hotel. In its day Bisbee was a rollicking mining town tucked in the canyons of the Mule Mountains—with its share of bitter labor disputes, cave-ins, tragedies, bandits, gunfights, and lynchings. Now it's a fun and funky collection of old hotels, knickknack shops, and odd little museums.

Highlights of a tour of Tombstone and Bisbee include a historic mining museum, an underground exploration of a 1,800-foot-deep mine, the titillating tour of a saloon where the working girls entertained in birdcages and the patrons often peppered the walls with .44 caliber slugs, the world's largest rose bush, and one of the most famous graveyards in the West.

Bisbee Mining and Historical Museum (all ages) 🏛️ 🔥

5 Copper Queen Plaza, P.O. Box 14, Bisbee 85603; (520) 432–7071; www.bisbeemuseum.org. Open daily 10:00 A.M. to 4:00 P.M. except Christmas and New Year's Day. $

Bisbee's glory days take shape as you stroll through this museum, tucked away in the old 1897 Copper Queen Consolidated Mining Offices. Mining dioramas, displays, and the mural-size 1908 photo of Bisbee give visitors a sense of this town's heyday. Children will especially enjoy sifting through a trunk of old-fashioned toys and games including clackers, an iron tractor, old jump ropes, glittering marbles, and wooden yo-yos.

Queen Mine Underground Tour (ages 3 and up) 🏛️

118 Arizona Street, Bisbee; (520) 432–2071 or toll-free (866) 432–2071; www.cityofbisbee. com/queenminetours.htm. Tours leave daily at 9:00 and 10:30 A.M., noon, and 2:00 and 3:30 P.M. Adults $$$, children ages 4–15 $. Under 4 free.

Before heading 1,800 feet underground, you and the kids will get geared up in a yellow slicker and a hard hat. And for good measure, you'll get belted with a battery-operated

Passport **Program**

If you're going to spend some time in Bisbee, it's well worth your while to purchase a Bisbee Visitor Passport ($$$), which offers admission to the Copper Queen Mine Tour and the Bisbee Mining and Historical Museum as well as discounts on other Bisbee attractions, lodging, and restaurants. Information: (520) 432–2071 or (866) 432–2071; www.cityofbisbee.com/start_passport.html.

light. Once the miner guiding you on this subterranean adventure is satisfied that you're ready, you'll load up in a ore cart, which snakes down into the mountain. During the seventy-five-minute tour, you'll explore part of the 143 miles of tunnels. The copper mine opened in the 1880s and ran for sixty years before closing down for good in 1943. Kids of all ages will enjoy hearing about the mining process, including blasting techniques, drilling, and ore processing. Make sure to wear a jacket as the tunnels stay at an even forty-seven degrees year-round.

Lavender Jeep Tours (ages 8 and up)
1 Copper Queen Plaza, 45 Gila Drive, Bisbee; (520) 432–5369. Call for hours. $$$$

Bisbee native Tom Mosier and his wife, Ginger, offer a different perspective of the back roads of Bisbee and the Sky Islands in a combination of jeep tours that even the locals enjoy. Mosier takes his passengers through Bisbee's back streets, regaling them with the history of the town and its buildings.

OK Corral (all ages) 🏛️ 🦪
308 East Allen Street, Tombstone; (520) 457–3456; www.ok-corral.com. Open daily 9:00 A.M. to 5:00 P.M. except Christmas Day. Adults $$, children under 6 free.

With the details still hotly debated between historians, the renowned 1881 gunfight between the Clanton gang and the Earps is reenacted daily at 2:00 P.M. at the infamous OK Corral. The gunfights and Western skits are popular with families, so be sure to get there early and get a seat. Other attractions at the OK Corral include a "historama" (part film, part diorama), a museum filled with artifacts from Tombstone's nefarious days, and several historic buildings, including a working blacksmith shop and an 1880s outhouse. Kids can pose for pictures with Wyatt Earp and the gang or on the stagecoach sitting on the dusty street. Before leaving, don't forget to get a copy of the *Epitaph*—a reprint of the original newspaper that came out the day after the fatal shootout.

Bird Cage Theatre (ages 5 and up) 🏛️ 📖

517 East Allen Street, Tombstone; (520) 457–3421. Open daily 8:00 A.M. to 6:00 P.M. Adults $$, children ages 8 and up $. Family package $$$.

Described by the *New York Times* in 1882 as "the wildest, wickedest night spot between Basin Street and the Barbary Coast," the historic 1881 Bird Cage Theatre boasts fourteen "birdcages" suspended from the ceiling, where prostitutes once plied their trade. Historic photos, displays of life in the Old West, and exhibits on Doc Holiday and Wyatt Earp are sure to entertain the whole family. Wander through this dance hall and see how many of the estimated 140 bullet holes, from sixteen different gunfights, you and the kids can find in the walls. You can also check out the horse-drawn hearse that carried Tombstone residents to their final resting place in Boot Hill.

Tombstone Courthouse State Historic Park (all ages) 🏛️ 📖 🚗

219 East Toughnut Street, P.O. Box 216, Tombstone 85638; (520) 457–3311; www.pr.state.az.us/Parks/parkhtml/tombstone.html. Open daily 8:00 A.M. to 5:00 P.M. except Christmas Day. Adults and children ages 7–13 $, under 7 free.

The 1882 brick territorial courthouse now boasts a museum chronicling the town's wild history with artifacts and photographic exhibits. Here you'll see the courtroom, a lawyer's office, and the assay office fully restored and ready for business—if it was 1900, that is. As you wander through the building you'll discover such things as mining picks, ore samples, guns, 1890s clothing, quilts, and children's dolls and toys. Outside you'll see the gallows, but the curator is quick to mention that public hangings in Tombstone are just the stuff of fiction today. Picnic tables make a great spot for lunch.

Amazing
Arizona Facts

Boothill Graveyard was the last stop for nearly 300 former rowdy residents of nearby Tombstone. Casualties from the OK Corral gunfight, famous prostitutes, and outlaws with "throat trouble" at the gallows have all been planted in the "bone orchard." Although many of the graves are unmarked, one of the remaining tombstones bears the famous epitaph of the luckless Les Moore:

> HERE LIES
> LESTER MOORE
> FOUR SLUGS
> FROM A .44.
> NO LES.
> NO MOORE.

Tombstone Epitaph Museum (ages 5 and up)

9 South Fifth Street, Tombstone; (520) 457–2211; www.tombstone-epitaph.com. **Open daily 9:00 A.M. to 5:00 P.M.** Free.

Pick up your own copy of Tombstone's *Epitaph,* the town's famous newspaper that John P. Clum founded in 1880. The office of this newspaper, which is still in business, offers free tours during which you can see the original printing press and other exhibits, including a copy of the front-page stories detailing the gunfight at the OK Corral.

Rose Tree Museum (ages 5 and up)

116 South Fourth Street, Tombstone; (520) 457–3326. **Open daily 9:00 A.M. to 5:00 P.M. except Thanksgiving and Christmas Day. Adults $, children under 14** free.

A rose to soothe a homesick heart takes on a delightful twist as visitors gaze at the world's largest rosebush, according to the *Guinness Book of World Records.* Covering more than 8,000 square feet, the Lady Banksia rose was sent from Scotland as just a root for a melancholy bride in 1885. The museum, housed in a historic adobe building, displays antiques and features several exhibits on the town. The best time to visit the museum is in April when the tree puts out white blossoms, in clusters of five to seven, which open to the size of a quarter.

Slaughter Ranch (all ages)

6153 Geronimo Trail, P.O. 438, Douglas 85608; (520) 558–2474. **Open 10:00 A.M. to 3:00 P.M. Wednesday through Sunday except Thanksgiving, Christmas, and New Year's Day. Adults $, children under 15** free.

A former Texas Ranger, John Slaughter rode into the area in 1884 and bought a lease to the San Bernardino Ranch, which is now a final testament to Arizona's great cattle-ranching days. For more than thirty years, Slaughter worked the 93,000-acre ranch while holding the office of sheriff of Tombstone. Visitors can take a self-guided tour through the restored ranch, which is located 16 miles east of Douglas. During the tour you and the kids will get a feel of early ranch life from territorial days. Along the way, you'll discover the ranch house and its outbuildings—the icehouse, commissary, washhouse, garage, and granary. You and the kids can stop for a picnic lunch and check out the ranch pond, which is home to endangered native fish. A nearby trail climbs up the hill to an abandoned U.S. Army post used during the Mexican unrest of 1911–23. At the top, a lookout provides great views of the San Bernardino National Wildlife Refuge, and you might just catch a glimpse of vermilion flycatcher, blue grosbeak, or blue heron streaking though the sky.

Douglas Wildlife Zoo (all ages)

4000 North Plantation Road, Douglas; (520) 364–2515. **Open 10:00 A.M. to 5:00 P.M. Monday through Saturday and 10:00 A.M. to 4:00 P.M. Sunday except all major holidays. Adults and children ages 3–12 $, under 3** free.

This zoo has a small yet satisfying collection of animals, including parrots, peacocks, emus, lemurs, apes, and jaguars. A small petting zoo brings kids up close to goats and deer.

Ghostly **Side Trips**

A great day trip for the kids in the vicinity of Tombstone is a ghost-town tour. Start your adventure by driving a leisurely 18 miles to Gleeson, a copper-mining town that flourished between 1909 and the late 1930s. The mine finally shut down in 1955, leaving the ramshackle remains of the town's jail, cemetery, school, and hospital. A mile east of Gleeson and 3 miles north, you'll find the old jail and some foundations that mark the spot where Courtland once marked the map. And 9 miles north of Courtland, you and the kids will find Pearce, named after the prospector Jimmie Pearce, who found gold here in 1894. Pearce sold his interest to the Commonwealth Mine, which operated until it was shut down in the 1930s. At one time Pearce supported 1,500 residents. Now all that remains is a few buildings and some tailings from the mine. Make sure to pack a lunch, plenty of water, and sunscreen. Stay away from the mine shafts, and keep a close eye on the little ones. For more information and a map of the tour, call the Visitor Information Center at (520) 457–3929.

Where to Eat

Big Nose Kate's Saloon. 417 East Allen Street, Tombstone; (520) 457–3107. Pizza, sandwiches, and quesadillas. Standard children's menu. $–$$

Brewery Steakhouse. 5 Brewery Avenue, Bisbee; (520) 432–3317. Serves up American fare in the 1905 Muheim Block Building, which once housed the Bisbee Stock Exchange. Children's menu. $$

Cafe Cornucopia. 14 Main Street, Bisbee; (520) 432–4820. This little cafe in Old Bisbee serves up some of the best soups, salads, and sandwiches in town. $

Cafe Roka. 35 Main Street, Bisbee; (520) 432–5153. Enjoy a four-course meal at this first-class restaurant on Main Street. $$$–$$$$

Grand Café. 1119 G Avenue, Douglas; (520) 364–2344. Standard Mexican and American food. $

Longhorn Restaurant. 501 East Allen Street, Tombstone; (520) 457–3405. Steak, burgers, and prime rib. $

Nellie Cashman's Restaurant. 117 Fifth Street, Tombstone; (520) 457–2212. Steaks, sandwiches, hamburgers, and salads served in the town's oldest restaurant, an 1879 boardinghouse. $–$$

Where to Stay

Bisbee Grand Hotel. 61 Main Street, Bisbee; (520) 432–5900; www.bisbeegrand hotel.com. This fully restored 1906 Victorian-style hotel features old-fashioned amenities like a Western saloon and a ladies' parlor. $$$–$$$$

The Bisbee Inn. 45 OK Street, Bisbee; (520) 432–5131 or (888) 432–5131; www.bisbeeinn.com. Known as one of the best bed-and-breakfast inns in town, this 1916 brick hotel is decorated in period antiques and features photos from Bisbee's past on the papered walls. Breakfast included. $$–$$$

Copper Queen Hotel. 11 Howell Street, P.O. Box Drawer CQ, Bisbee 85603; (520) 432–2216; www.copperqueen.com. This charming 1902 hotel once entertained notables like John Wayne, President Theodore Roosevelt, and Gen. John "Blackjack" Pershing. The hotel features a dining room, swimming pool, and "Old West" saloon. $$$–$$$$

Gadsden Hotel. 1046 G Avenue, Douglas; (520) 364–4481; www.theriver.com/gadsdenhotel. Established in 1907, the hotel's marble and gold leaf represent an elegant bygone era. The Gadsden offers several eating establishments, its own ghost, and the story of Pancho Villa's legendary ride up the hotel's marbled staircase. $$–$$$$

Holiday Inn Express. 630 South Village Loop, Benson; (888) 263–2283. Located off I–10 at exit 302, this standard motel is only 8 miles away from Kartchner Caverns. $$–$$$

San Jose Lodge. 1002 Naco Highway, Bisbee; (520) 432–5761. Family suites with kitchenettes, a restaurant, and a swimming pool. $–$$

San Pedro River Inn. 8326 South Hereford Road, Hereford; (520) 366–5532; www.sanpedroriverinn.com. This laid-back inn makes a perfect base for a weekend adventure exploring the San Pedro River, the last completely untamed river in Arizona. Accommodations in the adobe houses sit on twenty acres. Kids will enjoy playing in the property's tree houses and swinging on tire swings. $$$$

Shady Dell Vintage Trailer Park. 1 Douglas Road, Bisbee; (520) 432-3567; www.theshadydell.com. Stay in a restored 1950s aluminum travel trailer complete with period furnishings and dine at Dot's Diner, which is famous for its hearty meals and decadent desserts. $–$$

For More Information

Bisbee Chamber of Commerce and Visitor Center. 31 Subway, P.O. Box BA, Bisbee 85603; (520) 432–5421 or (866) 2–BISBEE; www.bisbeearizona.com.

Douglas Chamber of Commerce. 1125 Pan American, Douglas 85607; (520) 364–2477; www.discoverdouglas.com.

Tombstone Chamber of Commerce. P.O. Box 995, Fourth and Allen Streets, Tombstone 85638; (520) 457–9317; www.tombstone.org.

Annual Events

JANUARY

Wings Over Willcox. Willcox; (520) 384–2272. Third weekend in January. Sandhill crane celebration, guided tours, seminars, workshops, and field trips.

Sierra Stampede. Sierra Vista; (520) 378–3200. Third weekend in January. An all-women's professional rodeo featuring rodeo queens from across the state, the antics of rodeo clowns, and kids' horse rides.

FEBRUARY

Cochise Cowboy Poetry and Music Gathering. Sierra Vista; (520) 459–3868. Second weekend in February. A family-oriented celebration of Western culture, history, and folklore.

Territorial Days. Benson; (520) 586–2842. Second weekend in February. Reenactments from the Wild West frontier, wagon rides, carnival, toe sack races, and a petting zoo.

MARCH

O'odham Day Celebration. Ajo; (520) 387–6849. Third Saturday in March. Members of the Tohono O'odham tribe demonstrate basket weaving, traditional farming techniques, and storytelling at the Organ Pipe Cactus National Monument.

Ed Shieffelin Territorial Days. Tombstone; (520) 457–9317 or (888) 457–3929. Mid-March. Gunfight reenactments, an 1880 Arizona fire cart champion race, an all-pet parade, arts and crafts, and live entertainment.

APRIL

Pima County Fair. Tucson; (520) 762–9100. Last two weeks in April. 4-H exhibits, art displays, live entertainment, petting zoo, fair food, and games and rides at the County Fairgrounds.

MAY

Waila Festival. Tucson; (520) 628–5774. Mid-May. Tohono O'odham social dance performances, craft demonstrations, and native food.

Wyatt Earp Days. Tombstone; (520) 457–9317 or (888) 457–3929. Last weekend in May. Reenacted gunfights, saloon girls, a period fashion show, chili cook-off, and a parade.

JULY

Patagonia Fourth of July Celebration. Patagonia; (520) 394–0060. July 4. Parade, food, music, and fireworks.

AUGUST

Peach Mania Festival. Willcox; (520) 384–2084. First two weekends in August. You-pick peaches, all-you-can-eat peach

Winging **It**

Each winter sandhill cranes by the thousands from as far as Siberia flock to roost at the Willcox Playa, a giant lakebed south of Willcox. The playa, which covers 50 to 60 square miles, transforms into a shallow lake with the onset of the monsoons, giving these long-legged birds protection from landlocked predators such as coyotes. However, it doesn't save them from their airborne foe—the bald eagle. Every morning when the sun begins to peek over the Chiricahua Mountains, the cranes start shifting and vocalizing, and then, with a great burst of energy, they lift off in groups as large as 10,000 at the same time.

pancake breakfast, hayrides, peach-tasting pavilion, and outdoor craft festival at Apple Annie's Orchard.

Vigilante Days. Tombstone; (520) 457–9317 or (888) 457–3929. Second weekend in August. Gunfight reenactments, 10K run, and chili cook-off.

SEPTEMBER

Santa Cruz County Fair. Sonoita; (520) 455–5553. Last weekend of September. Exhibits, 4-H auction, carnival, and family entertainment at the Sonoita Fairgrounds.

OCTOBER

La Fiesta de los Chiles. Tucson; (520) 326–9686. Third weekend in October. An annual celebration of the chile pepper, with live entertainment, spicy cuisine, demonstrations, and children's activities at the Tucson Botanical Gardens.

Rex Allen Days. Willcox; (520) 384–2272 or (800) 200–2272. First weekend in October. A Professional Rodeo Cowboys Association (PRCA) rodeo, Western music, dances, golf tournament, and children's activities.

NOVEMBER

Tucson Celtic Festival and Scottish Highland Games. Tucson; (520) 743–9291. First weekend in November. Kilted bagpipe bands, clan tents, athletic competitions, sheep dog demonstrations, military reenactments, and ethnic food at Rillito Park.

Festival of Lights. Bisbee; (520) 432–6000. End of November. Parade, live nativity, and lighting of the streets in Old Historic Bisbee.

DECEMBER

Nogales Christmas Parade and Annual Christmas Tree Lighting. Nogales; (520) 287–3685. First Saturday in December. Santa Claus and his reindeer join the festivities, which include a children's parade and the lighting of a 30-foot Christmas tree.

Luminaria Nights. Tucson; (520) 326–9686. First weekend in December. More than 2,000 luminarias, holiday music, hot cider and cookies, holiday decorations, and live entertainment at the Tucson Botanical Gardens.

Old-Fashioned Christmas and Holiday Open House. Tucson; (520) 624–2333. Second Saturday in December. Take a trip into Christmas past at the Museum and Historic Block, which is decorated in the holiday style of early-1900s Tucson.

La Posada. Ajo; (520) 432–5421. Third Saturday in December. Join the procession in a one-night reenactment of the biblical story of Mary and Joseph's journey to Bethlehem and their search for a place to stay.

Other Things to **See and Do**

- **Ajo Historical Museum,** Ajo; (520) 387–7105.
- **Amerind Foundation,** Willcox; (520) 586–3666.
- **Arizona Cactus and Succulent Research,** Bisbee; (520) 432–7040.
- **Balloon America,** Tucson; (520) 299–7744.
- **Bisbee Trolley Tours,** Bisbee; (520) 432–7020.
- **Cabeza Prieta National Wildlife Refuge,** Ajo; (520) 387–6483.
- **Center for Creative Photography,** University of Arizona, Tucson; (520) 621–7968.
- **Colossal Cave Mountain Park Stables,** Vail; (520) 647–3450.
- **Frontier Relics,** Willcox; (520) 384–3481.
- **Golden Pin Lanes,** Tucson; (520) 888–4272.
- **H. H. Franklin Foundation Museum,** Tucson; (520) 326–8038.
- **Holy Trinity Monastery,** Saint David; (520) 720–4016.
- **Muheim Heritage House Museum,** Bisbee; (520) 432–7698.
- **Paintball Headquarters,** Tucson; (520) 293–5850.
- **Pharmacy Museum,** Tucson; (520) 626–1427.
- **Pimeria Alta Historical Society Museum,** Nogales; (520) 287–4621.
- **Postal History Foundation,** Tucson; (520) 623–6652.
- **Purple Mountain Pack Goats Family Adventure Tours,** Tucson; (520) 886–7721.
- **San Pedro Valley Arts and Historical Society Museum,** Benson; (520) 586–3070.
- **Singing Wind Bookshop,** Benson; (520) 586–2425.
- **Southern Arizona Adventures,** Bisbee; (520) 432–9058 or (800) 319–7377.
- **Tubac Center for the Arts,** Tubac; (520) 398–2371.
- **Tucson Sports Park,** Tucson; (520) 744–9498.
- **Walking Winds Stables,** Tucson; (520) 742–4422.

Arizona's
Coastal Country

There aren't many landlocked states that can boast of more than 1,000 miles of shoreline, but Arizona can and does. Most people are aware of the Colorado River's course through the Grand Canyon, but then it tends to get overlooked where it swings south and travels through a series of man-made lakes and dams along the state's entire western border. However, before it was tamed, the Colorado River reached up to 600 feet across in some places, making it a treacherous body of water for early travelers to cross. Today, the river separates Arizona from Nevada and California and creates a narrow, verdant path through an otherwise harsh desert. The Mohave Desert is the driest of the four deserts found in the state, with an average rainfall of only 4 inches a year. Even so, life abounds here, although even the plants seem hostile—prickly jumping cactus, the bayonet-tipped Joshua tree, and the spindly creosote bush. The northwestern edge at Lake Mead lies at an elevation of 2,000 feet and plummets to only 70 feet above sea level near the Mexican border outside of Yuma.

Carrie's
TopPicks for fun in Arizona's Coastal Country

1. Lake Mead National Recreation Area, Boulder City, NV

2. London Bridge, Lake Havasu City

3. Colorado River Indian Tribes Museum, Parker

4. Yuma Territorial Prison State Historical Park, Yuma

5. Yuma Crossing State Historic Park, Yuma

ARIZONA'S COASTAL COUNTRY

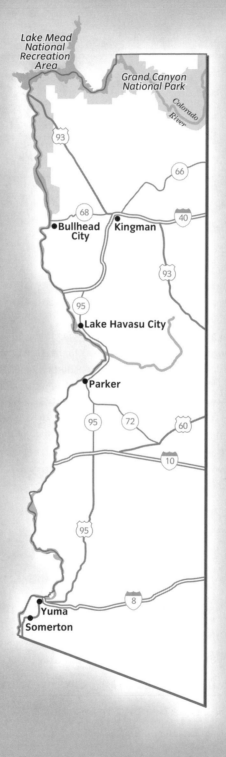

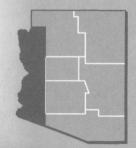

Because of the harshness of the desert, the few cities out here are generally concentrated near the river. There isn't much to see and do in this region, but you will find several wildlife refuges, some funky little museums, a territorial prison, three Native American reservations, abandoned mining towns, the world-famous London Bridge, and plenty of water-recreation opportunities. So break out your bathing suits and spend some time in the hottest corner of the state.

Kingman

Situated in the northwest corner of the state, Kingman makes a good base to explore this high desert region. Here you'll find Lake Mead, the lower Colorado River, Hoover Dam, the twin cities of Laughlin, Nevada, and Bullhead City, Arizona, the longest remaining stretch of Historic Route 66, and old mining communities. Kingman was named after a railroad surveyor who came through the area in 1880 in search of a right of way for the Atlantic and Pacific Railroad. The tiny railroad camp grew into a major mining, ranching, and transportation center, and in 1886 the county seat moved 15 miles south from Mineral Park to Kingman. However, the residents of Mineral Park weren't too happy about the switch and refused to turn over the county records. Kingman residents took it all in stride and in the middle of the night raided the offices in Mineral Park, stole the records, and transferred them to Kingman under the cover of dark.

You'll discover this tidbit and other local lore at the city's quirky museum. But that's about the only cultural experience you're likely to find out in this desolate stretch. Most activities are concentrated in Nevada's casinos and focus on water sports at Lake Mead and Lake Mohave. Because the lakes straddle the Nevada-Arizona border, you'll need a fishing license from one state and a special-use stamp from the other when fishing from a boat.

Mohave Museum of History and Art (all ages)

400 West Beale Street, Kingman; (928) 753–3195. Open 9:00 A.M. to 5:00 P.M. Monday through Friday and 1:00 to 5:00 P.M. Saturday except all major holidays. Admission $, children under 12 free.

Exhibits, dioramas, and murals at this little museum introduce visitors to the history of northwestern Arizona from prehistoric times to the present day. Here you'll find ranching and mining machinery, a 1923 caboose, a display on local movie star Andy Devine, and exhibits on the construction of Hoover Dam. You and the kids will also learn about turquoise mining, which is prevalent in the region. Native American artifacts on display include prehistoric pottery and baskets as well as modern Native American paintings and sculptures. Kids will especially enjoy taking a turn grinding corn on a stone metate and climbing aboard a historic caboose.

Mohave **Ghosts**

The Mohave Desert might seem fairly resourceless at first glance with its rough terrain and inhospitable climate, but the jagged mountains yielded a rich bonanza of minerals in the late 1800s, which led to a boom creating several towns. Many of these have since given up the ghost, drying up when the riches panned out, but a few tenacious survivors continue to hold on. Chloride, 20 miles northwest of Kingman, celebrates its history on Old Miners' Day, held the last Saturday of June. This town, which boomed in the early 1860s, is the oldest mining camp in northwestern Arizona. Some of the remaining structures you can see in this tiny community include an old miner's shack, jail, bank, and railroad depot.

Another nearby favorite for living-history buffs is the weather-beaten mining community of Oatman, which is located 28 miles southwest of Kingman. A few hundred people live in this town, named after the Oatman family—victims of a Mohave Indian attack in 1851. Several of Oatman's old buildings still hang on and are now occupied by gift shops and small cafes. Occasionally wild burros, descendants from the region's mining days, wander through the rough, cobbled streets.

Lake Mohave (all ages) Ⓐ ⊜ △ ⊛
Katherine Ranger Station, 1903 Katherine Spur Road, Bullhead City; (928) 754–3272 (ranger station). Open daily 8:00 A.M. to 4:00 P.M. Day use $$ for five days, $$$ annual pass.

Squeezed between canyon walls, Lake Mohave is 67 miles long but only 4 miles across at its widest point, making this narrow body of water seems more like a river than a lake. At Katherine Landing you'll find a white-sand swimming beach, picnic tables, a boat ramp, campground, and a lodge. To fully enjoy Lake Mohave you really need a boat, which you can rent from the marina. Fishing is a favorite activity here, and you'll find bass, trout, crappie, bluegill, and channel catfish. The bass are especially hot, weighing as much as fifty pounds. Waterskiing and swimming are other family favorites. Most hiking is pretty rough, but kids of all ages will enjoy the 1-mile round-trip trek to the Katherine Mine. The mine produced only about two million dollars in gold and silver before it played out, but the mill continued to process ore from other mines until it shut down in 1943.

Hoover Dam (all ages)

Boulder City, NV; (702) 294–3523, ext. 3; www.hooverdam.usbr.gov. Open daily 8:30 A.M. to 6:00 P.M. except Thanksgiving and Christmas Day. Dam admission $. Tours, adults $$, children ages 6–16 $.

In 1935 engineers created this immense concrete dam, which rises 726 feet above bedrock. The visitor center, accessed on the Nevada side, features historic exhibits, a viewing platform, an art gallery, historic photographs, and a thirty-six-minute video detailing regional history, dam construction, and the importance water plays in our lives. The dam is flanked by two winged guardians—bronze sculptures that tower 30 feet high. Children ages six and up can accompany adults on a ½-mile guided tour of the Nevada Power Wing and out onto the terrace for a spectacular view of the face of the dam.

Lake Mead National Recreation Area (all ages)

Highway 93 and Highway 166, Alan Bible Visitor Center, 601 Nevada Highway, Boulder City, NV; (702) 293–8990; www.nps.gov/lame. Visitor center open daily 8:30 A.M. to 4:30 P.M. except Thanksgiving, Christmas, and New Year's Day. Day use $$ for five days, $$$ annual pass.

This 110-mile-long lake, held back by Hoover Dam, is the largest artificial lake in the United States. Like at Lake Mohave, a boat is almost mandatory to fully enjoy the lake and the favorite sport here—fishing. To rent a boat, stop by the **Lake Mead Resort Marina** (702–293–3484 or 800–752–9669), where you'll also find a lodge, store, and restaurant. Other family activities include wildlife watching and desert recreation. The visitor center offers handouts on camping facilities and hiking trails and also carries a wide selection of nautical charts and topographical maps of the region.

Lake Mead Cruises (all ages)

480 Lakeshore Drive, Boulder City, NV; (702) 293–6180; www.lakemeadcruises.com. Open daily except Christmas and New Year's Day. Sight-seeing cruise $$$, children ages 2–11 $$, under 2 free.

The *Desert Princess,* a triple-deck steam wheeler, takes a ninety-minute trip up Lake Mead to Hoover Dam at noon, 2:00 P.M., and 4:00 P.M. In addition to the sight-seeing tour, the *Desert Princess* offers both a breakfast and a dinner cruise.

Amazing
Arizona Facts

The world's deepest dam, at more than 320 feet deep, is Parker Dam on the Colorado River.

Where to Eat

Calico's Restaurant. 418 West Beale, Kingman; (928) 753–5005. American-style entrees in a casual atmosphere. Children's menu. $–$$

Memory Lane Soda Fountain and Deli. 120 West Andy Devine, Kingman; (928) 718–2020. Sandwiches, hot dogs, and hamburgers in a 1950s diner. $

Mr. D'z Route 66 Diner. 105 East Andy Devine, Kingman; (928) 718–0066. Sandwiches, Mexican entrees, pizza, pastas, and salads. Children's menu. $

Where to Stay

Best Western Wayfarer's Inn. 2815 East Andy Devine, Kingman; (928) 753–6271. Microwave, refrigerators, deluxe breakfast buffet, pool, and spa. $$

Hotel Brunswick. 315 East Andy Devine, Kingman; (928) 718–1800; www.hotel-brunswick.com. Suites and a restaurant in a historic 1909 hotel. Under 10 **free.** $–$$$$

Hualapai Mountain Lodge. 4525 Hualapai Mountain Road, Kingman; (928) 757–3545; www.hualapaimountain lodge.com. Suites, RV park, restaurant, and a store in restored 1930s Civilian Conservation Corps camp buildings. $$$–$$$$

Area Campgrounds

Hualapai Mountain Park. Southeast of Kingman, Mohave County Parks Department, 3675 East Andy Devine, P.O. Box 7000, Kingman 86402; (928) 757–0915. Tent and RV sites with hookups. Small cabins, wildlife watching, forest hiking trails, and scenic views. $

For More Information

BLM Kingman Field Office. 2475 Beverly Avenue, Kingman 86401; (928) 692–4400; www.az.blm.gov/kfo/index.htm.

Bullhead Area Chamber of Commerce. 1251 Highway 95, Bullhead City 86429; (928) 754–4121 or (800) 987–7457; www.bullheadchamber.com.

Kingman Area Chamber of Commerce. 120 West Andy Devine Avenue, Kingman 86401; (928) 753–6106; www.kingman tourism.org.

Lake Havasu City

When children sing the ditty "London Bridge is falling down," they most likely don't realize that the famous bridge had been sinking down into the Thames River in England for centuries and that it now resides on the banks of the Colorado River in western Arizona. When **London Bridge** became too unstable to use, English officials decided to tear it down and put it up for sale. To the derision of many, California magnate Robert McCulloch bought the bridge in 1967 for $2,460,000 and then spent twice that having the 10,276 granite blocks shipped to Arizona, where he was developing a planned community. It took three years for the bridge to be reassembled, and then McCulloch had a channel dug beneath it.

It might seem absurd to see the London Bridge in the middle of a desert, but McCulloch's vision is now the second biggest tourist attraction in Arizona next to the Grand Canyon. While you're here, make sure to visit the quaint English Village, which has plenty of shops, galleries, and restaurants. Like most river towns, the biggest draw to Lake Havasu City is the water recreation. Lake Havasu, which is 45 miles long and 3 miles wide, offers plenty of boating, fishing, waterskiing, and swimming. Sailboat regattas add a splash of color to the water scene, and boat tours offer a relaxing way to explore the local waterways.

Lake Havasu State Park (all ages)

Windsor Beach, 699 London Bridge Road, Lake Havasu City; (928) 855–2784; www.pr.state.az.us/Parks/parkhtml/havasu.html. Open daily. Day use hours are sunrise to 10:00 P.M. Day use $$.

Located just north of London Bridge, this state park provides a multitude of outdoor activities, including swimming, picnicking, boating, fishing, hiking, and camping. From October to March the park offers interpretive programs of special interest to families, such as ranger-led tours of the desert gardens, presentations, and evening movies on desert plants and wildlife. But if you want to go on your own, try the 1½-mile trek along the Mohave Sunset Trail. This one-way trail offers great views of the desert and riparian habitats. About halfway along the trail you'll come across a botanical garden, which features native plants in a landscaped setting. If you want to try and tackle fishing, your best bet is to cast your line early in the morning during the summer months. If you're lucky, you'll pull out a catch of the lake's bass, crappie, catfish, and bluegill. Amenities at the park include restrooms, showers, and a fish-cleaning station.

Lake Havasu Museum of History (all ages)

320 London Bridge Road, Lake Havasu City; (928) 854-4938. Open 1:00 to 4:00 P.M. Tuesday through Saturday. Adults $, under 12 free.

This new addition to the Lake Havasu community traces the area's history from prehistoric times to modern day. Displays in the 3,000-square-foot museum include exhibits on the Chemehuevi Indians, the construction of Parker Dam, the region's mining activities, and information on London Bridge.

Roller Palace (all ages)

3539 North McCulloch Boulevard, Lake Havasu City; (928) 453-1553; www.therink.info/. Open 7:00 to 10:00 P.M. Friday and Saturday and 3:00 to 6:00 P.M. Sunday. $

Roller skating is the name of the game of choice at this open-air roller rink. The facility issues standard skates with admission, but for an extra fee ($) you can rent inline skates. Additional activities at this family fun center include rock climbing, laser tag, paint ball, and an arcade ($–$$$).

Blue Water Jet Boat Tours (ages 6 and up) ⌂ ⌂

501 English Village, Lake Havasu City; (928) 855–7171; (888) 855–7171; www.coloradoriverjetboattours.com. Hours vary. Closed June through August. $$$$

Choose from two different trips and enjoy the scenery from the climate-controlled cabin of the "Starship 2010." The two-and-a-half-hour narrated tour to Topock Gorge passes by the Havasu National Wildlife Refuge and other destinations along the Colorado River. The three-hour narrated tour heads 22 miles south of Lake Havasu on the Colorado River to the Bill Williams Wildlife Refuge, where you might even have the chance to see nesting blue herons.

Jerkwater Canoe and Kayak Co., Inc. (ages 6 and up) ⌂ ⌂ ⌂

P.O. Box 800, Topock 86436; (928) 768–7753 or (800) 421–7803; www.jerkwater.com. Hours vary. Half-day trips $$$$, under 10 $$.

This outfitter offers several trips ranging from easy half-day trips to overnight excursions. The best bet for families is the 12-mile paddling trip from Jack Smith Park in Needles to Park Moabi. The tour company will shuttle you to Needles from Park Moabi at 9:30 A.M. You can then take your time paddling back, exploring the Colorado River's hidden beaches and inlets as you go.

Dixie Belle Cruises (all ages) ⌂

1477 Queens Bay, Lake Havasu City; (928) 453–6776. Call for reservations. Adults $$$, children ages 4–12 $$, under 4 free.

These one-hour narrated tours travel the lake in a replica paddleboat. Tours run on weekends at 11:30 A.M. and 1:00 and 2:30 P.M.

Bill Williams River National Wildlife Refuge (all ages) ⌂

60911 Highway 95, Parker; (928) 667–4144. Open 8:00 A.M. to 4:30 P.M. Monday through Friday. Free.

With 6,000 acres situated along the lower 12 miles of the Bill Williams River, this refuge boasts the largest cottonwood-willow riparian area left along the lower Colorado River. A visitor center provides literature and wildlife exhibits on the refuge's programs, including one geared to increase razorback suckers and the bonytail chub—endangered native fish of the Colorado River. A scenic back road makes for a nice drive, and nature trails provide wonderful wildlife watching.

Cattail Cove State Park (all ages) ⊗ ⊜ △ ⊛

Fifteen miles south of Lake Havasu City on Highway 95, P.O. Box 1990, Lake Havasu City 86405; (928) 855–1223; www.pr.state.az.us/Parks/parkhtml/cattail.html. Open daily. Day use hours are sunrise to 10:00 P.M. Day use $$.

This 2,000-acre state park offers swimming beaches, boat ramps, fishing, picnicking, hiking, and camping. Interpretive programs are held year-round in the park's cactus garden. Tent and RV sites with hookups fill up fast and are offered on a first-come, first-serve basis. At the campground you'll find showers, restrooms, and a fish-cleaning station. To rent a boat, stop by the **Sandpoint Marina and RV Park** (928–855–0549). The marina also has a store and a cafe.

Buckskin Mountain State Park (all ages) Ⓐ ⊜ △ ⊛

5476 Highway 95, Parker; (928) 667–3231; www.pr.state.az.us/Parks/parkhtml/buckskin.html. Open daily. Office hours are 8:00 A.M. to 4:30 P.M. Day use $$.

Located 11 miles north of Parker, this is one of the most widely visited state parks in the region. Situated on a secluded bend of the Colorado River, the park features low cliffs, scenic river views, shaded picnic areas, swimming beaches, a boat ramp, campsites, and hiking trails. A playground, volleyball and basketball courts, and horseshoe pits add to this recreation wonderland. Interpretive programs and guided hikes are offered from January to April. Amenities include a marina, store, and cafe.

The World's Oldest **Living Plant**

The ancient reaches of Arizona's desert are mirrored in the lifetimes of the plants that make their home in these arid regions. Although several species of plant life, such as the lofty saguaro and flowering paloverde, live a couple of hundred years, the creosote holds status as the world's longest living plant—surviving several millennium in the form of clones. The creosote bush spreads out from a stem crown, sharing the root systems of its neighbors. When the crown dies, it leaves surviving plants, which break up into expanding circles. All the plants originating from the stem crown are identical to each other—clones of the original bush. The "King Clone" in the Mohave Desert, sometimes called the world's oldest plant, started from a seedling more than 12,000 years ago. But nothing in cloning is simple—the roots and stem of each separate bush are less than 200 years old, leaving one to ponder nature's mysteries and humanity's mishaps.

Colorado River Indian Tribes Museum (all ages) 🖼

Two miles south of Parker, Route 1, Box 23B, Parker 85344; (928) 669–9211, ext. 1335. Open 8:00 A.M. to noon and 1:00 to 5:00 P.M. Monday through Friday except major holidays. **Free.**

Several Native American tribes have historically lived on the banks of the ruddy Colorado River, including the Quechan, Cocopah, Mohave, Paiute, and Chemehuevi. The Colorado River Indian Reservation is home to several tribes and is one of three Native American reservations found along the lower Colorado River. Established in 1865, this 268,691-acre reservation spans the Arizona-California border and is home to Mohave, Navajo, Hopi, and Chemehuevi Indians. The museum here illustrates the history of the tribes now living on the reservation lands. Exhibits include native arts and crafts, traditional housing, Hohokam and Patayan artifacts, and a photographic display chronicling early reservation life.

Where to Eat

Bridgewater Café. London Bridge Resort, 1477 Queens Bay, Lake Havasu City; (928) 855–0888. American cuisine including steak, seafood, and prime rib. $$

Captain's Table. Nautical Inn, 1000 McCulloch Boulevard, Lake Havasu City; (928) 855–1897. Steaks, chicken, fish, sandwiches, burgers, and salads. Children's menu. $–$$

Max & Ma's. 90 Swanson Avenue, Lake Havasu City; (928) 855–2524. Fish, crab legs, shrimp, pasta, burgers, sandwiches, Mexican entrees, and a salad bar. Children's menu. $–$$

Papa Leone's Pizza. 304 English Village, Lake Havasu City; (928) 453–5200. Pizza, subs, pasta, and salads. $

Where to Stay

Bluewater Resort. 11300 Resort Drive, Parker; (520) 669–7000; www.bluewater fun.com. Four indoor pools, indoor water slide, beach, and miniature golf course. Children under eighteen stay **free.** $–$$

Havasu Springs Resort. 2581 Highway 95, Lake Havasu City; (928) 667–3361; www.havasusprings.com. Motel rooms, apartments, RV park, restaurant, swimming beaches, boat rentals, and an outdoor pool. $$

Island Inn. 1300 McCulloch Boulevard, Lake Havasu City; (928) 680–0606 or (800) 243–9955. Pool, spa, swimming beaches, and a restaurant. Children under sixteen stay **free.** $$–$$$

Sands Vacation Resort. 2040 Mesquite Avenue, Lake Havasu City; (928) 855–1388 or (800) 521–0360; www.sands-resort. com. Suites, heated pool, fitness center, spa, and a restaurant. $$$

Stagecoach Trails Guest Ranch. P.O. Box 580, Yucca 86438; (928) 727-8270 or (866) 444–4471; www.stgr.com. This family-oriented dude ranch offers horseback riding, hiking, cookouts, and a swimming pool. $$$$

Area Campgrounds

Crazy Horse Campground. 1534 Beachcomber Boulevard, Lake Havasu City; (928) 855–4033. Tent and RV sites with hookups. Showers, beach, pool, spa, store, and boat ramp. $

For More Information

BLM Lake Havasu Field Office. 2610 Sweetwater Avenue, Lake Havasu City 86406; (928) 505–1200; www.az.blm.gov.

English Village Information Center. 420 English Village, Lake Havasu City 86403; (928) 855–5655.

Lake Havasu Tourism Bureau. 314 London Bridge Road, Lake Havasu City 86403; (928) 453–3444; www.golakehavasu.com.

Parker Chamber of Commerce. 1217 California Avenue, P.O. Box 627, Parker 85344; (520) 669–2174.

Yuma

Yuma hasn't always gotten the best press. Some say that summer spends the winter here and Hell spends the summer. Yuma Territorial Prison carried the dubious nickname of the Hell Hole, and old Fort Yumers would say that in the summer chickens would hatch fully cooked. Today, residents just respond, "Where's your sense of Yuma?" With summer temperatures driving up to 120 degrees, Yuma is often the hottest place in the country. The tiny town came into existence as a ferry point for pioneers heading west during the California gold rush. Later it became a military depot and supply transfer point for materials shipped up from the Gulf of California on steamboats.

The people of Yuma have managed to make good use of their improbable climate and now successfully attract nearly 80,000 "snowbirds" (winter visitors), who travel from Canada and the Northwest to enjoy the warm winters. Surprisingly, agriculture flourishes here, giving Yuma the crown as the Lettuce Capital of the World. Down in these southern reaches of the state, kids will enjoy tours of a peanut patch and a walk though a citrus orchard, where a gardener enjoys sharing the fruits of his labor. Desert wildlife refuges near Yuma provide good wildlife watching and a chance to see bighorn sheep and migrating Canada geese up close. Whether you take a cruise up the river in a paddleboat, check out an old military fort, walk through a depot station, climb in a prison cell, or just lounge by the river, you'll find plenty of things to give you a sense of Yuma.

Quechen Indian Museum/Fort Yuma (all ages)

350 Picacho Road, P.O. Box 1899, Yuma 85366; (760) 572–0661. Open daily 8 :00 A.M. to noon and 1:00 to 5:00 P.M. Adults $, under 12 free.

Fort Yuma started out as a military camp in 1851 on the side of a hill near present-day Yuma, but after a disastrous flood in 1855 the camp relocated to its present site. The old fort is on the Fort Yuma Indian Reservation, home to the Quechan (Yuman) Indians. The

Roughing **It**

"Fort Yuma is probably the hottest place on earth. It is a US military post, and its occupants get so used to the terrific heat that they suffer without it. There is a tradition that a very, very wicked soldier died there, once, and of course, went straight to the hottest corner of perdition—and the next day he telegraphed back for his blankets." —Mark Twain, 1872

old buildings now house the Quechan tribal offices and a museum with displays on the history of Fort Yuma and Quechan Indian culture. The historic 1855 buildings, exhibits on the Quechan Revolt, and displays of military and native artifacts make this a satisfying stop.

The Farm (all ages)
2625 West County Seventeenth Street A½, Somerton; (928) 627–3631. Open daily 8:00 A.M. until dusk. Free.

This quaint two-acre farm provides a wonderful agricultural education in a small family farm environment. Darrel Wilson takes visitors on a tour of the orchards and pulls ripe fruit off the branches and cuts them up in quarters for the little ones. You won't have a problem hearing the kids fight over who got the most when this generous farmer is doling out the goodies. The Farm offers citrus (tangelos, oranges, lemons, and grapefruit) from December through April and stone fruit (apricots, plums, peaches, and nectarines) during May and June.

Yuma Territorial Prison State Historical Park (all ages)
One Prison Hill Road, Yuma; (928) 783–4771; www.pr.state.az.us/ Parks/parkhtml/yuma.html. Open daily 8:00 A.M. to 5:00 P.M. except Christmas Day. Closed at 2:00 P.M. on Thanksgiving and Christmas Eve. Adults and children ages 7–13 $, under 7 free.

Made famous by pulp fiction and Western flicks, this prison is one of the state's most visited state parks. It served as the Arizona territorial prison from 1876 to 1909, when the prisoners where transferred to new cells in Florence. Prisoners suffered the terrible summer temperatures of 120 degrees, and isolation meant spending time in a dark dungeon infested with scorpions. Despite this, it was known as a model prison in the nineteenth century and provided services no other penitentiary offered, including a library, school, hospital, and a workshop. The convicts built most of the prison, and photo-

Vacation **Values**

Visitors seeking a quick, discounted vacation are rewarded by visiting the Arizona Office of Tourism Web site at www.ArizonaVacationValues.com. The site offers visitors access to more than 200 discounts at Arizona attractions, hotels, resorts, golf courses, and airfare. Values range from 50 percent discounts to gifts with purchases.

graphs at the park illustrate their labors. Children especially enjoy climbing the main watchtower and wandering through the abandoned cells.

Yuma Crossing State Historic Park (all ages) 🏛 🛋 👪 🚗

201 North Fourth Avenue, Yuma; (928) 329–0471; www.pr.state.az.us/Parks/ parkhtml/yumacross.html. Open daily 9:00 A.M. to 5:00 P.M. except Christmas Day. Closed at 2:00 P.M. on Thanksgiving and Christmas Eve. Call for tours. Adults and children ages 7–13 $, under 7 free.

In 1864 this military depot was constructed as a supply distribution point for territorial outposts fighting the Indian Wars. River steamers would carry cargo from Port Isabel at the mouth of the Colorado River up to Yuma, where the material was then transferred out to the troops. The depot closed in 1883, but visitors to the park can see several of the restored buildings, including the U.S. Quarter Master Depot and the Commanding Officer's Quarters—an early adobe house built in the 1850s. In the warehouses you'll find an assortment of transportation-related items, including stagecoaches, mule wagons, and relics from century-old barges and steamboats. Outside, kids can climb into the cabin and ring the bell of the park's 1907 Baldwin steam locomotive, which was once operated by the Southern Pacific Railroad. A historic adobe corral, picnic tables, views of the Colorado River, a museum, and a visitor center complete the experience.

Amazing
Arizona Facts

The hottest day in Arizona's recorded history was June 26, 1990, when both Yuma and Phoenix reached temperatures of 122 degrees. The heat was so intense that Sky Harbor International Airport shut down.

Yuma River Tours (all ages) ⚠ 🍴

1920 Arizona Avenue, Yuma; (928) 783–4400; www.yumarivertours.com. Open daily. Call for reservations. Adults and children ages 4–12 $$$$, under 4 free.

Kids of all ages jump at the chance to explore the desert from the comfort of a jet boat on these five-hour narrated tours. Along the way you'll see scenic wilderness areas and have the chance for prime bird-watching. The tours, which include a box lunch, also make stops at an old mining cabin, petroglyph sites, and at Norton's Landing—a historic steamboat stopover.

Colorado King River Cruises (all ages) ⚠ 🍴

1636 South Fourth Avenue, Yuma; (928) 782–2412; www.coloradoking.com. Open daily. Call for reservations. $$$$

As early as 1852, steamboats plied the waters of the Colorado River. These river mainstays transported goods up from the Gulf of California to the river towns along the border of Arizona Territory. These queens of yesteryear stood up to three decks high, measured more than 140 feet long, and drew only 2 feet of water. Water traffic declined when the Southern Pacific Railroad made its way through Yuma in 1877, and by 1909 steamboats were a rarity.

Captain Ron brings back the steamboat's glory days with tours on his 57-foot-long paddleboat, the *Colorado King I*. These three-hour, narrated tours leave at 10:00 A.M. and 2:00 P.M. daily and can include lunch or dinner.

Camels in **the Desert**

In 1856 the first of two shipments of camels arrived in Texas as part of an army experiment utilizing camels to carry supplies in the arid Southwest. A happy-go-lucky caretaker named Hadji Ali arrived with the first shipment of thirty-three camels from the Middle East. The soldiers promptly changed his name to "Hi Jolly."

The camels, under the supervision of Hi Jolly, quickly proved their worth as pack animals, but the army officers and their mounts shied away from the strange-looking beasts. As a result, the experiment floundered, and the war department sold off many of the camels and released others in the Arizona desert. Hi Jolly, respected and honored for his part in the camel campaign, died in Quartzsite on December 16, 1902, at the age of sixty-four. His tomb, a monumental pyramid of quartz and petrified wood topped by a tin camel, honors his service to the army and his dedication to the camels of his own native deserts.

Century House Museum (all ages) 🏛️ 🖼️

240 South Madison Avenue, Yuma; (928) 782–1841. Open 10:00 A.M. to 4:00 P.M. Tuesday through Saturday except major holidays. Adults $, under 11 free.

Pioneer merchant E. F. Sanguinetti built this house and its colorful gardens in the 1870s. Today this historic home houses a branch of the Arizona Historical Society and a museum featuring period rooms and exhibits of Yuma from prehistoric times through the early 1900s. Here you'll discover the people of Yuma—Native Americans, missionaries, explorers, soldiers, miners, and settlers. The aviary, filled with flashy flowers and exotic birds, is a favorite with kids of all ages.

Yuma Valley Railway (all ages)

Located between First Street and Second Avenue, P.O. Box 10305, Yuma 85366; (928) 783–3456. Open weekends only. Adults $$$, children ages 4–16 $$, under 4 free.

This short excursion ride follows the Historic Yuma Valley Railroad line along the Colorado River. The narrated ride introduces passengers to local folklore and history as the 1922 Pullman coach and its 1941 diesel locomotive travel past Yuma's rolling farmlands.

Imperial National Wildlife Refuge (all ages) 🌼 ⚠️ 🚻 🐾

Forty-three miles north of Yuma off Highway 95, P.O. Box 72217, Yuma 85365; (928) 783–3371. Visitor center open 7:30 A.M. to 4:00 P.M. Monday through Friday and 9:00 A.M. to 4:00 P.M. Saturday and Sunday November through March. Free.

If you're visiting in the cool season, you'll have a good chance of seeing the Canada geese wintering on Martinez Lake. Other birds you might see include the great blue heron, great egret, and Yuma clapper rail. With more than 25,000 acres and 35 miles of river shoreline, the refuge provides plenty of exploration opportunities. Bird-watching, picnicking, hiking, fishing, and boating are the most popular activities here. The 1-mile loop, Painted Desert Nature Trail, is a favorite of families, especially in spring when desert wildflowers bloom in a riot of color.

Where to Eat

Britain Farms Chuckwagon. 4330 Riverside Drive, Yuma; (928) 782–4699. Western-style dinner, live entertainment, and stagecoach rides. Dinner served Wednesday through Saturday. Lunch also available. $$

The Garden Café. 250 South Madison Avenue, Yuma 85364; (928) 783–1491. Serving tri-tip steak, chicken, quiche, salads, and soups in a transformed carriage house surrounded by a lush garden. Open Tuesday through Sunday. Children's menu. $

La Fonda Restaurant & Tortilla Factory. 1095 Third Avenue, Yuma; (928) 783–6902. Authentic home-style Mexican entrees. $$

Yuma Landing Restaurant. 195 South Fourth Avenue, Yuma; (928) 782–7427. Steak, seafood, burgers, and ribs at the site of the first airplane landing in Yuma in 1911. Pictures from Yuma's past. Children's menu. $–$$

Where to Stay

Best Western Coronado. 233 South Fourth Avenue, Yuma; (928) 783–4453; www.bwcoronado.com. Family suites, two swimming pools, and a **free** buffet breakfast. Children under twelve stay **free.** $$–$$$

Clarion Suites. 2600 South Fourth Avenue, Yuma; (928) 726–4830. Family suites, continental breakfast buffet, heated outdoor pool, and spa. Children under twelve stay **free.** $$$–$$$$

La Fuente Inn & Suites. 1513 East Sixteenth Street, Yuma; (928) 329–1814 or (800) 841–1814; www.lafuenteinn.com. Continental breakfast, heated outdoor pool, and spa. Children under twelve stay **free.** $$$

Shilo Inn. 1550 South Castle Dome Avenue, Yuma; (928) 782–9511 or (800) 222–2244; www.shiloinns.com. Complimentary breakfast, restaurant, fitness center, heated outdoor pool, and spa. Children under twelve stay **free.** $$$–$$$$

Area Campgrounds

Fisher's Landing. Thirty-five miles north of Yuma at Martinez Lake; (928) 782–7049. Tent and RV sites with hookups, coin showers, restaurant, and marina. $

For More Information

Arizona Game and Fish Department. 9140 East Twenty-eighth Street, Yuma 85365; (928) 342–0091.

Bureau of Land Management. 2555 East Gila Ridge Road, Yuma 85365; (928) 317–3200.

Quartzsite Chamber of Commerce. 1490 Main Event Lane, Quartzsite 85346; (928) 927–5600; www.quartzsite chamber.com.

Yuma Convention and Visitor Bureau. 377 Main Street, Suite 101, Yuma 85364; (928) 783–0071 or (800) 293–0071; www.yumachamber.org.

Annual Events

JANUARY

Yuma Lettuce Days. Yuma; (928) 782–5712. Last weekend in January. Farm equipment displays, cabbage bowling, lettuce-box car derby, salad toss-off, petting zoo, arts and crafts, and live entertainment.

APRIL

Yuma Birding and Nature Festival. Yuma; (928) 367–4290 or (800) 573–4031. Second weekend in April. Nature lectures, photography workshops, a wild burro search, and a bat watch at Kofa National Wildlife Refuge.

SEPTEMBER

Andy Devine Days. Kingman; (928) 753–6106. Late September. Parade, rodeo, and festivities celebrating this local-bred Western movie star.

OCTOBER

Dia de los Muertos (Day of the Dead). Yuma; (928) 783–2423. October 30. An altar contest, calaveras readings (humorous poetry for the dead), Latin American music, and Mexican folklore dances.

London Bridge Days. Lake Havasu City; (928) 453–3444. Mid-October. Parade, contests, games, and live entertainment.

NOVEMBER

Greek Festival. Lake Havasu City; (928) 855–5208. First Saturday in November. Authentic food, Greek music, dancing, and exhibits in the lake's English Village.

Colorado River Crossing Balloon Festival. Yuma; (928) 343–1715. Mid-November. Sunrise balloon liftoff, sunset desert glow, fireworks, food, and entertainment.

DECEMBER

Christmas Bush Festival. Oatman; (928) 768–6222. Second week of December. Activities at this desert celebration include caroling, shopping, and a skit of the ghostrider gunfighters chasing the Grinch out of town.

Other Things to **See and Do**

- **Bonelli House,** Kingman; (928) 753–1413.
- **Captain Doyle's River Excursions,** Topock; (928) 768–2667.
- **Cocopah Museum,** Somerton; (928) 627–1992.
- **Colorado River Historical Society Museum,** Bullhead City; (928) 754–3399.
- **Crawdaddy's Kayak Tours,** Lake Havasu City; (928) 854–5377.
- **Dobson Museum,** Yuma; (928) 785–4013.
- **Gold Road Mine Tours,** Oatman; (928) 768–1600.
- **Havasu Hot Laps,** Lake Havasu City; (928) 505–7223.
- **Havasu Lanes,** Lake Havasu City; (928) 855–2695.
- **Historic Route 66 Museum,** Kingman; (928) 753–9889.
- **Kingman Army Airfield Museum,** Kingman; ((28) 757–1892.
- **Kofa National Wildlife Refuge,** Yuma; (928) 367–4290 or (800) 573–4031.
- **London Bridge Watercraft Tours and Rentals,** Lake Havasu City; (928) 453–8883.
- **Outback Off-Road Adventures,** Lake Havasu City; (928) 680–6151.
- **Peanut Patch,** Yuma; (928) 726–6292.
- **River Island State Park,** Parker Strip; (928) 667–3386.
- **Tyson's Well Stage Station Museum,** Quartzsite; (928) 927–5229.
- **Western Arizona Canoe and Kayak Outfitters,** Lake Havasu City; (928) 855–6414.
- **Willow Beach National Fish Hatchery,** Lake Mohave; (928) 767–3456.
- **Yuma Proving Ground Heritage Center,** Yuma; (928) 328–3394.

Index

About the Author

Back in college, Carrie Miner planned on seeing the world from an archaeologist's point of view. Then she discovered writing. As a freelance travel writer, Carrie now seeks out the past and the present through the art and culture of the people of the southwestern United States. She is a frequent contributor to *Arizona Highways* magazine, as well as a member of the Society of American Travel Writers.